"Ethiopia embraced Christianity earlier than many south Saharan African and European countries. Yet the cross-cultural mission involvement of the Church is not as strong as its long tradition and experience. In this book, the authors clearly emphasize the need for cross-cultural involvement and the necessary theoretical and practical steps to engage in cross-cultural mission. *Crossing Barriers for the Great Commission: An Ethiopian Perspective* can be used for Bible schools to prepare those who are training to be missionaries, for church leaders so that they can prioritize mission in their respective churches, and for missiologists and researchers to continue the discussion that these authors have started. I strongly recommend [this book] for all who are engaged in God's mission globally, but specifically for churches, Bible schools and missionaries in Ethiopia. It is a contextually relevant, ground breaking and timely book."

Ermias Mamo (PhD)
Chaplain and Mission Professor
Ethiopian Graduate School of Theology
Addis Ababa, Ethiopia

"I am extremely happy to see such a [book] focused on cross-cultural mission. I am thankful for the vision, commitment...and dedication of these authors, who took the initiative to produce this material. For me, this is the first...comprehensive document written on mission in the Ethiopian context....The authors do not [just have] a single way of doing cross-cultural mission, but they have genuinely addressed the challenges and obstacles, like lack of knowledge about cross-cultural missions, poverty, language barrier, etc....But as a solution for cross-cultural mission, the authors have indicated ways forward, like...missiological training within Ethiopia and beyond, strategies for sustainable funding and many others.

Therefore, I encourage all the evangelical church leaders, pastors, evangelists and lay ministers [to read this book]. Also I recommend [it] for Bible schools, seminaries and missionary training schools to enrich their training program and help those under them to be mission minded and mission practitioners."

Dr. Desta Langena Letta
Founder and International Director for AIPM

"*Crossing Barriers for the Great Commission: An Ethiopian Perspective*....focus[es] on the various methodological issues: proclamation, translation, campus ministry, evangelism, conflict-problems, and so on....This book will contribute to Ethiopia...for the Kingdom."

Chang Wun Charles Kim (PhD)
Good Shepherd Presbyterian Church, South Korea

"This [book] is indeed timely [for] maximizing mission endeavors in Ethiopia. It points to biblical and theological bases referring to...examples from both Old and New Testament stories with the need for proclamation....towards crossing beyond the barriers."

Esckinder Taddesse Woldegebrial (PhD)
Ethiopian Full Gospel Theological Seminary

"A powerfully thought provoking book that is full of insight and understanding of the history and future direction of the Church in Ethiopia. This book is relevant and practical in its approach as it ties in the history of Ethiopia, bible translation, persecution of the Church, the spread of the gospel and the unique position Ethiopians have in the spread of the gospel. Ethiopians need to raise up a healthy church, one focused on local and world mission, using their position of influence in order to cross the linguistic, cultural, historical, spiritual and theological barriers as they proclaim Christ in both word and deed. I would strongly encourage all Ethiopian believers, particularly church leaders, as well as those who have a heart for Ethiopia to read and meditate on what is written in this book. It is well written, easy to understand and challenging, as it gets to the heart of the some of the most relevant issues the Church is currently facing".

Tracie Herman
CCCI Africa Field Strategy - Jesus Film Project

"The authors of *Crossing Barriers for the Great Commission: An Ethiopian Perspective*...present a scholarly thesis of evangelization with a strategy specifically for Ethiopians living in Ethiopia and around the world. This book is an excellent treatise for the advancement of the Kingdom of God in Ethiopia and ...around the world."

Dr. Randy Delp
Dean of Students and Business Director CFNI

CROSSING BARRIERS
FOR THE GREAT COMMISSION

CROSSING BARRIERS
FOR THE GREAT COMMISSION

ABENEAZER GEZAHEGN URGA
GIRMA ALTAYE GEBREMEDHIN
JESSICA ANN UDALL
NAHOM TEGENE YEFRU

Crossing Barriers for the Great Commission: An Ethiopian Perspective

Copyright© 2016 by Abeneazer G. Urga, Girma A. Gebremedhin, Jessica A. Udall, Nahom T. Yefru. All rights reserved.
ISBN 978-0-692-59606-7
Cover Design: Bereket Tadesse
                contact@bekigraphics.com
                http://bekisquare.com

All emphasis in Scripture has been added by the authors.

Contents

ACKNOWLEDGEMENTS

CONTRIBUTORS

INTRODUCTION 1

CHAPTER ONE: A Biblical Theology of the Necessity of Proclamation in Crossing Barriers and Its Implications for the Ethiopian Context 3

Part I: Crossing Linguistic Barriers for the Great Commission 28

CHAPTER TWO: Bible Translation in Ethiopia: Theological and Missiological Impact 29

Part II: Crossing Theological Barriers for the Great Commission 50

CHAPTER THREE: Reasons, Principles and Strategies for Ethiopian Evangelicals Who Share the Gospel with Ethiopian Orthodox Adherents in Light of Jewish Evangelism in Luke-Acts 51

Part III: Crossing Cultural Barriers for the Great Commission 69

CHAPTER FOUR: Erecha and Spiritual Hunger: A Call to Cross Barriers to Proclaim the Gospel Contextually Among the Oromo People of Ethiopia 70

CHAPTER FIVE: Preparing Ethiopians for Barrier-Crossing Ministry: Maximizing Missionary Training for Great Commission Impact 88

CHAPTER SIX: Preparing Ethiopians for Barrier-Crossing Ministry: Survey of Missionary Preparation in Ethiopia and in Other African Countries 117

CHAPTER SEVEN: Ethiopian Immigrants as Cross-Cultural Missionaries: Activating the Diaspora for Great Commission Impact 143

Part IV: Crossing Geographical Barriers for the Great Commission 162

CHAPTER EIGHT: Connected Ethiopians Connecting the Lost to Christ: Harnessing Internet Technology to Cross Barriers for the Great Commission 163

Part V: Crossing Other Barriers for the Great Commission 168

CHAPTER NINE: Current Methods of Ethiopian Involvement in the Great Commission 169

CHAPTER TEN: Barriers to Great Commission Effectiveness Among the Ethiopian Mission Force 179

CHAPTER ELEVEN: The Antioch Model and Its Great Commission Implications for the Ethiopian Church 190

CHAPTER TWELVE: Ethiopia's Up and Coming Mission Force: Students and Graduates Crossing Barriers for the Great Commission 223

CHAPTER THIRTEEN: Sustainable Funding for Great Commission Involvement: Next Steps for Ethiopia 235

CONCLUSION 255

ENDNOTES 257

ACKNOWLEDGEMENTS

Thank you to Dr. Chang Wun Charles Kim, Dr. Esckinder Taddesse Woldegebrial, Cindy Udall, Dr. Christopher Little, Dr. Desta Langena, Dr. Edward Smither, Dr. Ermias Mamo, Dr. Randy Delp, and Tracie Herman, who read the manuscript and offered excellent constructive feedback.

Thank you to Dr. Enoch Wan, who gave several helpful suggestions for unifying the content thematically.

Thank you to our various professors on different continents, under whom most of this material was researched.

CONTRIBUTORS

Abeneazer Gezahegn Urga holds a B.A. from Hawassa University (Foreign Language and Literature) and a Masters of Divinity from Columbia International University. He has served with World Vision Ethiopia and the Evangelical Students' and Graduates' Union of Ethiopia (EvaSUE – IFES) and is currently a professor of Bible and Theology at Evangelical Theological College (ETC) in Addis Ababa. He is the author of *Prayer and Evangelism: Inseparable Elements in Furthering the* Gospel (2013); *A Reflection on Diaspora Cross-Cultural Evangelism: An African Perspective* (2015); *In Christ: An In-Depth Bible Study of Colossians for Theological Reflection* (2015); and *The Normal Christian Life in the Book of Daniel: A Guide to Theology, Mission and Spiritual Formation in the Everyday Life of Pilgrims* (2015).

Girma Altaye Gebremedhin holds a B.A. from Kotebe University (Geography), an M.A. from Indra Gandhi National Open University (Sociology), and an M.A. from Wheaton College (Evangelism and Leadership). He is serving with Great Commission Ministries Ethiopia (Cru) as the National Director for the Global Church Movement. He also serves as the Country Director for AWANA.

Jessica Ann Udall holds a B.Sc. in Biblical Studies and an M.A. in Intercultural Studies from Columbia International University. She has served as a cross-cultural trainer of short term missionaries to Ethiopia, has researched and spoken on Ethiopia for the Evangelical Missiological Society (EMS) national conference, and is the author of

Loving the Stranger: Welcoming Immigrants in the Name of Jesus (2015). She is married to an Ethiopian (Abeneazer Gezahegn Urga) and is a professor at Evangelical Theological College (ETC) in Addis Ababa.

Nahom Tegene Yefru holds a B.A. from Addis Ababa Bible College (Bible and Theology), an M.A. from Grace Graduate School with Vision International University (Christian Education), and a Masters of Theology from Presbyterian College and Theological Seminary in South Korea (Missiology). He has served as the Executive Assistant for the Christian Medical Doctors' and Dentists' Fellowship and as the Youth and Children Advisory Board Vice Chairman at Full Gospel Believers' Church Head Office. He is currently ministering in Dallas, Texas.

INTRODUCTION

Today in Ethiopia, the Evangelical Church has **more than doubled** since the fall of Communism. Though still a minority in the country, it continues to grow and is characterized by vibrancy, faith and prayer. Many advances toward Great Commission involvement are being seen.

Yet...

Today in Ethiopia, there are still **33 unreached people groups** made up of 24,000,000 who have yet to hear the Gospel. Many surrounding nations are considered to be mainly unreached as well.

How to reconcile these two seemingly contradictory facts? How can the vibrant Ethiopian Evangelical church connect to the unreached people groups in Ethiopia and beyond? *Through the cros sing of barriers that hinder the flow of the* Gospel, towards the end that every nation, tribe and tongue would worship God in truth.

There is great potential for the Ethiopian Church to make a Great Commission impact. There are also many barriers, whether religious, cultural, or practical, that stand in her way. This book is an attempt to brainstorm the way forward, strategizing how to cross these barriers for the glory of God and the joy of the nations. It is a compilation of several perspectives – from three Ethiopians and one American – considering how Ethiopia (and by extrapolation, other Majority World countries) could overcome barriers to become a key player in fulfilling the Great Commission.

These pages are a small contribution to a conversation that we hope will be lively and ongoing regarding Ethiopia's role in proclaiming the Gospel. Barriers must be crossed, even within one country, in order for all people to be reached. The Bible must be available to all peoples in their heart languages. The Gospel must be proclaimed relevantly to people from other faiths and from distinct tribal groups – this demands great discernment after beginning with a listening ear. The fact that missiological education must be available and contextual, with an awareness and sensitivity towards a non-Western orientation of the students in the choice of curriculum is emphasized. Ethiopians in the Diaspora are suggested as an underutilized key to reaching unreached people groups who have immigrated to Western countries. Current methods of Ethiopian mission are discussed and a helpful biblical model is recommended and applied. New digital strategies for proclamation are introduced and those working with university students are encouraged to equip and challenge them to continue mission work (conducted fruitfully during their school breaks) after graduation. Finally, overcoming the potential barrier of sustainable funding for Ethiopian barrier-crossing ministry is discussed and practical ways forward are suggested.

May this book be a conversation starter, a kindling, a catalyst for the barrier crossers all over the world to redouble their Gospel-empowered efforts. Let us join together to reach the unreached for Christ together, for the sake of His Name. He is worthy!

CHAPTER ONE

A Biblical Theology of the Necessity of Proclamation in Crossing Barriers and Its Implications for the Ethiopian Context

Growing up as an evangelical Christian in Ethiopia was not easy. Teachers, neighbors and classmates would throw hurtful words at me, and they did not want to socialize with me or my family. Being "Pente" – a short form of Pentecostal – is a derogatory term for all evangelical Christians. But these challenges did not stop me and my family from sharing the Gospel with my unbelieving friends, extended family members and some of our neighbors. Conversing with unbelievers was natural, because they would bring up the Gospel themselves in order to question our faith.

A few years ago I was working in a very unreached area with a Christian humanitarian organization that provided medication, school buildings, constructing bridges, giving away cattle and sheep, doing forestation, etc. The community was happy with all the physical support they received. But the humanitarian workers were not crossing the theological and spiritual barriers. The community was not hearing the Gospel, because we were *just* trying to convey the Gospel by deeds. When we realized this, a few colleagues and I started to do the work of evangelism along with three small local churches which consisted of around 150 people scattered among the 90,000 dwellers. The church members agreed to fast and pray for a few weeks and start preaching the Gospel everywhere at any time. A few people came to Christ in the midst of fierce persecution. Ten of my fellow brothers and sisters and I were imprisoned briefly. People who heard the Good News started to come to our office after walking three and four hours to receive the Lord. The school we built did not convert them to Christ, but the Gospel we preached drew them to him.

The Bible shows us various people sharing the mighty works of God in diverse contexts in redemptive history both in word and deed. Though word and deed should not be dichotomized, history teaches us that priority should be given to the proclamation of the Gospel verbally.[1] The Bible also asserts that we should prioritize the soul of man over his mere temporary needs (Luke 9:25).

Thesis

The thesis of this paper is verbal proclamation is significant in order for the Gospel to abound among the least reached, the unreached and the unengaged and to transform individuals and society for eternity. This theme is seen as a prevalent motif in various contexts in both Testaments (cf. Gen 12:1-3; 41:1-16, 25, 28, 32, 37, 39; Num 23:1-24:25; 1 Kgs 10:1-9; 17:7-16; 2 Chr 2:3-10; 9:1-8; Dan 2:27-28, 45b; 4:1-3, 34-37; Jonah 1:2, 6; 3:1-3; Luke 2:8-12; 9:1-6; John 4:1-42; Acts 2:1-41; 4:1-4; 7:1-53; 8:26-39, 40; 10:34-48; 13:7-12; 44, 48-49; 14:1-2; 17:1-4, 10-12, 16-34; 21:1-22:21; 24:10-21; 26:1-29; 28:23-31; 1 Cor 2:1-5; Gal 1:8-9, 11; 3:8; Phil 1:12-13; Col 1:3-8; 1Thess 1:4-6, 8; Phlm 10; 1 Pet 1:25; 2 Pet 2:5; 1 John 1:1-2; Rev 2:13; 11:1-7).

The whole counsel of God is filled with a steady stream of incidents that show that verbal proclamation of the Gospel and "the mighty acts of God" (Ps 64:9) are vital in order to "cross linguistic, cultural, historical, theological, and spiritual barriers."[2] Because the scope of this chapter cannot cover all the proclamatory events in crossing barriers that the Scriptures contain, four stories – two from the Old Testament and two from the New Testament – will be discussed in detail to support this thesis: Rahab and the nameless proclaimer, the slave girl and Naaman, Peter and Cornelius, and Paul with the Stoics and Epicureans.

The reason I am attempting to prove my thesis in such a way, by selecting representative incidents from both Testaments, is to display that proclamation does not just depend upon certain Old or New Testament passages as proof texts. The methodology I have adopted helps to avoid using Scripture as "a mine from which we extract our gems,"[3] or what David J. Bosch describes as the attempt "to extract our 'missionary' gold from it [the Bible]."[4] In this chapter, I will avoid "gleaning so called 'missionary texts' from the Bible"[5] and attempt to prove the motif of the *Biblical Theology of Proclamation in Crossing Barriers* by "[viewing the passages used in this study] within their own contexts and attempt to extrapolate [a Biblical] theology of [proclamation]."[6]

Biblical Motif of Proclamation in Crossing Barriers

Rahab the Prostitute and the Nameless Proclaimer

God promised he would deliver the Israelites from the strong hands of the Egyptians by his "outstretched hand" and would make them his own people (Exod 6:6-7). For this reason, God sent his servant Moses to Egypt to deliverer the Israelites. The ten plagues were sent through the agency of Moses so that Yahweh's identity and power might be known (Exod 7:17-21; 8:1-7, 16-19, 20-24; 9:1-7, 8-12, 13-26; 10:1-2, 21-29; 12:29-32).[7]

The Israelites left the mourning Egyptians behind and came to the Red Sea. Yahweh again intervened and dried the sea before them (Exod 14:21-25) so that they would inherit Canaan as it was promised to Abraham (Gen 15:12-16). These miracles served their purposes because the nations around them heard what Yahweh did for his people (Exod 18:10-11; Josh 2:8:13; 5:1; cf. Exod 15:14-16.)

Having given the law to the Israelites and having handed down his leadership, Moses died (Deut 31:1-3, 7-8; 34:1-9; Josh 1:9), and Joshua took the responsibility to take the Israelites into Canaan (Josh 1:1-3, 10-11). Before entering into the land, he sent two spies to scout the land and bring information (Josh 2:1-2). The two spies were helped by a prophecy as well as the mighty miracles of God that were heard by the people. Rahab stated that she knew "the Lord has given [them] the land" (Josh 2:9); the reason that Rahab and the other Canaanites had knowledge of Yahweh was that they "heard" what the Lord did at the Red Sea, and the battles the people of Israel won along the way (Num 21:21-35, Josh 2:10). She confessed that Yahweh was the Great God: "the Lord your God, he is God in the heavens above and on the earth beneath" (Josh 2:11). This is interesting, because someone had to proclaim to Rahab and to all the inhabitants of Canaan in order for them to know about Yahweh and his marvelous miracles as they did. The reason Rahab hid the two spies was because she believed in Yahweh's mightiness after hearing about his mighty deeds in Egypt, at the Red Sea and at the two battles with Sihon and Og. David M. Howard asserts the reasons why Rahab's confession is so profound:

> First, on its own merits, Rahab affirmed that Israel's God had dominion over the realms of the heaven and the earth – an extremely broad scope that surely encompassed the domains of many of the gods that her people worshipped....Second, Rahab stated that Israel's God, Yahweh, was indeed (the only) God...when Rahab stated that "Yahweh your God is God," she was stating that Baal, Asherah, and the rest were not true gods....Third, Rahab's words became even more significant when we realize that the last part of her affirmation – the phrase "in the heavens above and the earth below" – is found only three times prior to this, all

in contexts that affirm God's exclusive claims to sovereignty [Ex. 20:4; Deut. 4:39; 5:8].[8]

Rahab showed deep theological and personal knowledge of Yahweh and the Pentateuch.[9] But who proclaimed the Gospel to her and converted her?[10] Identifying the proclaimer might not be as vital as Trent Butler asserts, yet it is important to affirm the fact that there was a proclaimer in order for Rahab to hear the message.[11] There had to be someone to delineate what the Lord had done in the journey of the Israelites. Though one cannot identify the human agent by name, the proclaimer was successful in giving her the chance to embrace "saving faith" because of the news he or she brought to Rahab.[12] The goal of proclamation is and should be transformation of individuals and societies. The unknown proclaimer of God's miraculous intervention had significance in the life of Rahab and her family (cf. Josh 2:8-21).

First, the proclaimed message allowed Rahab to deny false gods and false worship and identify Yahweh as the only God who deserves worship and allegiance.[13] This points out that her confession and salvation was genuine, because James puts her on the same level "with Abraham" (Jas 2:23, 25).[14] The author of Hebrews indicates that she was a "prostitute," yet she obeyed Yahweh (Heb 11:31). Gareth L. Cockerill states that "calling Rahab 'prostitute'…makes it clear that one does not become or preserve as a part of God's people because of previous merit or birth."[15] John Hamlin also writes that "Rahab was a paradigm of hope, showing that the old idols, the old corrupt ways of the past, could be given up."[16]

Second, her genuine faith and transformation produced good work. James, in his argument that faith cannot be divorced from good works, uses Rahab as a role model along with Abraham (Jas 2:21-25).[17] It is important to notice here that her faith preceded her action, for the writer of Joshua shows this in her words, "the Lord your God, he is God in the heavens above and on the earth beneath" (Josh 2:11b).[18] Her genuine faith not only produced good works but risky good works, for she hid the two spies.[19] David Oginde comments:

> Why did Rahab risk her life this way? The fact that the king himself knew about the spies' visit put her in grave danger. But she had good reason to take the risk....Rahab had heard and believed [the proclaimed message]. What's more, her faith was not just a verbal confession. It was combined with action, and risky action at that. It was faith she was ready to die for.[20]

Third, she used the opportunity to save her family and herself from God's judgment (Josh 2:12-14; 6:22-25).[21] Rahab's receptivity toward the proclaimed message helped her to be a decisive instrument in saving the lives of her family from the judgment of God. Donald H. Madvig states:

> When Rahab requested that the spies "spare the lives" of her family, she may have been asking no more than that they be taken alive as prisoners...Eventually, however, they were assimilated into the nation (6:25). In Scripture salvation is frequently a family matter: the Israelites celebrated the Passover by families (Ex 12:3); Joshua decided for his whole family that they would serve the Lord (24:15; cf. "you and your household" in Acts 16:31). The family members would demonstrate their personal faith by gathering in Rahab's house and remaining there...The phrase "all who belong to them" is ambiguous in Hebrew and may refer to their entire households or to all their possessions or to both.[22]

Rahab's request was granted and they were spared (Josh 2:12-14; 6:22-25), yet the assertion that she requested that her family would be "taken alive as prisoners"[23] is weak in light of the statement, "Then they devoted all the city to destruction, both men and women, young and old, oxen, sheep, and donkeys, with the age of the sword" (Josh 6:21). Her request was a life and death issue (Josh 2:13). She knew what Yahweh did to the Egyptians, to Sihon and Og. She knew Yahweh would punish those who did not receive his people and their message. She knew that destruction and judgment was about to dawn on Jericho (cf. Josh 2:8-14).

As it can be seen in Rahab's speech in Joshua 2:9-11, all the inhabitants of the city were given an ample opportunity to hear the message through the nameless proclaimer. Nevertheless, it was only Rahab who responded to what she heard. The rest of the city refused and rebelled. They were even chasing after the two spies (Josh 2:2-3, 7; Heb 11:31). Donald Guthrie writes:

> The distinction between Rahab and the other inhabitants of Jericho is marked by the description of them as *those who were disobedient*. This implies that the people of Jericho, having heard of the exploits of God on behalf of his people, should have acknowledged these acts instead of resisting God's people. Certainly Rahab must have been prompted by such reports of God's dealings to lead her to give *friendly welcome to the spies*. She does not regard them as enemies, but as agents of God, and this perception is attributed to her faith.[24]

God judges sin and rebellion, yet he gives the chance to repent and turn to him (cf. 2 Pet 3:9). The people of Jericho worshiped false gods and idols and God was determined to destroy the nations around the Israelites (which included Jericho) and bring to the land the true worship of the true God (cf. Deut 12). The people of Jericho heard the message but refused to obey. God's judgment is inevitable and that is why proclamation is so vital. Peoples who live in sin by worshiping false gods and idols and by hardening their hearts to repentance will be judged and die eternally, unless the Gospel, which warns, instructs and saves is proclaimed among them (cf. Rom 6:23a; 2 Thess 1:7-10; 2 Pet 3:7).

Those who respond positively to the light and to the message will receive salvation and they will escape from eternal judgment and death that await them (cf. John 3:16; Rom 10:9-13; 1 Thess 5:9-10). But those who refuse and push the proclaimed message away will be judged and drink from the wrath of God and experience eternal damnation (John 3:36b; Rev 20:11-15). Paul Ellingworth asserts:

> Nothing in the OT account suggests that Jericho was destroyed because of its inhabitants' disobedience or unbelief; the reason is simply that "the Lord has given you [Israel] the city" (Jos. 6:16). Nor does the author of Hebrews draw a direct contrast between Rahab's faith and the other inhabitants' unbelief.[25]

This assertion has two problems. First, Ellingworth overlooks the fact that "the reason is [not] simply [about] the city."[26] Yahweh wanted to give the Israelites the city because the people were not worshiping Yahweh (cf. Lev 18:24-30; Deut 9:1-6; 18:9-13; Ezek 9:11). Yahweh's purpose was not just military conquest so that his people could occupy, control and enjoy the city. The reason was both theological and missiological: theological because God judges those people who do not worship him for who he is, missiological because Yahweh wants the nations including his chosen people to know who he is. Christopher J. H. Wright asserts: "The nations must know their Ruler, Judge and Savior." Yahweh acted as the "Ruler"[27] by guiding his people in the Exodus pilgrimage; he acted as the "Judge"[28] by bringing destruction on those who resisted him and his message; he acted as the "Savior"[29] for Rahab and her family through faith. Yahweh's concern was worship, not just giving a city or a land to his people, because the giving of the city was with a purpose: that Israel as well as the rest of the nations would know who Yahweh is (Lev 20:24).

The second problem with Ellingworth's assertion is related to the first one but more specific. Rahab was saved both physically as well as spiritually because of her faith, whereas the people of Jericho were slaughtered and destroyed because of their "disobedience or unbelief."[30] To begin with, Hebrews 11 talks about people who pleased, trusted and obeyed God. Rahab was one of them. Her faith produced good work, hence, she received the spies into her house (Heb 11:31). As James points out, Rahab's good works, which sprang out of her faith, made her righteous (Jas 2:25). Thus, in view of the whole context of Hebrews 11, faith is characterized by obedience. On the contrary, lack of faith is painted as "disobedience" (Heb 11:31). Therefore, "a direct contrast between Rahab's faith and the other inhabitants' unbelief"[31] is in view. Ralph Martin aptly says, "Rahab [is] a prize example of obedience."[32]

The implication of this is that lack of faith is "disobedience" (Heb 11:31), and this happens when an individual, a group or a people group rejects the proclaimed Word of God. This has eternal consequences: everlasting destruction and hell. Eternal destruction and judgment can only be reversed by responding to the proclaimed message like Rahab. This emphasizes that people must hear the message of Yahweh, the Gospel, in order to escape eternal damnation. This is a prime obligation of the church in any age because proclamation is "the bridge between God and humanity"[33]

As a result, Rahab's inclusion into the people of God can never be an indication of an "implicit" knowledge.[34] On the contrary, Rahab's response to the proclaimed message shows her explicit belief in Yahweh alone. This is seen in her words, "...the LORD your God, he is God in the heavens above and on earth beneath" (Josh 2:11b). It was faith in Yahweh alone that allowed her to be incorporated to God's people; salvation did not come through her old and false religion.

James as well as the writer of Hebrews does not see a distinction between Abraham's faith and Rahab's faith as "Christian" and "believer."[35] On the other hand, they show that both Abraham and Rahab believed "explicitly" in Yahweh and they were considered righteous as a result (cf. Rom 4:1-3; Gal 3:6-8; Heb 11:8-10, 31; Jas 2:21-25). [36] The connecting word "likewise" in James 2:25 draws "a parallel illustration"[37] between Abraham and Rahab, thus she "shared the same faith, the faith that expresses itself in action."[38] Because of this, the assertion that there is "explicit-implicit or ontological-epistemological distinction"[39] must be rejected, for it is not congruent with the teachings of Scripture.

In summary, Rahab escaped death, renounced false gods, did good works, became a worshiper of Yahweh, and saved her family because of her response to the proclamation she heard through the nameless proclaimer. Her life was transformed for the better both temporarily and eternally. Thus proclamation plays a significant role in transforming individuals as well as societies as they respond to the proclaimed message. It helps people to cross "theological and spiritual barriers."[40] That is why proclamation should be the primary task of the people of God.

The Slave Girl and Naaman

Mordechai Cogan and Hayim Tadmore state, "[2 Kings 5] contains more than just another miracle story."[41] Indeed, there is more to the story of the slave girl and Naaman and later Elisha. Syrians used to launch frequent raids on Israel and on one of these raids a little Israelite girl was captured and taken to Syria.[42] Though Naaman was an accomplished person, he had leprosy (2 Kgs 5:1). It created a significant need in Naaman's life; he would do anything to get rid of the leprosy (2 Kgs 5:5-6, 13).

Surprisingly, the slave girl who noticed the need of her master used the opportunity to tell Naaman's wife that there was a man of God who could heal Naaman's leprosy (2 Kgs 5:3). Humanly speaking, she was a little foreigner, a slave whose status was not equal to her master and mistress. Naaman "was a great man," (2 Kgs 5:1) yet he had a problem and was without God. Though the little nameless girl was enslaved, she had the knowledge of God. Considering her status, it is not an exaggeration to label her as extraordinarily bold and wise. Paul R. House notes the difference between her and Naaman: "she is an Israelite, he is an Aramean; she is a little maiden'…, he is a 'great man'…; she is a captive servant, he is a commander; he has fame in the king's estimation,…she has none, for she simply 'waited upon'…Naaman's wife."[43] She was bold in a sense that she was able to witness about God's work through his prophet, Elisha, in Israel. She was not complaining or sad about her situation. On the contrary, she talked about God by mentioning Elisha, the prophet of God. Walter Kaiser asks:

> What was the girl's name? We do not know. Where did she get such advanced theology? Did she not imply that he could heal Gentiles as well? Even one's enemy? And why did she think that Naaman, great as he was, must go and see this prophet in order to be healed? How could she think this when this God had not chosen to release her from her captors? Would this not be an impediment to her faith?[44]

The little slave girl crossed "linguistic, cultural, historical, theological, and spiritual barriers"[45] and told about her God by talking about God's prophet. She put aside her personal problem and condition and focused on communicating her God to the Gentiles. She did not go to Syria because she heard God's call to be his apostle; she was there because she was captured. Yet she was on a mission with God by proclaiming his mighty work. This indicates that Israel was fulfilling her missionary call somewhat involuntarily by proclaiming God's name among the nations, thus indicating a centrifugal mission (cf. Ps 105:1).

Regardless of her status and condition, "she [shared] the knowledge that her master needs most. Power and glory [could not] save Naaman, but this information [could]."[46] This implies that verbal witnessing is essential so that people can meet the Savior; for money, fame, status and success can never bring people to relationship with God. People can and will be saved when they know the Savior and call on his name (cf. Joel 2:32; Acts 4:12; Rom 10:13).

She was wise on how she communicated the saving message. Instead of conveying the report to Naaman directly, she witnessed first to his wife, for "she worked in the service of Naaman's wife" (2 Kgs 5:2b). Knowing that Naaman's wife would relay the information to her husband, the little slave girl used the opportunity to share about the God of Israel. Gina Hens-Piazza describes the little slave girl as "[an] agent of hope"[47] because she [provided] a piece of "decisive advice."[48] The reason why proclamation should be primary and essential is because eternal damnation is a reality.

The first consequence of her bold and wise verbal witnessing can be seen in the immediate response of Naaman. He took the report to the king, got a letter of recommendation from him, and made all the necessary preparations for the trip. In spite of her low status, the little slave girl's witnessing was influential and it went up through the ranks (2 Kgs 5:4).[49] The God of Israel was made known in Syria because of one faithful girl.

The second result of the girl's verbal witness was that Naaman encountered Yahweh through the miracle done unto him in the river of Jordan (2 Kgs 5:8-14). Naaman went to Israel to be healed by Elisha, and Elisha told him through a servant to "wash in the Jordan seven times, and your flesh will be restored to you and you will be clean" (2 Kgs 5:10). The esteemed captain of Syria became indignant and left (2 Kgs 5:11-12). Another wise servant, this time a Syrian servant who knew obedience very well, brought the simplicity of the required obedience to his master, which led Naaman to "[dip] himself seven times in the Jordan, according to the word of the man of God" (2 Kgs 5:14a). As soon as he obeyed, he was healed instantly (2 Kgs 5:14b). What he had heard from the slave girl, he now saw with his own eyes.

Naaman not only received healing from his leprosy but he also confessed, "Behold, I know that there is no God in all the earth but in Israel" (2 Kgs 5:15). His statements include his polytheistic view of gods becoming exclusive. The word "no" depicts that the gods he had known until the time of his healing could not be equal with Yahweh. There is a great shift in his knowledge of the divine, because he states: "Behold, now I know..." (2 Kgs 5:15, KJV). The Gentile received the blessing of salvation. House correctly states "...God desires to bless all nations through Israel. This ideal becomes a reality here due to the witness of the Israelite servant girl and the work of the Israelite prophet."[50]

Proclamation leads to the knowledge of the Savior and brings people into relationship with God, and that in turn results in obedience and true worship. That was what happened to Naaman. The girl witnessed, and as a result, he went to Israel and came to "know" that the God of Israel is the only One who could do mighty works. Now his "conversion...leads to some new commitments on his part."[51] He was transformed by the God of Israel, and "his recalcitrance is replaced by receptivity. Humility replaces anger. Gratitude supplants indignation."[52]

This transformation made him not only confess that the God of Israel was superior, but also that he would worship and devote himself to God alone (2 Kgs 5:17). His genuine conversion was reflected when he asked forgiveness from the Lord that he still had to work under the king of Syria and he might escort the king to the temple of Rimmon (2 Kgs 5:18). This shows that he understood that it was a sin to attach oneself to idols and false gods. Elisha simply said "Go in peace" (2 Kgs 5:19), because "the God who had brought this Gentile to faith, through however fragmentary or fulsome the testimony of the Israelite maiden, was able to bring this Gentile to spiritual growth."[53] Elisha's statement by no means indicates that he wanted Naaman to be a hidden believer, as those who advocate for Insider Movements among Muslims assert.

Proponents of Insider Movements use this passage as a proof text; however, it was obvious to everyone where Naaman went: to seek the prophet of God. The king of Syria, his wife, and the servants that accompanied him knew it all. More precisely, it was the king who wrote him a recommendation letter to ensure his good reception. Second, Naaman's profession of faith in the One True God was done before his servants. So he was not hiding his conversion at all. Third, Naaman clearly displayed an exclusive allegiance to Yahweh alone in his statement "Behold, I know that there is no God in all the earth but in Israel....from now on your servant will not offer burnt offering or sacrifice to any god but the LORD." (2 Kgs 5:15b, 17). Naaman declared that he would cut off his adherence to other gods and would never turn to them again. Fourth, he knew that there was something wrong with associating with other gods, specifically Rimmon. So he asked for forgiveness, for he would physically support his king who worshiped Rimmon by bowing down. But this does not mean Naaman was hiding his faith and bowing to God in his heart while physically bowing to Rimmon. He was only assisting the king of Syria, who was probably old and aged (2 Kgs 5:18).

In summary, the little girl's paradigm has depicted that faithful verbal witnessing in the *kairos* moment and through the proper channel is vital so as to cross barriers and make genuine disciples. It is the primary means to introduce people to the saving grace and knowledge of God. Had this little slave girl been quiet, being silenced by her situation and status, Naaman's wife, Naaman, the king of Syria and the king of Israel would not have heard about the God of Israel. Above all, Naaman would not have been saved. This nameless little girl played a significant role in this Gentile's conversion through verbal witnessing. Ultimately, God was known, was recognized, and received the glory (2 Kgs 5:15).[54]

Peter and Cornelius

Luke gives a convincing illustration to Theophilus as he writes his second evangelistic letter by inserting the story of Cornelius (cf. Luke 1:4; Acts 1:1; 10:1-48). "Cornelius was a Roman centurion and was a God-fearer who was engaged in a regular prayer…and many acts of charity among the needy of the Jewish people."[55] While he was probably praying at the ninth hour, the angel of God appeared to him and told him that his prayer and alms ascended to God (Acts 10:4).

As Peter explained this, "God shows no partiality, but in every nation anyone who fears him and does what is right is acceptable to him (Acts 10:34-35). Here the key word is "acceptable" in verse 35. As William J. Larkin attests, it does not mean Cornelius was saved, for Cornelius was told by the angel "to send for Peter"[56] and hear the Gospel message that would bring salvation (Acts 10:5, 22, 32;

11:13). Larkin continues: "That Cornelius or anyone else can be acceptable to God for salvation without hearing the gospel or confessing the name of Christ contradicts the angel's message and Luke's understanding of the way one comes to salvation through the gospel message (11:14)."[57] John Piper also agrees:

> The story of Cornelius the Gentile centurion could lead some to believe that a man can be saved today apart from knowing the gospel and just by fearing God and doing the good that he can....Acts 10:35 probably does not mean that Cornelius is already saved when it says that people in unreached ethnic groups who fear God and do right are acceptable to God. Cornelius had to hear the gospel message to be saved.[58]

As indicated above, Cornelius had to *hear* the Gospel. The Holy Spirit wanted Peter to be the proclaimer so that Cornelius and his household would be saved and cross theological barriers (Acts 11:14). The Gospel needs to be declared among those who have not yet heard and joined God's people.[59] John Stott also asserts the necessity of hearing the Gospel to be saved:

> [Cornelius the] devout, God-fearing, upright, sincere and generous man still needed to hear the gospel, to repent (11:18) and to believe in Jesus (15:7). Only then did God in his grace (15:1) save him (11:14, 15:11), give him forgiveness of sins (10:43), the gift of the Spirit (10:45; 15:8) and life (11:18), and purify his heart by faith (15:9). Moreover, only then was he baptized and thus visibly and publicly received into the Christian community.[60]

As was the case with Rahab, there is no way that Cornelius could be saved because of his "implicit"[61] knowledge based on the evidence seen in Acts 10-11. He had to hear that Jesus is Lord, that he died and rose and that he would judge both the living and the dead and that there is salvation through him (Acts 10:36-43). Cornelius heard *"salvation accomplished"* and experienced *"salvation applied."*[62] And then God confirms the salvation of Cornelius and his household by giving them the gift of the Holy Spirit as in the day of Pentecost (Acts 10:44-46), followed by water baptism (Acts 10:47-48).

The vital nature and prime importance of proclamation is indicated by employing a literary device called "functional redundancy,"[63] which means the repetition of an event several times, adds more information as the story is retold. The climax and the crux of the story is kept for the last retelling. Acts 11:13-14 narrates the importance of the declaration of the Gospel in the situation of Cornelius and his household coming to saving faith.

As a result, Peter, though reluctantly, crossed "linguistic, cultural, historical, theological, and spiritual barriers"[64] and proclaimed the Gospel. Because of this, Cornelius and his household were incorporated into the family of God. "The Cornelius Principle" is that God can work "pre-evangelistically" in unbelievers to respond to general revelation or some light positively, subsequently receiving more light through a human messenger to explain and declare the full-orbed Gospel in order that the hearers would receive salvation.[65]

Eckhard J. Schnabel points out the primacy of proclamation in the mission of God:

> God uses missionaries as his instrument, people who proclaim the message of Jesus Christ as he directs them....The proclamation of the word of God is of decisive significance in the communication of God's salvation: Peter speaks not about himself and his experiences but rather about God's revelation and action in and through Jesus.[66]

To sum up, the encounter of Cornelius and Peter shows that hearing the Gospel through the human medium is "decisive."[67] It points out that "The mission [of the church] is primarily to make disciples of all nations."[68] Unbelieving individuals or groups need to hear the Gospel and repent by calling the name of the Lord so as to be saved. The Church of Christ needs to proclaim the Gospel faithfully without replacing or shifting her focus from her prime and "decisive"[69] task. In doing so, the Gospel will breach various kinds of obstacles for the glory of God.

Paul with the Epicureans and the Stoics

Paul, having preached and made some converts in Thessalonica and Berea, was forced to leave these two cities and go to Athens (Acts 17:1-15). While he was waiting for Timothy and Silas in Athens, he noticed that "the city was full of idols" (Acts 17:16). None of Athens' glamour attracted or "struck" him.[70] "First and foremost, what he saw was neither the beauty nor the brilliance of the city, but its idolatry."[71] He saw that God was not glorified, but through idol worship Satan was. In order to bring God the glory through true worship, Paul started his preaching and reasoning with the Jews first,[72] then the Gentiles: the Epicureans and the Stoics.

He knew the only way to address the idol issue was by proclaiming "Jesus and the resurrection" (17:18). As a result, the people to whom he was preaching took him to the Areopagus to hear more from him (17:19). Paul presented a contextual Gospel through his proclamation in order to bring his audiences to the knowledge of Christ. He wanted them to cross every barrier that hindered their understanding of the Gospel.

The Epicureans "had a materialist metaphysics"[73] and believed "the gods to be so remote as to take no interest in, and have no influence on, human affairs."[74] Therefore, "the concept of bodily resurrection [was] laughable"[75] for them, whereas the Stoics were "materialist Pantheist, [who] identified the divine as the principle of reason pervading all and, in the form of fate governing all."[76] Their "eschatology was cyclic."[77] They also "[emphasized] fatalism, submission and the endurance of pain."[78] Paul had two different audiences who emphasized two different belief systems. Yet he proclaimed Christ in a proper way to both.

Before addressing each group's worldview, he made sure that they both understood that God "does not live in temples made by man," (v. 23) which is an ingenious assertion to keep the Gospel's "integrity and [separate] it from Stoic and Epicurean thought."[79] Paul understood that it would help avoid "syncretization,"[80] because he knew that they perceived that he was talking about "foreign divinities" (v. 18).[81] Interestingly, Paul seemed to use Old Testament background when talking to his pagan audiences (cf. Deut 4:32-39; Isa 45:56).[82] He also stated that God is the one who made everything (cf. Ps 146:6; Isa 42:5).[83]

The Epicureans, who "[emphasized] chance,"[84] heard that everything did not come by "chance,"[85] but from God. The Stoics who emphasized cultural homogeneity heard that God created various nations from one man (v. 26).[86] Again, the Stoics were challenged through Paul's proclamation that their understanding of "God within,"[87] that is, humanity should seek God and realize that the Pantheist understanding of God within is incorrect.[88]

The Epicurean worldview that God was distant and unconcerned with humanity was also challenged when Paul said, "he is actually not far from each one of us" (v. 27) and he in fact cares for humanity (v. 25). He then quoted their own poets and affirmed their understanding as correct (v. 28) that God is the Father of humanity.[89] Thus, he proclaimed that God can be known; he is concerned and involved in everyday life and he is personal. Then he called for repentance, because God "will judge the world" through Jesus whom he "raised...from the dead" (v. 31). "Paul's missionary preaching to Gentile audiences concentrates on the proclamation of repentance and forgiveness which flows from the resurrection."[90] Paul's proclamation included "both the warning of judgment and the promise of salvation blessings."[91]

His proclamation resulted in having three kinds of responses: those who rejected the claims of Paul with regard to "the resurrection of the dead" by mocking (v. 32a), those who became interested to hear more from Paul (v. 32b), and those who "joined him and believed" (v. 34).[92] His responsibility was to proclaim the truth in a relevant and contextual manner, yet it was new for them, for they said: "May we know what this new teaching is that you are presenting?" (v.19). He did not shy away from stating the truth of the Gospel.[93]

While he could have engaged the Epicureans and the Stoics in a religious dialogue that promoted tolerance by avoiding assertive religious absolutes and dogmas, he did not. He did quote some of their poets, but he did not spend that much time searching for "common ground"[94] or taking the "similarity approach."[95] In fact, Paul's audience noticed that he was talking about "foreign divinities" (v. 18). He was not preoccupied in "...discovering redemptive analogies and what [Don Richardson] calls 'eye-openers'...that will enable non-Christian peoples to understand the gospel."[96] Instead, he preached "Jesus and the resurrection" (v. 18) from the outset. Religious dialogue without a call to repentance is meaningless and unscriptural.[97] As David Hesselgrave notes, "It seems safe to conclude that interreligious dialogue is a questionable means of establishing common ground."[98] After all, the reason biblical Christianity emphasizes evangelization of people from other religions is because it asserts that the people from other religions are lost. Thus it exclusively claims and also presupposes that biblical Christianity is the only true religion and others are false, for biblical Christianity[99] offers *the* way to God *through* Christ.

Paul has shown that proclamation or verbal witnessing is primal in order to bring people from "ignorance" (v. 30) to the knowledge of God so that they repent and cross over from death to life (cf. John 5:24). Though he respected and acknowledged their culture and religiosity, he did not hesitate to confront their idol-saturated worldview and lifestyle. He did not tolerate the rampant idol making and worshiping customs; instead, he preached Jesus, the resurrection, God's judgment and salvation blessings. Consequently, they all heard the Gospel through special revelation and some believed. Here Paul crossed "linguistic, cultural, historical, theological, and spiritual barriers"[100] and made disciples.

Implications for the Ethiopian Context

Rahab's transformation shows us that as the Gospel is preached, it has the power to change lives. The Ethiopian Protestant Church has been faithfully preaching the Gospel and as a result, many were able to embrace the Gospel. Many, especially in the Southern part of Ethiopia, renounced their false gods and false worship. Yet there are a number of Rahabs who are marginalized and who are living for the god of sex. The church needs to engage prostitutes in Bole, Merkato, 22 Mazoria, and Megenagna areas. Being a prostitute is a serious cultural taboo, and as a result, prostitutes in Addis are pushed to the periphery of society. The Church should come out of her comfort zone and engage these lady outcasts with the Message of the Gospel so that they could cross spiritual, cultural and social barriers. As we have seen in Rahab's life, the Gospel has the power to renew, change, and transform anyone who responds positively to the proclaimed Gospel. In order to avoid temptations and Satan's trap of sexual immorality, the Ethiopian Evangelical Church can train female evangelists who understand the world of these prostitutes and send them to preach the Gospel.[101]

The other area in which the Ethiopian Evangelical Church needs to be intentional and proactive is equipping those Christian females who are emigrating for domestic work to the Arab World. There are hundreds of thousands of female Ethiopians in the Arab World who are involved mostly in domestic work, and there are also a few who are involved in the import and export business. Though they were not taken as captives like the little slave girl from Israel, the economic, social and personal pressures have forced most to leave the country. Despite the problems, Christian female workers can use this opportunity to reach Arab women in the houses where they work. Typically it is difficult for missionaries to spend time with Muslim women in the Arab World, yet there is an ample opportunity for Ethiopian Christian domestic workers to share Christ passively (Col. 4:6) and also with words as opportunities arise, as the little Israelite girl did with Naaman and his wife. The Ethiopian Church both in Ethiopia as well as in the Arab World needs to encourage these young Christian female workers to be bold, wise and intentional.

The Ethiopian church could learn from this little girl that even though she was not a prophet, a priest or a clergy per se, she used the ample opportunity and her God given platform to communicate about God's prophet and what God would do through him. In other words, the church should cease the false dichotomy or polarization that witnessing or proclamation is for "fulltime" ministers and that the rest of us are spectators. The little slave girl's intentionality should burn in the long term memory of the Ethiopian evangelical church so that it makes clear to its members that the mission of God belongs to the whole church and all of us are called to be witnesses in our God given contexts.[102]

The story of Peter and Cornelius urges the Ethiopian Church to do a cross-cultural ministry within Ethiopia. Ethiopia has currently more than eighty million people, of which only 18% are evangelical believers. The country has 33 unreached people groups, most of which are tribal Muslim-Animist peoples. In some areas, the church is plagued with tribalism and ethnocentrism which put a cultural barrier between various tribes. As a result, the same churches are tribe-based, lacking a cross-cultural motivation for mission.[103] Like Peter, most church members are reluctant to engage and serve people groups who are different from them.

The other reason the churches are not engaging these people groups is that they are in remote, undeveloped rural areas. Evangelists and preachers do not want to go to such areas, for they are not as "civilized" as Addis Ababa or Hawassa. Though urban ministry is essential in Ethiopia, it is also imperative to focus on rural area, for that is where 84% of the population lives. The mass exodus of ministers from villages is affecting the expansion of the Gospel in rural areas.

The Church needs to cross cultural, tribal and economic barriers in order to introduce the lost people groups of Ethiopia to the King of Kings. Ethnocentrism, tribalism, pursuing fame, "civilization," and prosperity are slowing the progress of the Gospel in Ethiopia. The church must fight these distractions and fulfill the Great Commission unflinchingly. The Oromo Christian tribe should put their historical scars behind them by the power of the Holy Spirit and cross every barrier to share the Gospel with the Amhara tribe; the Gurage tribe should engage the Sidama or Wolayta tribe with the Gospel of Christ. In doing so, the Gospel will run unhindered, and all people groups in Ethiopia will hear the Gospel, and lives will be transformed. When Jesus alone is worshiped and glorified and not angels, demons, or people, the lost people groups in Ethiopia will experience salvation blessings.

The evangelical church in Ethiopia should also engage those who affiliate with the Coptic Church (EOC) and claim to hold to the tradition of the church but who do not have a personal relationship with Christ. This is not to say that no EOC members are believers. There are some who have placed their faith in Jesus Christ and who are following him wholeheartedly, but by and large, most Copts in Ethiopia believe that salvation can be earned through good works, prayer, and almsgiving. Some, if not all, are truly seeking God in this way. As it has been shown in Cornelius' story, salvation cannot come even through sincere good works. It seems that many Copts are responding to the preevangelistic light that they see, so the Church needs to proclaim, explain, and offer salvation blessings to these God-fearing Copts in Ethiopia, thereby providing them with more light. The Evangelical Church, instead of looking down on them, should associate with them and gently explain the truth as Peter did. In so doing, many can and will come to the saving knowledge of the Gospel.[104]

The other area the Evangelical Church of Ethiopia needs to engage with the Gospel is the universities. The two big university student movements – Great Commission Ministry Ethiopia (Cru) and the Evangelical Students' and Graduates' Union of Ethiopia (EvaSUE) – have been playing a significant role in the lives of university students throughout the country. Thousands of students have come to the Lord through these ministries, yet the Church as a whole seems to be one step behind in engaging the Ethiopian intellectuals.

Most students are exposed to various ideas, worldviews and religions through their education, their personal reading and their interactions with various people. The Ethiopian

Evangelical Church needs many more Pauls who understand the students' philosophical, intellectual, theological and sociological world and who can engage and mentor them with the Gospel. The diverse worldviews and intellectual orientations on campus call the Ethiopian Church to assert and proclaim Christ in a relevant way so as to impact the students. It is recent history how the church during the period of the communist regime reached as well as nurtured the youth in the universities that enabled the students to withstand the ideology of Marxism and Leninism. Some leaders of the church, like Gudina Tumsa, understood "that the battle for souls was going to be fought in the hearts of young Ethiopians."[105] He strove to assist them "to be fully armed in every possible way to stand firm in the face of the growing influence of atheism and to provide aggressive testimonies of their Christian faith in word and deed."[106] By the same token, the evangelical church should catch the same vision to reach, equip and send the students to their own friends and beyond by understanding their current intellectual milieu, which includes postmodernism and the relation between faith and science to name two. One strategy the church could employ is technology. Most university students spend much of their time on computers, iPhones, or iPads. Thus, the Church should use this opportunity to share the Gospel through the internet. Recent initiatives like Global Media Outreach and Habeshastudent.com (in Amharic) should be encouraged and supported so long as they address issues with which Ethiopian university students grapple.[107]

Part I:

Crossing Linguistic Barriers

for the Great Commission

CHAPTER TWO

Bible Translation in Ethiopia: Theological and Missiological Impact

Introduction

This chapter will demonstrate how Bible translations in Ethiopia into vernacular languages have made a decisive impact on the theological landscape and on the missiological understanding and praxis of the Ethiopian churches by crossing linguistic barriers.

The theological impact of Bible translation in Ethiopia will overview the church's fresh and biblically informed understanding of Christ as the high priest, God-Man, and unique mediator. The priesthood of the believer– which explains Christians' practice of directly accessing God through prayer, personal Bible reading and the asking of forgiveness for actual sins committed by individuals without going through a mediating priest at a local church, and also the nature of worship without centering on the *tabot* (the ark) as seen in the Old Testament but centering on Christ and the Holy Spirit.

Regarding missiological understanding and praxis, this chapter will articulate how bible translation reawakened the urgency and the mandate for mission. The chapter will also depict how this missiological understanding assisted in defending and proclaiming the gospel message in the face of severe persecution in the Ethiopian church throughout history. Besides this, another discussion will be included of how the vernacular Bible in Ethiopia informed and enabled Christians to contextualize, interpret and deliver the gospel message stripped of the unnecessary garb of a Western hermeneutical grid which is plagued by rationalism and the excluded middle.

Before embarking on the discussion of the theological and missiological impacts of Bible translation in Ethiopia, it is both appropriate and necessary to give an overview of the history of Bible translation in Ethiopia.

Overview of the History of Bible Translation in Ethiopia

The specific timeline of the introduction of Christianity into the territory of Ethiopia has been a matter of difficulty for scholars.[108] Some associate the coming of the Gospel to Ethiopia through the Ethiopian eunuch,[109] and some others through Apostle Matthew, and others with more force and evidence associate the time with Frumentius (*Abba* Selama) and Aedesius, who were captured at the Red Sea after their ship encountered catastrophe in the 4th century.[110] Henceforth, Christianity began to spread throughout Ethiopia under the patronage of the Aksumite kings and through monasticism, especially through the Nine Saints (*Tsadiqan*) and through the apostolic authority of the Alexandrian Church as well.[111] "Christian merchants" also played a significant role in propagating the Christian faith in Ethiopia as Frumentius had urged and encouraged them to do so.[112] Christianity became a state religion and Ethiopian kings oversaw and took responsibility in propagating, developing, and at times defending the religion throughout the country by any means[113] until King Haile Selassie, the last king from the line of the Solomonic dynasty, was deposed by the Communist regime. Thus, the "throne-altar and crown-clergy relationship" ended.[114]

Tibebe Eshete, however, asserts that before organized Christian religion came to Ethiopia, the Christian faith was already in the country.[115] Though King Ezana promulgated the Christian faith as the state religion of his kingdom, Christianity was already introduced through "merchants [who] transacted, settled and commingled with the local people, thereby forming communities of believers in major urban cities, such as Axum and Adulis."[116]

Bible Translation into Ge'ez

Another area scholars debate regarding the Christian religion in Ethiopia is the time "when the Scriptures were translated into Ge'ez, by whom, from what language or languages, and which versions at what period sponsored a series [of] versions and corrections."[117] It is asserted that the Greek language was spoken in Ethiopia before the third century, but later Ge'ez took its place.[118] As a result, many scholars believe that the Ge'ez (Ethiopic) Bible was rendered from the Greek Septuagint. But others believe that not only the Greek version but also the Hebrew and Syriac texts were employed in the translation process.[119] *Abba* Selama (Frumentius) is considered to be the one who began the translation of the Bible into Ge'ez immediately after the conversion of King Ezana.[120] The process was then continued by the Nine Saints.[121]

The time of the completion of the first Ge'ez Bible varies and scholars put it between the middle of the fourth century and the middle of the seventh century.[122] Later in the Middle Ages, the Ge'ez Bible was revised based on the Arabic and Hebrew texts by *Abba* Selama "'the Translator'" as opposed to *Abba* Selama "the Illuminator" (Frumentius).[123] However, some argue that the Septuagint was also used in revising the Ge'ez Bible in this period.[124] With regard to specific books of the Bible in Ge'ez, the book of Psalms[125] and the Gospel of Matthew were popular. It appears that *Abba* Libanos translated the Gospel of Matthew into Ge'ez.[126] The Psalter has been the most favored and famous book of the Bible in the history of Ethiopia; in-depth research is needed to probe its historical, theological as well as missiological impact on the Ethiopian Church.[127]

Bible Translation into Amharic

Peter Heyling, the ephemeral German missionary to Ethiopia, translated "the Gospel of John in[to] Amharic."[128] Afterward, the Gospels were translated in 1824 and they were available for distribution by the CMS missionaries in Ethiopia.[129] Martin Flad, a missionary to the *Bete* Israel (Felashas) and many other Western missionaries tried to reach Ethiopians by translating Scriptures into Amharic, for the Ge'ez had become foreign and incomprehensible to many.[130] Abu Rumi, otherwise known as Abraham, translated the Amharic Bible for the first time in 1840 in its entirety.[131] Johann Krapf, along with Mikael Aragawi, revised Abu Rumi's translation, which later played a significant role in the Ethiopian church.[132] It was the Amharic Bible translated by Abu Rumi that "elicited widespread interest in reading the Holy Scriptures and eventually led to the formation of an Evangelical church."[133] In 1930, Emperor Haile Sellasie ordered another translation of the Bible into Amharic. Eshete states:

> The Emperor was wise enough to appreciate the fact that the Bible, or versions of it so far translated into Amharic, had not been accepted by the priests, who looked down on it as the product of foreigners....The emperor [as a result], organized a team of scholars, composed of twelve Ethiopians and six expatriates with scholarly and technical expertise, to translate the Bible into Amharic.[134]

The emperor went so far as to purchase a printer for the success of the translation. Nevertheless, "the Italo-Abyssinian war broke out and the work was held up indefinitely."[135] This translation was eventually completed and published, first the New Testament in 1955 and then the whole Bible, in 1962.[136] Since then, the Amharic Study Bible was translated from the NIV in 2001.

Bible Translation into Tigriña[137]

Yet another vernacular language which the whole Bible was translated into was Tigriña.[138] But before the appearance of the whole Bible in Tigriña in 1956,

> St. Mark and St. John [were translated] by Nathaniel Pearce who had accompanied Henry Salt and lived in Ethiopia from 1805 to 1819. His rendering was written 'in English characters' and conforms with the notions of traditional English spelling.[139]

Other Tigriña portions of Scriptures also appeared in later years. For instance, "the rendering of St. John's Gospel commissioned, in 1830s, by Samuel Gobat... [which consisted] of 140 pages"[140] appeared simultaneously with "the four Gospels [that would be] translated by Däbtära Matewos of Adwa."[141]

Spencer J. Trimingham also mentions that "Psalms and Isaiah were printed in 1949" in Tigriña. The tireless Bible translator of the Swedish Evangelical Mission, "Mrs. Elsie Winquist, [was] engaged at the age of 86 in the revision of the Old Testament" including the former two portions.[142]

Bible Translation into Afan Oromo

The Gospel of Matthew and the first five chapters of the Gospel of John were the first Afan Oromo translations.[143] Johann Krapf believed that reaching the Oromo people was decisive in reaching the continent of Africa; thus he devoted himself to bringing this vision to realization through translating the Scripture into Afan Oromo.[144] Ruufo, a trilingual Ethiopian, also assisted Krapf in the translation project. Ruufo translated "the Acts of the Apostles and Paul's Epistles to the Romans."[145] Together with Krapf, he then translated "the Gospel of Luke in Oromo,"[146] and continued assisting "in revising [Krapf's] twenty-year-old Oromo translations of the Gospel of Matthew and several chapters of John."[147] Simultaneously, Zännäb, also known as Johannes Meier, "translated the New Testament" into [Afan Oromo]" along with an Oromo speaking Ethiopian called Waaree.[148]

Another former slave, Hiikaa, otherwise known as Onesimos Nesib, would translate "the first complete Bible into the Oromo vernacular language in 1899 using the Sabean/Ethiopic."[149] However, this frontline evangelist did not translate the Bible into Afan Oromo by himself. An evangelist and a compiler of the Afan Oromo dictionary, Aster Ganno, helped greatly in the completion of the Oromo Bible translation project.[150]

Bible Translation into Other Ethiopian Vernaculars

Though the Amharic Bible was available in some parts of Ethiopia, some found it difficult to read and comprehend the Amharic texts since it was not their mother tongue.[151] Though there are many other tribal languages in Ethiopia, the Ethiopian government declared that "all literature printed and published in the country [was] to be done in Amharic language…to unify the country and peoples by the use of one official language."[152] As a result, it was an arduous task to obtain Scripture in other tribal languages. For instance, the Gospel of John was available in Wolaitta, which was translated by Walter Ohman.[153] He also translated the Gospel of Mark into a dialect of Wolaitta called Gofa,[154] which "was often laboriously copied out by hand – costing in this form a considerable sum of money."[155] Duff and Couser Clarence were also able to translate portions of Scripture into the Hadiya language.[156]

The Communist regime (the Derg) issued a decree that gave an opportunity for "minority languages" to be ennobled so that speakers of those languages would back up its socialistic ideology.[157] SIM took the opportunity "to translate selected portions of the Bible into seven local languages"[158] that are spoken mainly in the southern parts of Ethiopia.[159] Trimingham points out that there were portions of the Bible, specifically the Gospels, which were translated into Sidama, Gudeila, Somali (the four Gospels), and Agaw/Quara (the Gospel of Mark).[160] Paul Balisky lists some of the vernaculars that have the Bible in Ethiopia:

> Full Bibles are now available in Wolaitta and Chaha Gurage. New Testaments are available in Aari, Bench, Burji, Kafa, Maali, Arsi, and Sidama. Work on the New Testament is in progress in Basketo, Kullo Konta, Hamer/Bunna, Koyra, Me'en, and Mursi. And full Bible translation projects are under way in Aari, Gamo, Gofa, Kafa, Maali, Arsi, and Sidama.[161]

The Theological Impact of Bible Translation in Ethiopia

The Bible appearing in various Ethiopian vernaculars has brought about unprecedented impact on the theological understanding, reflection and expression of Ethiopian Christians. Christ, the Priesthood of the believer and the nature of worship are the main areas where Bible translation has impacted the church's theology.

Christology

The Ethiopian Orthodox *Tewahedo* Church (EOTC) has historically held and continues to hold one nature Christology, otherwise known as monophysite or "*miaphysis*," that is, a "'composite of unity'...[which] emphasize[s] that Christ's deity and humanity preserved their essential attributes in the union of the two natures."[162] Though EOTC theologians stress the existence of the two natures, Steve Strauss shows that the lay members of the EOTC overemphasize the one nature of Christ:

> Christ's humanity was transformed by his deity; his humanity became a divine humanity. The EOTC believes that only by means of an absolute unity that made every part of Christ's person divine could deity die and so bring divine salvation to humanity…Though they maintain that 'neither of the natures was assimilated by the other,' they also insist that his "flesh was made divine' so that every part of Christ's person would be God, enabling him to provide perfect salvation for the whole world.[163]

Thus, the EOTC falls into the category of the Alexandrian school of theology that overemphasized Christ's divinity. Bryant M. Litfin states:

> The Christological tendency at Alexandria was to think of the Logos as so all-encompassing that Jesus, the earthly man, basically disappeared. In its most extreme form, the Alexandrian theology did not even consider Jesus to be a true man at all. He was not exactly like us in every way. Rather, he had a special kind of super-soul which ruled the body with complete mastery. The Alexandrians were so keen to elevate the heavenly, other-worldly aspect of the Logos that they often disregarded or downplayed Jesus' earthly life [humanity]. To them he was a great mystical power, totally in control all the time – not a man who truly suffered and felt weakness, a man with whom we can identify.[164]

Since the EOTC was theologically as well as ecclesiastically connected with the Alexandrian Church, it naturally reflects the Alexandrian theological position with regard to Christ.[165] Steve Strauss' findings indicate that,

"Ethiopian theologians and laypeople [of the EOTC] sometimes make statements that seem to indicate that Christ's deity so absorbed his humanity that his humanity was distinctly different from that of other people."[166] The EOTC staunchly held the monophysite doctrine declaring "Christ was *from* two natures which effected a perfect union (Ge'ez, Tewahedo)."[167] The reasons the EOTC gives for holding a monophysite Christology are, first, that Chalcedonian Christology seems to threaten "the salvific effectiveness of Christ's death"[168] by "elevat[ing] the humanity of Christ at the expense of his deity, the ultimate concerns of the EOC's non-Chalcedonian Christology."[169] Second, they say that Chalcedonian Christology, according to the EOTC, suggests "a degree of subordination in the persons of the Holy Trinity, and, moreover, tended to open the way for a continuing distinction between the divine and human natures in Christ."[170] Both Protestant and Catholic missionaries holding the Chalcedonian Christological position that stressed Christ's two natures in one person, came to Ethiopia in various periods and challenged especially the EOTC "in the mid-sixteenth century."[171]

European missionaries were adamant in asserting the Chalcedonian Christology. Yet they focused on emphasizing the humanity of Christ, which made them fall under the Antiochene School of theology. Even today, Westerners emphasize and overemphasize the humanness of Christ. This makes them functional monophysites, though of a different type than their Ethiopian counterparts. In other words, though Western theologians and missionaries affirm the Chalcedonian Creed stating that Christ is the God-Man, in their actual theological expression – in hymns, preaching, teaching and articulation of the atonement – they "[overemphasize] Christ's humanity."[172] This is what it means to be a functional monophysite.

It is at this juncture that the Scripture translated into the Ethiopian vernaculars played a decisive role. The Evangelical Christians of Ethiopia, wanting another option besides the Christology of the EOTC and the Christology of the Western missionaries, used their Bibles to develop a nuanced and balanced Christology indigenous to the Ethiopian context.[173] This represented a monumental shift: the Ethiopian Evangelicals, now equipped with Scriptures in their language, could read, reflect and theologize on the biblical teachings of Christ. They indeed benefitted by taking advantage of the two Christological positions which they had been placed in between – examining the strengths and weaknesses of each in the process of developing their own interpretation.

It is common for Ethiopian Evangelicals to declare "*Iyesous Geta new*! (Jesus is Lord!)," emphasizing Jesus' divinity, his victory over death, sin and the devil, and over any difficulty they face, through their songs, preaching, witnessing and prayers. They also emphasize Christ's mediation and high priesthood with regard to salvation. Strauss observes:

> [I]n the Ethiopian context, overemphasis on the deity of Christ at the expense of his humanity has led to the strong sense that other mediators are necessary to approach God. Several subjects even linked the importance of approaching God through saints and angels to the fact that Christ was not only fully human.[174]

The Ethiopian Evangelicals have corrected this by their fresh understanding of Christ using their Bible. This has led them to largely affirm what the Western missionaries have taught regarding Christ as penal substitute.

The Ethiopian Evangelicals as well as some EOTC members "stressed personal salvation centered on faith [in Christ] and grace rather than work."[175] The translated

Scriptures enabled many to reject Mary's and saints' mediation as well as "practices such as *tezkar* [commemoration of the dead] and a Mass for the dead, believed by the Orthodox Church to have the power of redeeming someone from *seol* [Sheol]."[176] The Bible informed, corrected and assisted a number of Ethiopians to believe "that it is only the work of Christ that provides complete redemption and a guarantee to heaven."[177]

Priesthood of the Believer

An understanding of Christ as God-Man, Mediator and High Priest played an indelible role in the understanding of the place of born again individuals before God. Ethiopians who have encountered Christ and embraced salvation through Christ's sacrificial-victorious work have made a great leap forward in their orthodoxy as well as orthopraxy.

The Ethiopian Evangelicals, who formerly belonged to the EOTC, as well as those from a Muslim and Animist background, have used the opportunity of the translated Bibles to critically reflect on their belief as a result of their personal Bible readings in Amharic, Afan Oromo and other vernacular languages.[178] Just as it did during the Protestant Reformation in Europe, the Bible in the vernacular allowed Ethiopians to engage in grassroots level, lay hermeneutics.[179] The EOTC, like the Catholics of Europe, discouraged the reading of the Bible by lay people, because "the bible contained things difficult to understand, left only to the priests, teachers in whom Christ dwelled, who had received the Holy Spirit, and who had been appointed in place of the Apostles. Christians were henceforth deterred from reading and interpreting the Scriptures by themselves."[180] In addition to this, "[A]ll services [in the EOTC] had for centuries been completely unintelligible to the ordinary people and the ancient language [Ge'ez] had become vested with a kind of sanctity."[181] But Bible translations into the vernaculars went against the tradition and shook the theology of the EOTC that was taught for centuries: that people had to go through the clergy of the church to reach God. As F. Peter Cotterell states, with the advent of God's Word into the vernaculars, "The Bible became an open book. The hold which the thousands of often ill-educated priests [of the EOTC] had had on the people began to loosen."[182]

This has given the lay members of the EOTC and other Christians the opportunity to read their Bibles and obey what they read,[183] "apply[ing] it [to] their daily life situations."[184] They were also able to instruct others without the mediation of a member of the clergy from the EOTC.[185] What John Mbiti asserts regarding the ownership of the Bible by Africans can be vividly seen in Ethiopia today: "They now have full access to the word of God. Now God speaks their language – and the Bible is now their Bible. They are at last freed to take it seriously and apply it in ways they understand."[186] The late Kwame Bediako was also right when he stated that "the existence of vernacular Bibles not only facilitates access to the particular communities speaking those languages, but also creates the likelihood that hearers of the Word in their own languages will make their own response to it and on their own terms."[187]

The translated Bible also played an invaluable role in helping Ethiopians understand that they could have direct access to God through prayer as well as through Bible reading. This was a veritable fact especially among the Ethiopian youth who were frustrated with the traditional church.[188] Eshete notes that, "[The youth] read voraciously from the Bible about [the Holy Spirit] and ceaselessly prayed that they might experience the power of God....they desired to experience God directly, personally, and more powerfully."[189]

In the EOTC, "When the faithful fall into sin, they go to a priest when he is alone and tell him the sins they committed, all that they have done whether great or little, and the priest, considering the number of their sins, whether a large number or a small, gives them a penance; this penance is fasting, prayer, prostrations or alms."[190] This is not inherently wrong, for it is committing to restitution for a sin committed. Yet the theological problem found in such a case is that the sinner cannot ask God for forgiveness directly; it is the priest who has the power to "absolve" so that the sinner could be forgiven.[191] Nevertheless, the reality of the "open book"[192] has brought a clear grasp of the priesthood of the believer, encouraging Ethiopians to approach God for mercy and forgiveness without a middle man, because of Christ, their great High Priest.

Worship: "Tabot-Centred" Versus Christ-Centered

In order to understand the impact of Bible translation, it is vital to look at how the Old Testament has influenced the liturgy and worship of the EOTC as well as the Evangelical Church of Ethiopia. The Hebrew Bible has a great place in Africa.[193] In Ethiopia this is crystal clear.[194] As a result, the Old Testament has impacted the liturgy and worship of the EOTC as well as the Evangelical Church of Ethiopia. Scholars estimated that it is probable that the Hebrew Bible (probably the Septuagint) had already impacted Ethiopia before the arrival of institutionalized Christianity with Frumentius and Aedesius.[195] Then the translation of the Hebrew Bible into Ge'ez/Ethiopic strengthened its impact on theology and missiology.[196]

Kebra Nagast (The Glory of Kings) "recounts the story of how the ark of the covenant [sic] was brought from Jerusalem to Ethiopia."[197] As a result of this document, the kings viewed Ethiopia as the New Jerusalem which connected the bloodline of the Ethiopian kings to the Solomonic Dynasty.[198] Edward Ullendorf states that "the concept and function of the *tabot* represent one of the most remarkable areas of agreement with Old Testament forms of worship."[199]

"[T]abot-centered worship"[200] is still prominent in the liturgy of the EOTC. In fact, there are forty-four *tabotat* (arks).[201] Ullendorf notes that,

> [T]he genuine Ark is supposed to rest at Aksum; all other churches can only possess replicas. In most cases they were not, however, replicas of the whole ark but merely of its supposed contents, i.e. the tablets of the Law or the covenant….The veneration accorded to the *tabot* in Abyssinia up to the present day, it's carriage in solemn procession accompanied by singing, dancing, beating of staffs or praying sticks…, rattling of sistra, and sounding of other musical instruments remind one most forcefully of the scene in 2 Samuel 6:5, 14-16, where David and the people are dancing around the Ark.[202]

But this long held tradition that centers and revolves around "*tabot*-centered worship"[203] would not go unchallenged. As Ethiopians started reading their Bibles and found out that the other half of the Bible (the New Testament) gives flesh and bone to the shadow, they started to confront, challenge, and correct the object of worship. This would be one of the dividing theological issues that came into existence between the EOTC and the Evangelical Church of Ethiopia.[204] Some EOTC members shifted their focus of worship to Jesus and began closely resembling the Evangelical Christians in terms of Christology, but the majority remained staunchly opposed to this theological shift.

The place of the New Testament in Evangelical circles and its interpretation and appropriation have enabled the

Evangelical Church to point out that the *tabot* was a shadow pointing to the Messiah, and its fulfillment is seen and taught in the God-Man Christ. Thus the Gospels and the Epistles, especially the Book of Hebrews, would play a major role in correcting the focus of worship of the EOTC.

The Missiological Impact of Bible Translation in Ethiopia

As seen above, the Bible in the vernaculars have allowed the Ethiopian churches (both the EOTC and the Evangelical churches) to grasp the proper theological teachings of Scripture. This in turn would affect the missiological understanding and practices of the Ethiopian Christians for the better.

Persecution

The new theological understanding of the Ethiopians was not received well by the kings, clergy and adherents of the EOTC nor by politicians. The EOTC felt threatened and betrayed when its long held tradition with regard to Scripture reading by the laity was shaken. As seen earlier, the EOTC strongly asserted:

> Those who have authority to interpret the Holy Bible and to take out of it the ordinances of the Church are priests, doctors and teachers who have received the Holy Spirit, in whom Christ dwells who have been approved in the place of the Apostles who Christ appointed in the place of the Apostles who Christ appointed with the words, 'Go round all the world and teach,' who succeed one another until the Advent.[205]

The clergy's authority was undermined when people started to read, interpret and apply the word for themselves. Cotterell states that, "The persecution has invariably originated from the hostility and suspicion of the Orthodox Church....Tragically, instead of recognizing the immediate need for reform, the Orthodox Church persecuted the new Christians."[206] The brief Italian occupation of the country also created antagonism toward Protestantism; both because Protestantism was linked to countries like Britain and America and also because Italy wanted Catholicism to spread.

Even as little as eight pages in some areas of the vernacular Bibles helped "believers through the times of persecution."[207] The Church endured public ridicule by turning to their Bible, reading it and defending the truth.[208] But in some areas the EOTC members "burnt Scriptures"[209] because they considered the Bible of the Evangelicals to be altered and twisted. Indeed, the Orthodox and Evangelical Scriptures are different in a way, "for the Orthodox the books of the Bible number 81, including the Apocryphal books, known as [the Book of Canon], while Protestants accept only 66."[210]

Tsega Endalew also notes that the Protestants' view of the Bible and their Bible-centered teaching made them susceptible to persecution in Ethiopia.[211] But the Evangelical church stood firm in the storm of persecution, for it was equipped with God's Word. When Marxism-Leninism became prevalent in Ethiopia, it was the Bible that sustained university students to withstand the Communist anti-Christ and anti-God propaganda.[212] The defense of the Gospel was also carried out by evangelical singers. These "songs were virtually taken from the Bible and became a source of great encouragement for Christians under stress."[213] Consequently, the church was able to resist the pervasive indoctrination, persecution and oppression of the Communist government. Eshete notes:

> The Church became one of the biggest roadblocks to the creation of 'socialist man' and a 'socialist culture' that sought to stress that evangelical Christianity places on the new birth experience was a challenge to the socialist metaphor of a 'new man.'[214]

"The Gospel for Ethiopians by Ethiopians"[215]

The positive side of the persecution both during the Italian occupation as well as during the Communist regime was that it brought an Evangelical unity which could not be achieved in the presence of the missionaries.[216] This period also allowed "the Ethiopian evangelical churches to emerge as indigenous."[217] The unity of the Evangelical church coupled with the reawakened passion to reach the nation of Ethiopians with God's Word in their language facilitated for the expansion of Evangelical Christianity. The Gospel spread like a wildfire in the country through "local missionary-evangelists who traveled far and wide, cutting across various tribal groupings to preach the gospel to diverse communities, supported by their local congregations."[218] The EOTC emphasized that the preaching of the Gospel should be done by priests;[219] now the Evangelicals would defy that since they grasped that the Great Commission was the task of the whole body of Christ. Most of the local missionaries were "farmers."[220] The translated Bible in the hands of the lay people had become "an effective tool to transmit the gospel to the Ethiopian people at large."[221]

The vernacular Bibles were instrumental in equipping Ethiopians to fulfill God's mandate by conveying the message of Christ. Eshete observes: "The Ethiopians wanted to share their newly embraced religious convictions with the rest of Ethiopia."[222] Indigenous missions were already in play. For instance, the Mulu Wongel Church

> set a new precedent of being a national mission-sending agent independent of any foreign financial assistance....the Pentecostals expanded their sphere of missionary activities....They accomplished this by

mobilizing local missionaries, mostly men and women serving as government employees in different parts of Ethiopia, and by organizing self-support revivalist meetings.[223]

Contextualization

The persecution periods also provided enough time for Ethiopians to contextualize the Bible and its message independent of the missionaries. In some areas, "the only Scripture they had was a copy of the translation of the Gospel of Mark."[224] Even with only one portion of the Bible in the Wolaitta area, the church exploded with thousands of converts. The reason was that "the messages of the Bible were appropriated and contextualized, at times with the risk of some theological errors."[225]

The expulsion of the missionaries and the availability of God's message in the vernaculars assisted the Ethiopian missionaries in addressing the excluded middle. Local evangelists addressed fetishes, demons, witchcraft, and other related issues which were neglected by the missionaries who had "a Western intellectual mind-set, [who] had not encouraged" the locals to address them.[226] Philip Jenkins points out the negligence of such an issue from the missionaries' praxis on the mission field in general:

> Pagan and primal religions teach the existence of spiritual menaces facing society, but they also provide means to combat those dangers. A crucial flaw of early white missionary activity in Africa and Asia was that it forbade these solutions, whether amulets, fetishes, spells, charms, or ceremonies, since all were conspicuous symbols of pagan practice. At the same time, though, missionaries rarely offered plausible spiritual resources to combat what were still universally seen as pressing menaces.[227]

Not only the content but also the method of preaching was contextualized. Eshete notes:

> The local missionaries also developed an indigenous style of preaching where they narrated gospel stories applied to the situation of listeners through responsive chants. Their method of communicating the gospel was simple enough to be understood by the ordinary man, for they were unencumbered by a sophisticated theology. Primarily, they preached messages that attacked sin and the devil and insisted on repentance and return to God to avoid eternal suffering and damnation. Messages presented through songs and repetition of words were easy to remember and compatible with oral culture characteristic of preliterate societies.[228]

The vernacular Bibles in many instances helped the missionaries of the Ethiopian Evangelical Church to contribute to the growth of the Church in every direction.[229]

The reading of the Bible, specifically the New Testament, convinced most Ethiopian Evangelicals that its teachings could be applied and practiced. For instance, the book of Acts was not considered to be merely descriptive but also prescriptive and normative.[230] Thus they found that most of the missionaries neglected the role of the Spirit and the gifts of the Spirit, but then the Ethiopians corrected this hermeneutical negligence by "[challenging] the established theology of mainline churches by its pronounced espousal and bold exercise of the gifts of the Holy Spirit."[231] Tilahun Haile states:

> It took us a long time to understand the [Pentecostal] movement since we did not have a good grasp of its theological underpinnings. We had basically no sound teachings, coming either from the historic church or from the churches of mission background, concerning the power of the Holy Spirit and gifts of the Spirit and its

workings, or at least the subject was under-emphasized. We saw the fruits of Pentecostalism as young people faithfully witnessed and extended their faith and as a result brought many of their equals into transformed lives. Consequently, we had to introduce a change of perspectives."[232]

The book of Acts was therefore not confined to its historical and cultural context; neither its authorship nor its authenticity was questioned. Far from engaging in higher criticism, naturalism, Enlightenment thinking and fear-based hermeneutics, the Ethiopians embraced its message as God's message *for* and *to* them in order to finish the work of evangelists. These indigenous missionaries who took God at His Word faithfully and relevantly share the Gospel, at times at the cost of their lives. As a result, many have become children of light.

Conclusion

This chapter has traced and depicted the history of Bible translations in Ge'ez/Ethiopic, Amharic, Tigriña, Afan Oromo and other vernacular languages. Since the introduction of the institutionalized Christianity into the country, the translated Scripture either full Bible or portions have played a significant role in shaping the theology of the EOTC as well as the Evangelical church of Ethiopia.

As seen earlier, the Bible in the vernaculars has brought about a significant understanding of Christ as the unique, God-Man mediator between God and humanity. Ethiopians have been assisted through missionaries and local evangelists in what it means to be followers of Christ. The understanding of Christocentric salvation has led many to draw closer to God in private and in public through prayer, reading the Bible and worship. Thus the long held teaching of the EOTC that asserted the necessity of human or angelic mediation in approaching God for confession and prayer have been abrogated as people encountered and embraced God's Word in their own tongues.

The word of God in the vernaculars has also enabled Ethiopians to realize and carry out the mission of God within the country. It indeed empowered them to be strong in the face of stern persecutions done against them. Ethiopian Christians were also able to appropriate the gospel message so that their neighbors could understand and embrace it. Hence, they were able to address issues the missionaries, whether knowingly or unknowingly, overlooked.

To conclude, Ethiopian Evangelicals owe much of the formation of their theology, of the expression of their faith in a contextual way, and of their afresh and deepened relationship with God to the Word of God that was made available by both Western and local missionary translators. The vision of the translators and the missionaries came to reality for the Word of God was able to penetrate various tribes and languages of Ethiopia and inform, correct and reform.

Part II:

Crossing Theological Barriers for the Great Commission

CHAPTER THREE

Reasons, Principles and Strategies for Ethiopian Evangelicals Who Share the Gospel with Ethiopian Orthodox Adherents in Light of Jewish Evangelism in Luke-Acts

Introduction

Why and how can one present the Gospel to Ethiopian Orthodox adherents? Is it really necessary to present the Gospel to followers of the Orthodox faith? Is this not "'evangelizing the evangelized'?"[233] Are not the Evangelicals committing a huge mistake by sharing the gospel with the already Christian people?

This chapter attempts to address the above mentioned questions along with other issues by exploring Jewish Evangelism as seen in Luke-Acts. Yet it is essential to insert a caveat at the outset of this chapter. The author does not state that all adherents to the Coptic Orthodox faith are unbelievers, just as all Evangelicals are not necessarily so by claiming that they are believers or by mere association.[234] Indeed, it was the Ethiopian Orthodox Tewahido Church (EOTC) that spread Christianity within the country. This chapter does not attempt to quibble about the form of Christianity. To deny diversity in the expression of faith in various contexts is to commit a serious error. In his article *"The Orthodox-Protestant relationship in Ethiopia: a glimpse on interaction, attitude, causes of disharmony, consequences, and some solutions,"* Mersha Alehegne states:

> When the Ethiopian Orthodox Church was established there were no European missionaries in the country. having unfettered access to the vast interior of Ethiopia

and the Horn, the Church was therefore able to preach the Gospel throughout the region. Thus, historically, Ethiopian society developed a predominant adherence to the Orthodox faith. However, recently, the challenge presented by the activities of Protestant missionaries has alarmed the Orthodox faithful. Serious conflicts, replete with derogatory attitudes and ostracization, involving sometimes the loss of property and even life, have taken place, showing that this ecumenical encounter has not been an easy one.[235]

Is there a biblical answer to Mersha Alehegne's concern? Are there some practical solutions that Ethiopian evangelicals can glean from the Bible? Were the Evangelicals challenging their Coptic Orthodox neighbors for the sake of challenge or did they have a gospel-driven reason? Was the challenge only from the Evangelicals, or were there some challenges from within the EOTC itself, from those who saw theological deviation from its original teachings?

The Reasons for "evangelizing the evangelized"

Though there is a lack of consensus on when Christianity was introduced in Ethiopia, there is a general agreement "that the Aksumite kingdom adopted Christianity in the fourth decade of the fourth century A.D"[236] during the conversion of Emperor Ezana through "Frumentius, who later became the first bishop of Axum under the name of Abba Salama."[237] In the following century, Ethiopia received other missionary monks from Syria. These monks were avoiding the maltreatment and persecution imposed "by the Romans because of their anti-Chalcedonian theological stance."[238] Another caveat is imperative to mention at this juncture. It is not the intention of this chapter to argue whether Christ has one or two natures, for it is not the nature of Christ that is at stake here, but the role of Christ.

Ethiopian Church history depicts that the Christianity which expanded during the Aksumite kingdom through evangelism, monasticism and Bible translation, continued to make an impact until the first quarter of the fifteenth century. In all those periods and even after them, the kings were highly involved in Christianizing the idol worshiping peoples in Ethiopia.[239] But it was Zara Yaqob,[240] who, unlike other kings, "adopted an aggressive policy of evangelization."[241] During the reign of Zara Yaqob, the Ethiopian Orthodox Tewahido Church's theological position was impacted positively as well as negatively. Tibebe Eshete gives an excellent summary of Zara Yaqob's missiological and theological influence on the Orthodox Church:

> [Zara Yaqob] instituted rules for regular and ceremonial readings from the *Book of Miracles of Mary* in all churches and inaugurated a large number of holidays to various aspects of life. During his reign, the cross assumed centrality, both as a metaphor and as a powerfully effective symbol to fight evil spirits. He used such visual symbols as a pragmatic approach to address his illiterate, largely un-Christian subjects with Christian messages. The king deemed visual symbols able to transcend local rivalries and appealed to diverse people as a habitual nonverbal pattern of religion. He was even reported to have imposed upon his Christian subjects as well as new converts the branding of the right arms with words like, "I deny the devil," or "I am a slave of Mary." The custom of tattooing crosses on hands and over the foreheads also appears to have been inaugurated during his period. Zara Yaqob took steps toward the eradication of magical practices, though his motives may have been questionable.[242] The emperor was also instrumental in publishing numerous hagiographical works dealing with Mary and miracles of saints that have been incorporated

into the theology of the Orthodox Church and which affected its ritual practices. These measures taken by the monarchy left indelible marks on the religious traditions and spirituality of the Ethiopian society.[243]

Eshete's summary of Zara Yaqob's impact can be seen in three categories. First, though Zara Yaqob stressed the cross, it is clear that *Mary* was the center of his worldview. *Mariocentric* theology and devotion was then propagated through the writings, confessions of faith and celebrations revolved around Mary. But nowhere in Scripture do we see the apostles Paul and Peter and other disciples exalting her in that matter. Today the Orthodox Church follows *Mariocentric* hermeneutics in both the Old and New Testaments.[244] The legacy left by King Zara Yaqob has plagued the Ethiopia Orthodox Church. Thus in the present day, Mary is viewed as the mediator even though it is Jesus who died on the cross. Mary is the one who forgives. She is the one who stands between men and God. Indeed, Mary does deserve respect and proper esteem, and most Ethiopian Evangelicals wrongly ignore her as a reaction against *Mariocentrism*. But it is a vivid fact that *Mariocentric* theology puts Jesus' role at stake. If it is accurate, then why did Jesus die, and what role did he play?

Second, not only Mary but also saints took an extremely large amount of Zara Yaqob's attention, and this caused the Ethiopian Orthodox Church to lose its focus on Christ and his work. The introduction of various extra-biblical writings that do not align with the teachings of Scripture made inroads. As a result, Christ has been deemphasized in the EOTC today. Most Orthodox Church members give scant attention to the Bible.[245] When they do give attention to it, they usually focus on certain favorite topics like angels,[246] Mary or salvation by works[247] by employing an isolationistic interpretation of each verse and imposing their theology on the interpretation.

Third, Zara Yaqob's method of evangelism parallels that of the *conquistador* or the crusaders from Western Christendom, which Eshete labels as "the 'garrison model.'"[248] Evangelism was carried out using military power in most parts of Ethiopia, which, like Constantinian Christianity, opened the door widely for a syncretistic kind of Christianity. Girma Bekele rightly asserts:

> [T]he missionary movement within the EOTC lived its history primarily as the religious wing of imperial expansion, rather than as an ecclesially driven, evangelistic, missionary movement. It lacked charismatic relevance, and as such its movement into new territories under the shadow of imperial expansion, was either resisted as the religious hegemony of the ruling elites or was applied like a veneer over the pre-existing cultural milieu, resulting in a theologically uncritical syncretism.[249]

As a result, the Church struggled to get "faith [to take] deep root in the lives and culture of the new converts."[250] The evangelists of the Orthodox Church

> also ignored for a time such folk practices as witchcraft, magic, or devotion to household spirits....such accommodations trespassed into the more substantive tenets of Christian worship and faith, which in the long run undermined the basic foundations on which the Christian Church rests and deprived much of the Christian content of the Ethiopian Church.[251]

In summary, much is at stake when considering Ethiopian Orthodox theology. As said before, the form of Christianity or the one or two natures of Christ, or missionary methodology is not what is at stake here. It is the nature of *soteriology*, that is, how can one be saved? Who is the mediator: Mary, angels, saints or Christ? Are good works the basis for salvation?[252] The above historical glimpse has shown us that this theological deviation from central biblical teachings has resulted in the fifteenth century with King Zara Yaqob.

So what is the solution for these questions? The answer lies in the gospel: preaching the gospel, living out the gospel and making disciples with the gospel. And this gospel is Jesus Christ, who is God-Man. So long as this biblical tenet is central, the form of expression of Christianity is a secondary issue.

Contrary to Mersha Alehegne's accusation, the Protestant missionaries challenged the status quo in the Ethiopian Orthodox Church which neglected the evangelistic mandate for God's people as well as strayed in its theology. The challenge was not only from the exterior but also from the interior. There were EOTC groups who opposed the theological divergence of the Orthodox Church under King Zara Yaqob.[253] Saint Estifanos (Stephen) was "very critical of some of the positions of the Ethiopian Orthodox Church, particularly the fusion of royal ideology with Christology and some of the tenets of the Church that granted undue emphasis to angels and saints."[254] Estiphanos and his followers gave primacy to biblical teachings and practices. He was also "remembered [more so] in the hagiographic tradition as a man who was vehemently opposed to some of the practices related to the veneration of the Mother Lady."[255] His theological stance put him in sharp conflict with the king. He was labeled along with his followers, as a heretic and "faced severe persecution".[256]

Girma Bekele describes another group that tried to reform the Orthodox Church from within:

> Various attempts to purify the faith by detaching the church from its dependence on hagiographical tradition (Zar'a Ya'aqobism) were suppressed as antithetical to Orthodoxy. A notable recent example is the *Mahibere*

> *Bekur* (Society of the First Born), which was founded by *Aleqa* Meseret (1926-1996)....He grew discontented after struggling in vain to reconcile his best understanding of the doctrine of salvation, gained from reading Scriptures, with his church's traditional hagiographical teachings and beliefs about asceticism and prayer for the saints' intervention in absolution of sin. His passion led him to debate with various monastic leaders in an attempt to learn more about the Orthodox roots of his church. He came to believe that most of his church leaders knew that the church has been derailed from the faith of its first few centuries, but either found it too overwhelmingly difficult to bring about reformation or have felt that reformation might mean losing economic and social power.[257]

Later *Aleqa* Meseret was expelled from the church. However, groups and individuals who seek for the Ethiopian Orthodox Tewahido Church to be restored to its biblical and historical foundation have not stopped emerging here and there throughout the centuries in spite of the fierce opposition they face.

Before turning to Luke-Acts, it is imperative to consider some of Mersha Alehegne's concern with regard to Evangelical arrogance in his article. Here is what he listed in reference to how the Evangelicals feel about the Orthodox:

- They [the Orthodox] are not enlightened.
- They suffer from a lack of knowledge and false pride
- They have a spirit that prevents them from coming to Jesus.
- They rely more on cultural norms than biblical norms.
- They refuse those people who teach the Bible.
- They honour creatures more than the Creator.[258]

There is an Evangelical pride that looks down upon the Coptic Orthodox in Ethiopia. This Evangelical pride and some of the generalized assertions against all adherents to the Orthodox faith should be corrected. Instead, Christ-like character towards them should be displayed. This would promote ecumenical harmony. But ecumenism that annuls *Christocentric soteriology* is unorthodox orthodoxy and orthopraxy that defies the mandate, the motive as well as the message that is outlined in Scripture is heterodoxy. Though form and other non-essentials can be compromised on, one cannot and should not sacrifice truth (that peoples are lost and that they need to be rescued through the hearing of the gospel) on the altar of ecumenism. At the *parousia*, it is not ecumenism that will save people from eternal damnation, but Christ, the High Priest and the Victor, the God-Man.[259]

Scriptural Solution

Doctor Luke delineates how the Jews were evangelized in Luke-Acts. There are a number of invaluable principles on how to carry out gospel proclamation among the Jews. But one might question the parallel between Judaism and the Orthodox faith, for there are some significant differences between the two. For instance, followers of Judaism reject the fact that Jesus is the Messiah while the Ethiopian Orthodox Church accepts it. Jews only acknowledge the Old Testament as authoritative, whereas the Orthodox Church acknowledges the New Testament as being the continuation of the Old.

One needs to factor in the fact that though there are significant chasms between the two groups, the Ethiopian Orthodox Church has been impacted by Judaism. In fact, the Ethiopian Orthodox Church gives more emphasis to the Old Testament than the New. Regarding the influence of the Old Testament as well as Judaist culture on Ethiopia,

Edward Ullendorff in his book, *Ethiopia and the Bible: The Schweich Lectures* asserts:

> Old Testament influences and reflections had probably reached Ethiopia even before the introduction of Christianity in the fourth century and before the translation of the Bible. Monophysite Christianity, once it had taken root, became not only the official religion of the Ethiopian empire but also the most profound expression of the national existence of the Ethiopians. In its peculiar indigenized form, impregnated with strong Hebraic and archaic Semitic elements as well as pagan residua, Abyssinian Christianity constitutes a storehouse of the cultural, political, and social life of the people.[260]

Philip Jenkins also comments that, "The Ethiopian Church [the EOTC] has many aspects…that stem from Judaism."[261] These common factors will allow room for applying the principles, strategies and tactics employed in Luke-Acts in an effort to convey the liberating and redeeming work of Christ to the mere followers of the Orthodox faith specifically, and to any group of people in general. Unlike the pagans, the Jews had prior knowledge of half of the Bible, Yahweh, the Messiah and the need for salvation.

Luke and Jewish Evangelism in Luke-Acts

The Gospel of Luke

Luke gives us various principles and strategies which are applicable to doing evangelism in a Coptic Orthodox context. He starts with the angel's announcing the birth of Messiah to a Jewish young girl named Mary. The angel Gabriel explained the identity of the Messiah, how and why he would be born. Luke depicts how the Gospel or "salvation [to be] accomplished" is delivered to Mary (cf. Luke 1:26-38).

First, he used Old Testament references (1 Sam 7:13, 16; Pss 2:6-7; 89:26-27; Isa 9:6-7). This indicates that Gabriel was using Mary's previous knowledge of the Hebrew Bible concerning the coming Messiah (cf. Luke 1:32-33). Second, he used another proof that she could test his declaration as true, through the pregnancy of her relative Elizabeth. Thus he employed a sign as a referent for his proclamation (cf. 1 Cor 1:22).

Luke again proceeds to show how an angel preached the Good News to the shepherds that were in Bethlehem tending their flock. The angel announced that the one who was born is a Savior (showing that the motivation for Jesus' birth is salvation), Christ (the Messiah that was prophesied about in the Hebrew Bible), the Lord (who is to be worshiped and obeyed), that this is Good News for all (the extent of the salvation blessings is universal and that its end goal is to bring praise and glory to Yahweh (Luke 2:8-14)). The angel used the same methodology, that is, he first appealed to prior knowledge, alluding to the Old Testament (cf. Mic 5:2; Isa 7:14; 53:12). He also used a sign or proof: "You will find a baby wrapped in swaddling clothes and lying in a manger" (Luke 2:12).

John the Baptist, though he had a mixed audience, was also involved in Jewish evangelism (Luke 3:3), confrontation and warning (Luke 3:7-9). In his proclamation, he quoted the Hebrew Bible (Isa 40:3-5; 42:16; 52:10). His quotation and his warning regarding the claim, "We have Abraham as our Father" indicates that he assumed prior Scripture knowledge in his evangelism and pointed to the Jewishness of the context in which he proclaimed (Luke 3:4-6, 8).

Returning to Jesus, he used synagogues to teach and proclaim. He also quoted the Hebrew Bible in his proclamation. He did not hesitate to challenge the Jews about their wrong perceptions and understanding (Luke 4:17-30). He also engaged the Jews in a question and answer dialogue (Luke 5:33-6:11; 10:25-37; 17:20-21; 20:1-9), through private social encounters (Luke 7:36-50; 19:1-10), through parables (Luke 8:4-18; 13:18-30; 15:1-32; 20:9-19), through warnings (Luke 11:37-54; 13:1-9), and through confrontations (Luke 13:10-17; 14:1-6; 19:45-48).

The Book of Acts

In the book of Acts, we see Jewish evangelism performed in various ways: Peter addresses the confused gatherers at Pentecost and clarifies what is going on by quoting and alluding to the Hebrew Bible (cf. Luke 2:14, 17-21, 25-28, 34-35; Isa 53:10; Pss 16:10; 16:8-11; 110:1; Isa 44:3; 57:19; Joel 2:28-32). Peter also appeals to his ethnic relation with Jews when he addresses them in his apologetic as well as evangelistic preaching: "Men of Israel" (Acts 2:22), "Brothers" (Acts 2:29), and "…the house of Israel" (Acts 2:36). Peter again proclaims that he and John did not heal the lame beggar – God did – to show that Jesus is the only way for salvation (Acts 3:11-4:20). The apostles employ proclamation in evangelizing the Jews even in the midst of persecution (Acts 5:17-32) and Stephen exposits the entire Hebrew Bible in defense of the truth to the Jews (Acts 7:1-53).

Paul proclaimed Jesus as God's Son in Jewish synagogues by building upon their prior knowledge of Scripture (Acts 9:20; 13:5, 14-43; 14:1; 17:2-4a, 10-12a; 18:5-6, 19; 19:8). Paul used *apologia* against the charges the Jews made as an opportunity to declare the Gospel. But he did it in a respectful way as Peter did in Acts 2 by addressing the Jews as "Brothers and fathers," and "Brothers" (Acts 22:1-21; 23:1-6). Apollos also publicly defended Jesus as the Christ using the Hebrew Bible when dealing with the Jews (Acts 18:27-28).

Principles for Sharing the Gospel with the Coptic Orthodox

Luke-Acts provides a number of principles for Ethiopian Orthodox evangelism for our day. The principles provided below could be used in any evangelistic effort but because of the scope of this chapter the principles will be applied in a narrower sense.

1. The use of the Old Testament

The angel, John the Baptist, Jesus, Peter, Paul and Apollos used the Old Testament in preaching, persuasion, and defending the Gospel. This principle rightly assumed prior knowledge of God's Word by the Jews in Luke-Acts. The Jews knew, revered, and accepted the Old Testament. What was lacking was the right hermeneutic, which would unveil and exposit the plan of Yahweh from *the* Book of Yahweh by separating it from man-made tradition that defected from the revelation of Yahweh.

2. The use of the Synagogue

Jesus, Peter, the apostles and Paul frequented the synagogues both in Israel and in Gentile areas because that was where the Jews gathered to hear the Torah, fellowship, and worship. That is where the people were.

3. Proclamation

Whether in a synagogue or outside of a temple, or in public areas, proclamation was used to convey the message of the Gospel. The proclamation can be exposition, defense (*apologia*), reasoning or warning with boldness. John Stott asserts that proclamation should "focus on Jesus."[262] He then provides a "framework"[263] for the declaration of the gospel in four categories: *"the gospel events," "the gospel witnesses," "the gospel promises,"* and *"the gospel conditions."*[264] In giving further delineation to his frame work, Stott states:

> Here, then, is a fourfold message- two events (Christ's death and resurrection), as attested by two witnesses (prophets and apostles), on the basis of which God makes two promises (forgiveness and the Spirit), on two conditions (repentance and faith, with baptism). We have no liberty to amputate this apostolic gospel, by proclaiming the cross without the resurrection, or offering forgiveness without the Spirit, or demanding faith without repentance. There is a wholeness about the biblical gospel.
>
> It is not enough to 'proclaim Jesus'. For there are many different Jesuses being presented today. According to the New Testament gospel, however, he is *historical* (he really lived, died, rose and ascended in the arena of history), *theological* (his life, death, resurrection and ascension all have saving significance) and *contemporary* (he lives and reigns to bestow salvation on those who respond to him). Thus the apostles told the same story of Jesus at three levels – as historical event witnessed by their own eyes), as having theological significance (interpreted by the Scriptures), and as contemporary message (confronting men and women with the necessity of decision). We have the same responsibility today to tell the story of Jesus as fact, doctrine and gospel.[265]

Stott's assertion strengthens the principle that proclamation is necessary and should always revolve around Christ and his work whatever form the proclamation takes.

4. Proof or sign

The angel of the Lord appealed to prior miracles or events. Paul used his personal conversion and call as a proof. What God has done in one's own or others' lives can be used as an evangelistic tool. Miracles, produced by God, can also be used in such a way.

5. Respect, honor and identification

Paul and Peter are seen using this approach in their encounter with the Jews. It is biblical and appropriate to display respect and honor to the Coptic Orthodox adherents as they are engaged by Christians in evangelism. Disrespect, pride and a "know-it-all" attitude will not attract people to Christ; on the contrary, it will be a hindrance for people from seeing and embracing Christ.

6. Dialogue

Listening, answering questions, and good asking questions are vital in Coptic Orthodox evangelism. Listening is vital in order to understand what exactly they believe and where they are. By answering thoughtfully their questions and asserting the necessity to be saved can play a significant role in reaching out to the Coptic Orthodox adherents. This dialogue will help the evangelist find out whether a Coptic Orthodox adherent has a personal relationship with Christ. As mentioned earlier, it is a huge mistake to consider all Copts as having no relationship with Christ, for there are some who are living by the Book.

Strategy[266]

In light of the Luke-Acts principles, the following strategies might be helpful in efforts to share the gospel with the Ethiopian Coptic Orthodox adherents.

1. The use of the Whole Bible

Most evangelical Christians focus on the New Testament and refer to it most frequently. It is important to use both Testaments especially Psalms when interacting with Ethiopian Orthodox Tewahido adherents, because it helps to avoid contemporary Marcionism.[267]

A tactic to apply this would be to show them that Jesus is the Mediator, the High Priest, the Substitute, the Advocate, and the Victor God in the Old Testament and then move into the New Testament. It will give them a full-orbed understanding of who Jesus is according to the whole counsel of God.

2. Listen, Answer, Ask

Evangelicals are known for their arrogance because they do not have the patience to listen. Instead, they rush to answer and fix people. While the intention and the eagerness to share the gospel is commendable, it should be noted that they are conversing with people who want to be listened to, respected and accepted. Evangelicals can make a far-reaching impact, by the power of the Spirit, in the lives of their Orthodox neighbors, friends and relatives just by listening, answering and asking gently rather than dumping one's theological dogmas haughtily onto their listeners.

A tactic to implement this would be to listen to them attentively and answer their burning questions, and also to ask good questions. This will help the unbelieving Coptic Orthodox adherent to understand the Gospel and help them see the real Gospel and its call to commitment. It also helps the evangelist to know where people really are.

3. Proclamation

This is an essential part in evangelizing the Jews. They need to hear the Gospel so that they can embrace Jesus the Messiah as their only Savior. A tactic to apply this would be to use the Old Testament first, and then the New, showing that Jesus is the only Mediator and High Priest, the Only One who can save them. The use of appropriate literature that is contextual is essential to effectively reach Coptic Orthodox adherents. By making the Bible available, especially the New Testament, one could play a significant role in the dissemination of the gospel. When proclaiming to, warning and confronting people with the Gospel, it is essential to talk about sin and the need for a Savior. One principle the Evangelicals cannot emulate from Jesus, Paul, Peter or Apollos is that of entering the "synagogue" or for the current context, entering Orthodox churches. This is forbidden by the law and considered provocative. Hence it is essential to obey this law and respect the jurisdiction of the Orthodox Church. But evangelicals should encourage their believing Orthodox friends and relatives to talk about the Bible, Jesus and his finished work in the compounds of the Orthodox churches, for those who believe the Bible already make up part of the membership of the Orthodox Church and there is no law that forbids them to preach the gospel.

Conclusion

Ethiopian Coptic church members and ministers should not consider an explicit declaration of salvation blessings only through an active faith in Christ Jesus as foreign and unimportant. In fact, the EOTC should clearly and boldly teach this very doctrine *if* the church really holds to the apostolic faith of the gospels. The truth should resound as often as possible so that church members cannot forget the essential truth of the gospel faith.

But since much of the church forgot her task in asserting the *Solus Christus*, it is essential to preach the gospel to members of the Coptic church of Ethiopia. The EOTC should let go of some of its extra-biblical teachings on salvation and its meritorious approach to the free gift of God and instead embrace God's mercy and grace. The EOTC should also put blessed Mary in her proper place in the progress of redemption rather than making her the center of worship as well as the mediator between God and men.

The Evangelical church of Ethiopia should strive to share the gospel with nominal Orthodox adherents and with those who confess that they are "Christians" (because their parents were Christians but who lack personal relationships with Christ) with humility and listening ears; in so doing, they can introduce the Copts to the saving knowledge of Jesus Christ.

The Evangelical Church should not shy away from communicating the gospel to the Copts in spite of their so called claim of allegiance to Christ. The inclusivist claim of some Western missionaries' and a few seminary trained Ethiopians should not discourage the church from preaching the gospel so as to bring about an explicit confession of faith in and allegiance to Christ. As seen in the corpus of Luke-Acts, the apostles did not hesitate in sharing the gospel respectfully with those who had a partial understanding of the gospel. The EOTC adherents should not be treated as pagans or adherents of other religions, for they acknowledge most of the tenets of Christianity.[268]

Though it is encouraged to share the gospel with the Copts, Evangelicals should avoid the assumption that all Copts have no personal relationship with Christ. That is why it is vital to ask questions and to probe their understanding in a subtle and respectful way to grasp their spiritual contour and stance with Christ. Many Evangelicals in Ethiopia have made a grievous error by assuming all Copts are lost and they know nothing about Christ.

Part III:

Crossing Cultural Barriers

for the Great Commission

CHAPTER FOUR

Erecha and Spiritual Hunger: A Call to Cross Barriers to Proclaim the Gospel Contextually Among the Oromo People of Ethiopia

Introduction

Erecha is a religious festival celebrated in Ethiopia by many Ethiopians every year at the end of September. The participants come mainly from the Oromo people group, which is the largest single people group in Ethiopia with a population of 30 million, constituting 34.5% of the total population.[269] September is when Ethiopians celebrate the New Year and it is the end of the rainy season. *Erecha* is celebrated in September because this is the end of the rainy season ("the dark times" according to the participants of the festival). It is a thanksgiving ceremony celebrated at different locations of the country but formally observed near Horra Aresede Lake in the town of Bishoftu, near Addis Ababa. The celebrants carry flowers and fresh grass and go to mountaintops, the seaside or riverbanks to perform prayers and have times of thanksgiving. Historically, *Erecha* was celebrated twice a year: before the beginning of the rainy season as a prayer ceremony for good harvest and at the end of the rainy season to give thanks to *Waaqa*, the Oromo god. In the modern day, however, the prayer before the beginning of the rainy season is performed at the family level and does not have a national magnitude.[270]

Erecha has been practiced for many years among the Oromo people. There is no general agreement whether this festival was officially banned during the Communist regime like other religious activities or not, but it certainly was not as widely and openly celebrated as it is now.

Since recent years, especially with the coming to power of the current Ethiopian government, which constitutionally supports the freedom of religion, the *Erecha* festival is gaining a national magnitude and attracting millions of participants of varying socio-economic statuses. According to Ethiopian Television (ETV) News (aired October 2, 2010), the festival generally attracts around 3 million people to the national celebration at Bishoftu Town. Top government officials, including the president of the Oromia Regional State, were present at that year's festival. According to Addis Neger News, the attendees of this festival come from different religions, including Islam, Coptic Orthodoxy and Evangelical Christianity. Tesfaye describes the diversity:

> "Today the day is Teklehaymanot's! May Teklehaymanot fulfill your wishes!" says an old [Ethiopian Coptic Orthodox] man giving his blessings. A lady standing in the middle of the water sprinkling ceremony prays in a broken, confessional tone, "Oh, Lord Jesus, this is my culture!" While others chant "*Aselam aleyka*" to the "Arabic speaking' spirits."[271]

In this chapter, I will focus on five major areas. First I will trace the historical roots and meaning of *Erecha*. Second, I will look into the global and local factors contributing to the revival of traditional religious practices in Ethiopia in general, placing the celebration of *Erecha* into its wider context. Third, I will evaluate spiritual, cultural and historical issues related to *Erecha*. Fourth, I will evaluate the barrier-crossing implications of *Erecha* for mission in Ethiopia. Finally, I will suggest what ought to be a missional response: how the spiritual hunger being expressed by those participating in *Erecha* celebrations can be turned in to an opportunity to cross religious and cultural barriers to share the life-giving message of the Gospel.

Historical Roots and Meaning of *Erecha*

Erecha can be best understood in relation to *Gada*, the traditional democratic government system of the Oromo people. According to Asafa Jalata,

> the traditional *Gada system*, developed by the Oromo organizes and orders society around political, economic, social, cultural and religious institutions. We do not know when and how this system emerged. However, we do know that it existed as a full-fledged system at the beginning of the sixteen century.[272]

Gada has three interrelated meanings. First, it is a system used to govern all aspects of the Oromo people from birth to death. It linked political, social and religions lives of Oromo people. Second it is an age grading system for all male Oromo. Upon birth all Oromo male enter in to an eight year peer grouping. Every male born within a certain generation of eight years belongs to the same *Luba* (peer group). An Oromo male passes through eleven such age grouping in his life span. Each generation assumes a certain responsibility in the society, and the transition from one stage to another is marked with a religious ceremony. Third, *Gada* is related to an eight year span where elected officials in the society assume power.[273]

In the *Gada* system, all officials were democratically elected with the participation of all male members of the society. The officials stayed in power for a term of eight years. The criteria for election to office included bravery, knowledge, honesty, public service and demonstrated ability. There were three leading officials in the *Gada* system: the *Abba Bokuu (Abba Gada)* who is the top official, the *Abba Dula* who is the war minister[274] and the *Abba Muuda* who is the highest spiritual leader in the system.[275] The *Gada system* had a general assembly called *Cheffe*, which met every eight years.[276] In the

Gada system, *Waqafana/Waqaffata* (the belief in *Waaqa*, the traditional Oromo god), is considered to be the religion. The *Qaallu* were spiritual experts or clergy who took their blessing from the *Abba Muda*, the spiritual leader of the society.[277]

The *Gada* System is still practiced in some parts of Ethiopia. *Erecha*, therefore, is a spiritual festival related to *Waqafatta*, the traditional Oromo religion. It is not a new festival being developed in this age but existed as part and parcel of the *Gada system*.

In the 16th century, the Oromo were able to control large areas in the South, Southwest and Central regions of Ethiopia through war and conquest. Indigenous people were assimilated into the traditional Oromo system, and worshiped the Oromo god. Therefore, the Oromo traditional religion, *Waqafatta*, was able to expand into the conquered lands.[278] However, with the territorial expansion of Menilik II, the Ethiopian king from the north, which lasted from 1870-1900, the Oromo lost control over their territory. King Menelik II, a Coptic Orthodox adherent himself, gave the Ethiopian Orthodox Church the mandate to willingly or forcefully convert the people in the newly conquered lands. Therefore, some Oromo converted to Orthodox Christianity because of pressure from the ruling class and because of the benefits attached to conversion to Orthodox Christianity. On the other hand, many Oromo converted to Islam as a resistance to the pressured Orthodox conversion.[279]

Waqafatta, therefore, lost its centrality among many Oromo communities with the conversion of Oromo to Christianity and Islam. It did not totally lose its importance in their daily lives, however. In fact, in many parts of Oromia, *Waqafatta* coexisted with Christianity and Islam.[280] Many Oromo openly identified to be Christians or Muslims but continued the practice of worshiping *Waaqa* in their private lives. Even today, "their worldviews are still hidden under the surface. Oromo prayers, greetings and blessings manifest Oromo worldview."[281]

In recent years *Waqafatta* is regaining wide acceptance in the Oromo community. *Erecha* is a manifestation of the returning of many Oromo to their traditional religion. The number of attendees of this religious festival is increasing from year to year. In September of 2010, approximately 3 million people attended the ceremony in Bishoftu Town alone. That was almost 10% of the total Oromo population in one location! From a missiological point of view there is a need to examine the reasons behind and the renewed commitment of such huge numbers of the Oromo population to the traditional religion of *Waqafatta*, with *Erecha* as one of its outward manifestations. The irony is that, increased numbers of Evangelical Christians are also attending the yearly festival. In my opinion, the attendance of *Erecha* festivals is going to increase in the coming years, attracting many more Oromo from all religious groups, including Evangelical Christians.

Factors Contributing to the Revival of Traditional Religions

The Oromo are not the only people group in Ethiopia returning to their traditional religion. There are many Ethiopian tribes reviving their long forgotten or once undermined religious ceremonies. The Sidama tribe in the south is a good example. I will not go in to detail in this area as I want to focus on the *Waqafatta* of the Oromo people. But I will briefly discuss a few of the global, continental and local factors contributing to the return to traditional religions in Ethiopia.

Globalization versus Localization

Globalization is a complex process of integration at the global scale. Thomas Friedman described it as the "inexorable integration of markets, nation states and technologies to a degree never witnessed before in a way that is enabling individuals, corporations, and nation states to reach around the world farther, faster, deeper and cheaper than ever before."[282] Globalization is a process where the relationships between people are being intensified because of the advancing of communication and transport technologies. With globalization the impact of other culture on African countries has been huge. "[G]lobalization has its own dominant culture, which is why it tends to be homogenizing."[283] Therefore, "the challenge in this era of globalization, for countries or individuals, is to find a healthy balance between preserving a sense of identity, home and community and doing what it takes to survive within the globalization system."[284] The process of globalization therefore, often prompts an increasing identity quest at local levels. I believe that *Erecha* is one of the results of the globalization versus localization tension.

The African Renaissance Movement

The African Renaissance movement aspires to political, cultural, scientific and economic renewal of the continent. The concept was first introduced by Anta Diop and popularized by the former South African President Thabo Mbeki during his time in office. In a 1998 speech, he paints a picture of an African Renaissance as a response to globalization:

> ...as the process of globalization develops apace...it is necessary that, acting together, we ensure that Africa,

like other regions of the developing world, occupies her due place within the councils of the world....out of Africa reborn must come modern products of human economic activity, significant contributions to the world of knowledge, in the arts, science and technology, new images of an Africa of peace and prosperity.[285]

The African Renaissance, among other things, tries to restore African traditions and customs which were undermined during the colonial era. In line with this movement, some scholars in Ethiopia advocate the return to traditional African religions. Some of the organizers of the *Erecha* celebration are scholars from higher learning institutions, who advocate the African Renaissance ethos.

The Constitutional Provision of Religious Freedom in Ethiopia

During the Communist regime in Ethiopia, many religious activities were officially banned. Traditional religions also lost their public celebrations during those years. The current Ethiopian government supports freedom of religion. In relation to this freedom, many traditional religious festivals are regaining prominence and attracting attention.

The Tourism Value of Traditional Religions

Another reason for the growth and expansion of traditional religions is the media coverage they get from government and private media outlets and the support they get from federal and regional administrative bodies for their tourism value.

Environmental Issues

Because many traditional religious celebrations like *Erecha* are performed in places like mountaintops, river banks, seaside and forested areas, they give attention to the protection of the natural environment. Therefore, many scholars in Africa today advocate the continuation of traditional religions because of their sensitivity to the natural environment.

Issues Related to *Erecha*

The above are few of the factors related to the general revival of traditional religions in Ethiopia. However, there are specific issues related to the *Erecha* festival and its growing magnitude. These issues related to *Erecha* can be classified into three broad categories: spiritual, cultural and historical.

Spiritual Factors

Some scholars argue that *Erecha* is purely a cultural event. It is undeniable that *Erecha* has a cultural aspect. But according to many scholars who have studied *Erecha*, and also listening to the testimonies and rituals of the attendees and looking into the historical roots of *Erecha*, we can understand it is worship of a deity. It is a festival related to the traditional religion of *Waqafatta*, which is the worship of *Waqqa*, who manifests through different *Ayaanas* (spirits). *Waqafatta* has a clergy man/woman called a qallu (male) or qality (female). The temple of *Waqafatta* is called *Gelemma*. *Erecha* is a religious festival in the *Waqafatta* religion.[286] Therefore, many of the participants attend *Erecha* as a spiritual pilgrimage. *Erecha* is a clear sign of spiritual hunger among the Oromo. When one finds more than 3 million attendees of a spiritual ceremony in a location, the majority of them with the intention of worship, it cannot be anything else than spiritual hunger. "Is the celebration of *Erecha* satisfying this spiritual hunger?" is a question to be answered.

Cultural Factors

The growth of *Erecha* is closely related to Oromo nationalism. Some of the attendees of the ceremony go to the festival for the sole purpose of identifying with the Oromo culture. An Addis Neger news reporter described his observation during the 2010 celebration of the festival in the following words:

> The multitudes waving national and regional flags lend additional color to the festivities. T-shirts, scarves, banners and other articles of clothing printed in the colors of the flag add to the vibrancy. One can easily see the emotions behind the banners: "*Erecha* is our culture!" and, more frequently, "*Waaqeffetaa Ta'uun of tauudha!*" (Literally meaning, "being a *Waqefeta* is being oneself!").[287]

In addition, Brita Marie Servan writes:

> My impression is that *waqqaffana* is given a central position in the political discourse of the Oromo culture....The celebration of *Erecha* in Bishofti (Debrezeit) is a popular event with clear tendencies of Oromo nationalism.... In recent years, this celebration has been dominated by young and urban participants, which sing nationalist songs and wear t-shirts with the Oromo flag and map of Oromia.[288]

Identity is one of the issues behind *Erecha*. Not all the participants of *Erecha* are interested in the issue of spirit worship but they are looking for a religion that can allow free expression of their cultural identity. The Addis Neger news reporter quoted one of the parliamentarians who was in attendance of the festival in 2010:

> Tesfaye Fufa, Parliamentary representative of the Oromo Federalist Congress, has another argument. 'Yes, many Oromo show the inclination to follow their traditional religion.' But, he says, 'What is expressed in these festivals is a quest for identity.' Tesfaye cites his reason, remarking, 'Most people who participate in the festival are followers of different religions. Most of the people who go to the festival go just to visit their fathers' religion–no more than that.' In Tesfaye's opinion, the festival coordinators share this motivation.[289]

Historical Factors

When understood from a historical point of view *Erecha* is the rejection of forced conversion. Many Oromo still adhere to Ethiopian Coptic Orthodoxy, Evangelical Christianity or Islam. However, significant numbers of Oromo are going back to their ancestral religion as a rejection to the forced conversion to Ethiopian Coptic Orthodoxy or Islam. As I mentioned above in this paper, many Oromo converted to Islam as a resistance to the pressure from the Ethiopian Orthodox Church, which operated closely with the conquering forces of King Menilik II. In his sociological article, "Oromo Peoplehood," Asafa Jalata wrote:

> Without fundamentally changing their traditional religious perceptions, northern Oromo began to accept Islam during the eighteenth century, albeit mainly for political reasons. To protect themselves from incorporation into Christian Abyssinia and maintain

their identity, a few Oromo groups - the Raya, Azabo, Yejju and Wallo - in addition to armed resistance, embraced Islam during the 18th century.... For the same reason, some Oromo in Wallaga, Illubabor and other regions preferred Islam to Orthodox Christianity. However, there were Oromo who were forced to accept Orthodox Christianity after their colonization. The remaining Oromo have continued to practice their Oromo Religion. Generally speaking, both Islam and Christianity have been gradually grafted on Oromo religion in many Oromo regions. Although Christian and Islamic religious philosophies did not provide superior explanations to that of the Oromo for the functioning of the complex world, they were mainly imposed on Oromo by the gun and sword. Some Oromo nationalists are engaged in rediscovering the original Oromo cultural traditions and are trying to reconcile them with the borrowed cultural elements that penetrated Oromo minds and society through these religions.[290]

Implications of *Erecha* in Evangelizing the Oromo

As explained above, *Erecha* has spiritual, cultural and historical aspects, and many of these erect barriers to a true embrace of Christ as one's primary identity. Spiritually, it should be understood as worship of a deity other than Yahweh and a return to ancestral religion; culturally, it is closely tied with the question of Oromo identity; historically, it is a clear rejection of the forced conversion ordered by King Menilik II.

Now we will turn to the examination of the challenges and opportunities for Christian mission in Ethiopia in relation to the revival of the Oromo traditional religion. When looked at from a spiritual point of view, *Erecha* depicts that there is a huge need for evangelization among the Oromo. Even if they are looking for a solution from wrong sources, those who attend *Erecha* are looking for a spiritual solution. In many societies around the world today, spiritual solutions are being ruled out. On the contrary, many Oromo are actively seeking a spiritual solution. *Erecha* can be positively understood as a spiritual hunger.

Looking at the growth in magnitude of the *Erecha* celebration, one may think the Oromo are drifting away from God. But *Erecha* can be a good indicator that the Oromo are still open to spiritual matters. It is usually difficult to preach the message of the Gospel to communities who are spiritually cold. But people groups like the Oromo are open to spiritual conversation. True Christians and missionaries need to intensify coordinated evangelization among the Oromo people. They need to take the opportunity to connect these people to the one true God. The call of Jesus would be: "Look, I tell you, lift up your eyes, and see that the fields are white for harvest" (John 4:35 ESV). The Oromo are not spiritually cold but they are seekers of spiritual reality. What may at first seem like a huge spiritual barrier actually has a bridge built over it for Gospel-carriers to cross! Surely, the time presents a huge opportunity for anyone interested in evangelizing Ethiopia because the Oromo, who are the biggest people group in the country, are open to spiritual matters. It is an incredible opportunity, which, if seized, will impact the whole nation with the true message of the Gospel.

Whoever goes first with humility and genuine intentions and also with a contextualized presentation of the message can get the attention of the Oromo people. One may argue that the Oromo people already quenched their spiritual hunger through spiritual practices like *Erecha* or through their connection to their traditional gods, but I believe that true spiritual hunger will only be quenched when the people connect to the one true God who is the source of every life.

Culturally, the Gospel in Ethiopia faces the challenge of syncretism. Syncretism "refers to the replacement of core or important truths of the Gospel with non-Christian elements.[291] A related and equally concerning issue is that of lack of discipleship. Many Christians who claim to be born again attend the *Erecha* festival every year. This can lead to the blending of Biblical Christianity with the Oromo traditional religion. After her interviews among Oromo Diaspora in Norway, Servan observed that some of the Oromo who participated in the *Erecha* festival believed that *Waaqa*, the Oromo god and the Christian God are one and the same:

> Gemechu and Taddesse emphasize how they consider practice to be what differ between the disparate religions among the Oromo: God is only one God ....if you follow traditional way or that way or that way, you believe in one God, but the way you exercise differ (Gemechu).When I asked Tadesse about what he understands to be the difference between the concept of God in the different religions he answers: the difference is not that big, the difference is only how one pray to God.[292]

This is an indication that there is a widespread theological confusion in understanding the *Erecha* festival and the worship of *Waaqa*. As *Erecha* presents an invaluable opportunity for evangelization among the Oromo and also exposes a huge need to intensify discipleship among believers in the Oromo people group. If those who attend church or call on the name of the one true God start mixing the worship of the one true God with traditional religious and cultural elements, it presents a clear danger for the true Gospel. Teaching the true meaning of Christianity or the true identity of God as expressed in the Bible is crucial in Oromo churches. There is a possibility that many young people may continue to be torn between Christianity and the Oromo traditional religion and that in turn will lead to the loss of the true meaning of Christianity.

Historically, the Evangelical churches in Ethiopia stand in a unique position in relation to the Oromo society, because there is a general openness towards the Evangelical church among Oromo scholars. The barriers are low. There are two main reasons for this: first, many Oromo converted to Evangelical Christianity through the peaceful preaching of the faith (in contrast to the forced conversions of other religions). Second, many Oromo scholars believe that the Evangelical churches in Ethiopia are helping in the process of answering Oromo identity questions. Asafa Jalata wrote: "Despite the fact that a few Oromo groups were forced to accept Ethiopian Christianity [that is, Ethiopian Coptic Orthodox] and the Amharic language, the majority of Oromo accepted Islam and other forms of [Evangelical] Christianity in opposition to the Ethiopian colonizing structures."[293] Discussing Oromo conversion, Servan concludes the following, based on literature reviews and direct interviews with several Oromo scholars:

> Seemingly, the evangelical Christianity movement has been important to the development of Oromo identity, especially concerning the development of written Afaan Oromo ....The evangelical churches in Ethiopia have been some of the fastest growing in Africa....Both evangelical Christianity and Islam could be seen a critical response to Amaharisation as well as to communism.[294]

Evangelical Christians and missionaries should take this strategic evangelistic opportunity that they have to cross low barriers. It is obvious that God does not support one form of Christianity over the other as long as it is in line with His ways as revealed in the Bible. However, people may prefer one form of Christianity over another based on their own historical and social realities. In this regard, Evangelical missionaries have a unique opportunity for presenting the Gospel in our generation. But we should not forget the reasons why Evangelical Christians are being accepted here. While preaching the Gospel, they are also helping in the building of Oromo cultural elements such as developing the language of the people. In addition, there is no historical incident that associates Evangelical missionaries with forceful conversion of the Oromo. Therefore, it is important to capitalize on this and continue to approach the people lovingly and peacefully, contextualizing the Gospel to the culture of the people. But this does not mean every cultural element needs to be welcomed without critical evaluation in light of the Bible.

However, it may mean to accept those cultural elements that are not necessarily condemned by the Bible and to lovingly correct or transform those that need to change. Missionaries and teachers must walk alongside the people as they learn how to hold onto their cultural identities in appropriate ways while practicing true Christianity and finding their ultimate identity in Christ. There are numerous Biblical examples that support this culturally contextualized yet biblically faithful approach. Historically, such approaches were effective in the rapid expansion of the Gospel among people groups. One biblical example we have in this regard is the decision passed by the Acts 15 council of the Apostles. After that decision was made to accept Gentiles without forcing on them any foreign cultural practices, the Gospel began spreading like wildfire. We see the need for the same kind of decision to be made as we seek to expand the Gospel among the Oromo, allowing people to practice their cultural elements as long as it does not conflict with biblical teachings. The return of many Oromo to their traditional religion is calling for a contextualized approach for the Gospel. When a people group is looking for a religion that allows a free expression of identity, whoever answers the question first can win the hearts and minds of the people.

What Should the Response to *Erecha* Be?

Evaluating the challenges and opportunities that have come with the revival of the *Erecha* festival, which is basically a manifestation of return to Oromo traditional religion, the churches in Ethiopia should respond in a manner that will help the expansion of the kingdom of God. It takes wisdom, neutrality and the upholding of kingdom values to appropriately respond to such trends as *Erecha*.

In his book, *Culture Making: Recovering Our Creative Calling*, Andy Crouch wrote that Christians often respond to culture in a counterproductive manner. They may condemn, critique, copy or consume a cultural product. But according to Crouch, "The only way to change culture is to create more of it."[295] Christians need to engage in the business of creating alternative cultures instead of simply condemning, critiquing, copying or consuming culture. The churches in Ethiopia should give a timely response to the growing trend of returning to traditional religions in general and to the revival of Oromo traditional religion in particular. Therefore, I recommend the following as a barrier-crossing response to *Erecha* (one of the outward manifestations of the revival of *Waqafatta*).

Theological Response

Churches and Christians in Ethiopia should give a clear theological response to *Erecha*. They have to clear up the confusion being created among many Oromo believers in understanding the difference between the Christian God and the traditional Oromo God, *Waaqa*. Churches also need to educate their members regarding the clear difference in the worship of the Christian God from the traditional

Oromo god. This clear stand will help the church in protecting the Christian faith from syncretism and will also pave the way for future evangelization among the Oromo.

Strategic Response

The Evangelical churches should take advantage of the historical unique position they have among the Oromo communities. Because of this, they need to strengthen strategic evangelization among the Oromo. Crossing barriers to evangelize the biggest people group in Ethiopia will certainly be key to the expansion of the kingdom of God and the preservation of Christian heritage in the Horn of Africa.

Cultural Response

"Culture is what we human beings make of the world."[296] Everyone is born into a culture and highly influenced by it. No one is free from the influence of culture. "The beginning of culture and the beginning of humanity are one and the same because culture is what we are made to do. There is no withdrawing from culture. Culture is inescapable."[297]

In Luke 24:46-49 and Acts 1:8 the mandate is about reaching all geographic territories starting in Jerusalem. In Matthew 28:17-20, Jesus is referring to all peoples in a more particular sense, not just geographical regions but specific cultural groups within those regions.

The Great Commission of Jesus Christ clearly has a cultural dimension. Mission activities without the consideration of the culture of the local people are not effective. Knowingly or unknowingly, mission efforts in Ethiopia, including local and international initiatives, have practiced cultural hegemony, which is the forcing of another culture upon converts, instead of allowing the Gospel itself to righteously transform a local culture. They should not be expected to cross cultural barriers into another culture; that is the Gospel messenger's job. If people groups realize that they are being forced to accept another culture along with the Gospel, sooner or later they will reject the idea of cultural hegemony and, together with it, the Gospel. A clear demonstration of this is the recent return to traditional religions among many Oromo communities. The rejection of cultural hegemony may not necessarily indicate the rejection of the Gospel but the victimization of the Gospel by being associated with cultural hegemony.

The longing of many Oromo today is to find a faith that allows the expression of their cultural values. The Evangelical churches in Ethiopia should realize this need and intentionally work towards contextualizing the Christian Gospel into the Oromo culture by affirming the cultural values that are in line with the Biblical values and wisely transforming those cultural values that need to change. This task is not going to be an easy one. First, it is a process; second, it takes openness of the heart and the mind; third, it takes neutrality: the commitment to Jesus of Evangelical leaders over and above loyalty to their cultures; and, finally, it takes a coordinated effort. When people groups reject a form of Christianity or return to their traditional practice, it is usually easy to look for explanations and solutions from elsewhere, but the biggest problem and the best solution usually lies within the Church itself.

CHAPTER FIVE

Preparing Ethiopians for Barrier-Crossing Ministry: Maximizing Missionary Training for Great Commission Impact[1]

As of 2005, missionaries from the majority world have moved to center-stage as the majority of the 21st century mission force.[298] These men and women who are called to reach the unreached hail from various countries and cultures, but all can be loosely categorized as non-Western. This non-Western identity is a boon in many regards – it allows these missionaries to gain entrance into countries which have closed their hearts, their borders, or both to Westerners. It also often gives them commonality with those whom they are called to reach: many aspects of values and worldview are relatively consistent across otherwise diverse non-Western cultures, so the barriers are lower for them than for Western missionaries.[299]

Despite the fact that non-Western Christians make excellent candidates to be barrier-crossing missionaries among the unreached, they are all too often under-utilized and inadequately trained. This may seem surprising due to the above-mentioned statement that non-Western missionaries make up the majority of the missionaries in the world today, but this fact must be considered in light of the wider global context if it is to be properly understood. The booming mission force from the Two-Thirds world is a result of the booming church growth in the "Global South."[300] It is right and logically follows that when the

---

[1] Chapters five and six are adapted from the following: Jessica A. Udall, "Preparing Ethiopians for Cross-Cultural Ministry: Maximizing Missionary Training for Great Commission Impact" (master's thesis, Columbia International University, 2013).

Church in a given location grows, its mission force will grow as well. While it is laudable that so many non-Western missionaries have been sent out, one must also realize how many more could be sent out if the global Church was mobilized for mission and if specific training for barrier-crossing ministry were more available to non-Western missionary candidates.

There are a growing number of missions-training schools in the non-Western world, but the availability of the training they offer has often being outstripped by the demand.[301] Worse, there is sometimes a lack of awareness within the Church that such training or that mission in general is needed – thus, Christians are not challenged to even consider reaching the unreached through cross-cultural missionary work.[302] Insularity is a human malady, and it infects non-Western Christians as much as Western Christians.

Need for and Purpose of this Study

This study will focus on Ethiopia – a country which is gradually waking up to her enormous potential to contribute in the area of world mission. The time for harvesting harvesters has arrived, and strides are being taken to begin missionary mobilization. In light of the admirable work already being done, this study will analyze what challenges must be overcome by the Ethiopian Church in the area of barrier-crossing ministry training in order for her to become a major missionary sending nation in the near future. It is hoped that what is shared will also have applicable value to other African nations and other non-Western countries who desire to become more involved in fulfilling the Great Commission.

Ethiopia has the potential to be a key player in strategic world evangelization and also has some unique obstacles standing in her way. She has never been colonized by an outside culture (the Italians who occupied some of her major cities for five years were driven out before getting a firm foothold),[303] and the national culture and way of life have been fiercely protected by patriotic rulers with isolationist tendencies throughout the ages.[304] These factors contribute to the healthy patriotism and positive self-image of the majority of Ethiopians, but they also mean that Ethiopians have had very little opportunity to interact with foreigners. Most have seldom or never had a meaningful encounter with people who are different from them. This has put Ethiopians a step behind some other non-Western countries when it comes to preparing to serve as barrier-crossing missionaries.

This barrier of lack of exposure to other cultures does not seem so daunting, however, when considered in balance with the many factors which make Ethiopians particularly well-suited to being barrier-crossing missionaries. First, the intense persecution that came upon the Church under the recently overthrown Communist regime has forged strong and faithful soldiers for Christ who accepted suffering as part of following their Savior and who now teach their disciples to do the same. The Ethiopian Church is a Church which has counted the cost. They are ready for the hardship, persecution, and trials that inevitably come when seeking to reach the unreached, because they can look back and see how God sustained them and their forefathers through the difficult recent past.[305]

Second, Ethiopian university students have been extremely effective within their own country on short-term evangelistic trips to rural areas which are unreached by the Gospel. Far from "spiritual vacations," these trips, taken during school breaks, have brought hundreds into the Kingdom of God in 2012 alone.[306] These Ethiopian young people, if properly mobilized and trained, are poised to be ideal barrier-crossing missionary candidates as they graduate from university and look to begin their life's work.

Third, it should be noted that this aforementioned vibrant and faithful Church in Ethiopia is strategically located on the fringe of the 10/40 window (the northern half of the country is even considered part of the window).[307] Beyond geographic proximity – which is certainly helpful – Ethiopians have open doors to enter countries where few Westerners can tread (Saudi Arabia, Yemen, Oman, etc.).

Despite her incredible potential, only 3% of the Ethiopian Church is considered "missions mobilized."[308] Though a few brave and zealous Ethiopians have for decades been going to far-flung places such as "India, Pakistan, and Sudan" for the purpose of reaching the unreached,[309] their numbers are a miniscule compared to the total number of Ethiopian believers.[310] This problem of ratio is a microcosm of the general problem facing the global South – while any number of missionaries being sent out is praiseworthy, it is troubling when the number is so small a percentage of the whole *potential* mission force (which includes every follower of Christ in Ethiopia or in the Global South).

Study of the challenges and opportunities facing the Ethiopian Church as she seeks to maximize her involvement in barrier-crossing ministry is immediately necessary. Ethiopia is experiencing unprecedented opportunity to be a major contributor in global evangelization, but she stands in danger of missing the opportunity if the process of becoming an Ethiopian missionary is not streamlined. If Ethiopian missionaries are trained and sent, taking advantage of the current opportunities, there will be huge impact on the Kingdom of God as droves of uniquely well-equipped laborers are sent out into the hardest harvest fields. If this happens, Ethiopia stands to benefit because of the principle that sending some out and staying connected to those sent ones serves to strengthen and broaden the prayer-horizons of the whole Church. Beyond national blessing for Ethiopia, the whole global Church, the body of Jesus Christ, stands to benefit from the influx of new brothers and sisters that these Ethiopian laborers will bring—brothers and sisters from hard-to-reach but beloved-by-God tribes and tongues and nations from around the globe.

Given the strides that Ethiopian evangelicals are taking toward greater involvement in fulfilling the Great Commission, this chapter and the next will investigate what steps can be taken to encourage Ethiopia's further development into a major missionary sending nation. Several related questions will also be explored. First, what barrier-crossing ministry training is currently available for Ethiopians who want to take the Gospel to the nations, and how can this training be expanded and enhanced for maximal effectiveness? Second, what barriers stand in Ethiopia's way that keep her from using her great potential in global missionary service, and what steps can be taken to remove those barriers? Third, in terms of missiological education, what have other African countries done to cross barriers and to become major missionary sending nations, and how might Ethiopia incorporate some of these factors into her own efforts in preparing missionaries?

Scarcity of barrier-crossing (often known as "missiological") education is certainly not the only challenge that Ethiopians mention when pondering what is holding them back from being intensely involved in fulfilling the Great Commission among the nations. Beyond lack of adequate training, they also speak of poverty and lack of infrastructure due to the recent fall of the Communist Regime. This study will not deal extensively with these factors, except to note the inspiring example of South Korea, who rose to become a major missionary sending nation out of the ashes of war-weariness and extreme poverty.³¹¹ God delights to use His servants mightily despite obstacles and lack of resources. Throughout the Bible, He has used the weak things of this world to show Himself strong, and where He has commanded, He will supply what is needed to fulfill that command if His children will step forth in faith.

This study will also not be focused on training Ethiopians for ministry work within their own cultural context. The Ethiopian Church as well as several Bible schools and seminaries are doing excellent work in this area. Evangelism is strongly encouraged, especially among university students, and ministries that care for street children, prostitutes, and other outcasts of society are growing and flourishing. That the Church is rapidly growing in Ethiopia is a testimony to two things: God's Spirit is at work there and His people are fulfilling their roles well as His messengers in monocultural settings.³¹²

Precedent Research

As the Church has begun to understand the burgeoning growth of the missions movement in the Global South, much has been written on the topic of missiological education for this "new breed of emerging mission[aries]."³¹³ Before embarking on the investigation of missionary training opportunities in Ethiopia and in other African countries, it will be helpful to review the current standard literature on this topic in order to understand three things: first, why there is such a need for barrier-crossing ministry education; second, why contextualization of curriculum and application of learning is of vital importance; third, what is accepted by the global Church as adequate and effective contextualized barrier-crossing education (this will be used as an objective standard when evaluating schools in Ethiopia and in other countries in Africa).

Ben Naja emphasizes the urgency of this preparing and sending of Two-Thirds World missionaries when he describes the decline of the Christian population of the West and the concurrent growth of the Christian population in other parts of the world. He concludes: "To reach the billions of people of our generation, millions of workers are required, and these workers can be found nowhere but in the Global South."[314] If the churches of the Global South are not "catalyze[d]…to take the gospel to nearby unreached people groups…Global South mission enterprises are doomed to fail."[315]

Naja referred in general to the Church in the Global South becoming active in sending barrier-crossing missionaries, but Theodore Williams becomes a bit more specific about what should be done to prepare the missionaries if they are to be effective on the field. He laments that there are so many "drop outs" in the Two-Thirds World missions force, and attributes this high attrition rate largely to lack of appropriate barrier-crossing training. Williams goes on to concede that this problem is well known and is being addressed, but most of the resulting "training programmes…are just in the early stages of development."[316]

Howard Brant's article on emerging missions movements makes this problem of Two-Thirds World missionary attrition even more disturbing, since availability of the kind of training they need to ensure their longevity as missionaries is so rare. He explains:

> If we look at Christian education in the majority world we will quickly find that the Bible schools, theological colleges, and seminaries are largely committed to training Christian workers for work in their own context.…Few are committed to giving their students the tools they will need to become cross-cultural workers in distant parts of the earth.[317]

Though theological education is certainly important and seminaries should continue to be established and enhanced, specific preparation for barrier-crossing ministry is also essential if the 2 Timothy 2:2 dynamic is to be continued across borders and in other languages toward the ultimate fulfillment of the Great Commission.

As we consider the need for training for Two-Thirds World Christians and specifically missionaries, several authors caution that we must be careful to avoid the temptation of a quick-fix importation of ready-made theology and missiology. William A. Dyrness advocates for those in the Two-Thirds world to be allowed to do theology for themselves, lamenting the "misconception that good theology has already been discovered and developed (usually in the context of Western Christianity), and it needs only to be exported and taught in Third World training schools."[318]

Howard Brant lists "Appropriate Training" as one the "Seven Essentials of Majority World Emerging Missions Movements" and elaborates on what Dyrness began to explain about the detrimental effects of importation. He explains that when missiological education is available, it is all too often "reworked lessons from the Western gurus of contextualization" who, though eloquent and excellent at connecting with Westerners, are inadequate to "dig down into the kinds of contextual issues that are faced by this new breed of emerging missions."[319]

In his book, *The Theological Task of the Church in Africa*, African theologian Tite Tiénou, reflects on the need for training in contextualization for Africans in general – how much more for Africans who desire to serve the Lord cross-culturally! His findings are significant for missiological educators who want to emphasize crossing cultural barriers in their classes. Tiénou speaks of both ethnocentrism and escapism as challenges for the African Christian. Tribalism – leading to ethnocentrism – is ingrained and must be intentionally addressed and eradicated by the cleansing power of the Holy Spirit if African missionaries are going to be effective as they seek to cross barriers to love and share with people who are different than them. The tension of living "in the world" (Jn. 17:11) but not being "of the world" (Jn. 17:16) has also led many Africans to isolate themselves in "cultural ghettoes" to avoid interaction with those whose beliefs and lifestyles are different than their own.[320] This recoiling reaction to differences is natural, but God calls His children to a higher standard, made possible by the blood of Christ which "has destroyed the barrier, the dividing wall of hostility" (Eph. 2:14). Tiénou charges Africans to face their avoidant tendencies head-on by developing a viable "theology of culture."[321] This will not only be helpful with engaging their own neighbors, but will also exponentially increase their effectiveness in barrier-crossing ministry throughout the globe. Specifically, Tiénou suggests that missionary training schools should "make…students aware of the cultural conditioning of all theologies…[and] make them aware of the fact that cultures are not bad in themselves."[322] Though he is from a different country in Africa, Tiénou's words ring poignantly true in Ethiopia – both ethnocentrism and escapism are being used by Satan to hold Ethiopians back from actively being involved in fulfilling the Great Commission by crossing cultural barriers. If these barriers are overcome through the power of the barrier-breaking Gospel and through contextualized curriculum designed to produce skilled cross-cultural contextualizers, the Ethiopian Church stands poised to reach some of the most unreached places in the world through her witness.

Ayuk A. Ayuk, a Nigerian missionary, agrees with Tienou on the importance of contextualization in African education, saying:

> Western theologians have written a lot of theological books; but, perhaps only a handful of professional theologians are interested in what has been said by these very articulate theologians...Theology is [only] relevant when it answers the questions of the context in which it is done. There is nothing that makes the Word of God more relevant than a proper understanding of the language and culture of a people.[323]

If Africans are trained in a Western way, they have an additional barrier to cross when going to another (likely non-Western) culture. If, on the other hand, Africans are trained in a way that is in relevant to their own culture, they will likely be able to develop the self-understanding that is necessary to then make the Gospel relevant to another culture when they heed the call to go to the nations. Since they have understood the Gospel in their heart-culture, they will be equipped to help others understand the Gospel in another heart-culture. Let us not erect more barriers for the swift spread of the Gospel than already exist!

Dr. Sarojini Nadar, in her article entitled "Contextual Theological Education in Africa and the Challenge of Globalization," gives an eloquent caution from an African perspective decrying the detrimental effects of globalization on theology. She shows the need for barrier-crossing training to be contextual in order to produce people who will effectively "*do*...contextual theology" rather than "merely being...scholar[s] of contextual theology."[324] She calls for African theologians to use their theology to transform their communities, not to merely speculate in ivory towers – something that many in the Western academy are guilty of doing. Though Nadar does not directly mention missiological education in her article, missionary trainers can glean much from her plea for contextual theology, for missionaries must be some of the most adept contextual theologians, becoming God-glorifying change agents not only their own context but also the context of those they go to. If Nadar's ideas are true for a theologian within his own culture, they become doubly true for a theologian (which every missionary is) crossing barriers to bring the Gospel to another culture.

R. Paul Stevens and Brian Stelck, Westerners with experience in Africa, write in a similar vein as they "critique...fascination with Western theological education"[325] in their article entitled "Equipping Equippers Cross-Culturally: An Experiment in the Appropriate Globalization of Theological Education." Like Nadar, Stevens and Stelck caution against "globalization without contextualization."[326] Though most Africans unconsciously agree that the Western degree is the ultimate credential, the authors lament: "In this mess of pottage, the Two-Thirds World sells its inheritance," because the problems of Western education come along with the credentials.[327] All too often, the West has "infected younger churches with arid intellectualism lacking spiritual power."[328] The reason for this stems from the fact that for many years "in Western education, there [has been] no clarity about how theory and practice should relate."[329] Western-style schools have become places where information is pondered but not applied outside the walls of a classroom. Especially in theological and missiological schools, this is a death-sentence to effectiveness in future ministry, because there is a lack of connection and continuity between what is learned in class and what is applied on the field. In a search for a better alternative, Stevens and Stelck suggest something very similar to what was previously mentioned by Ferris, Brynjolfson and Lewis, and Nadar. *"Theoria"* – the type of education associated with most classrooms – is a component, but it is combined with *"poiesis,"* which is the imaginative and creative expression of what has been learned in a way that will connect with others, as well as with *"praxis."*[330] Two-Thirds World missionary training schools – most of which are still young and flexible – have the opportunity to correct course and to bring back the clarity of the relationship between *theoria*, *poesis*, and *praxis*. This can only happen if the illusion of Western superiority is broken and the value of contextualization is realized through the voices of the astute authors mentioned in this paper as well as others. Ben Naja adds:

> The [W]estern missionary is, in most cases, oriented towards the intellect. To him being a missionary means to verbally spread the biblical message. His mission is completed when his counterpart intellectually understands his message. However, most unreached people groups are much more oriented towards experience.... In such a context, demonstrating power is much more important than demonstrating knowledge.[331]

Coming from a non-Western, power-oriented culture will be a great boon for Majority World missionaries, because they will intuitively understanding the worldview and longings of the people whom they serve and will therefore be able to say, "Our gospel came to you not simply with words but also with power" (1 Thess. 1:5). Their innate grasp of their hearers point of view makes the barriers lower for them than for Western missionaries taking on the same task.

The idea of power being a major aspect of the worldview of Two-Thirds World cultures is interesting when paired with the fact that "Pentecostalism is the predominant characteristic form of Christianity on the African continent." [332] This brand of Christianity has historically had the tendency to eschew theological education, but in recent years "are becoming increasingly aware that they stand in danger of misappropriation or misuse of scripture if their preachers are not properly trained. As a result, since the 1980s, there has been a growing desire for Pentecostal theological training in Africa."[333] Perhaps Pentecostal Africans will lead us down a balanced pathway of neither idolizing nor ignoring education, due to their recognition of their need for education but their reticence to trust in it. Karl Barth remarked that perhaps Africa is the "hope that the deficit [of Western theology in the areas of "spiritual experience and power"] could be mitigated."[334] Specifically related to the doctrine of the Holy Spirit, Omenyo quotes Cheryl Johns to make the incisive point that the Holy Spirit plays a major "pedagogical role" in education, suggesting that perhaps the "Pentecostal experience is the 'epistemological key' that 'radically alters traditional forms of theological education.'"[335] In contextualized theological and missiological education in Africa, knowledge and power to apply that knowledge will go hand in hand due to the positive influence of Pentecostalism on the continent.

Tite Tiénou has additional wisdom to add to the ideas that the above-mentioned authors have introduced about theology that leads to powerful action. In his essay, "The Training of Missiologists for an African Context," he strongly argues that "[m]issiologists trained for twenty-first century Africa will need to develop and sustain intellectual probity." By this, he means that missionary training schools should not exist merely to "satisfy people's need and desire for degrees and other credentials."[336] Rather, these schools should be the hotspot of prayerful discussion and brainstorming in order to "deal seriously with the specific issues of Christian mission in Africa."[337]

Dr. Robert Ferris' *Establishing Ministry Training: A Manual for Programme Developers* is a ground-breaking work designed to "walk educators and trainers through the path to start new ministry training programmes, as well as to strengthen existing ones."[338] They helpfully lay out ten "Biblical-Educational Commitments to Guide Missionary Training" in the appendix of the book. Training, according to this list, should be "church related." Actual "require[ments] for effective service" should determine the curriculum, and everything about the set-up of the school should be designed to help students toward living in a way that meets these requirements. Training should be contextualized in a way that works with the students' natural "ways of thinking and learning" and should have "the learner's experience" as a significant foundation and referent. All that is taught should be "validated by Scripture and by general revelation," and all that is learned should be put into practice. Both "skills....character qualities and values" should be not only be taught, but also "model[ed]," "practiced," and "reflect[ed]" upon in order for true learning to take place. Finally, "training equips the learner for effective ministry and continuing growth."[339]

As the editor for *Diversified Theological Education: Equipping All God's People*, Ross Kinsler has provided a complementary perspective showing how similar concepts could be conveyed through the Theological Education By Extension (TEE) and/or Diversified Theological Education (DTE) methods. He describes three components of the holistic training program: first, students "study...appropriate materials"[340] which might take "written...audio or visual" form;[341] second, students work out what they have learned in practical settings within their "local church and/or community" in order to "test" what they have learned; third, students gather "to review, clarify, and discuss the material studied in the local church and/or community." [342] In this way, the knowledge the students gain is put into action immediately and then is reflected upon, creating a cycle of transformation in their communities.

In their book, *Integral Ministry Training: Design and Evaluation*, editors Robert Brynjolfson and Jonathan Lewis, acknowledging a debt of gratitude to the above-mentioned two books,[343] elegantly restate and clarify the components of missiological education. They describe that students should be helped to grow in the areas of "understanding," "character growth,"[344] and "skills development."[345] In this way, the "whole person" is trained.[346] Like Ferris, Brynjolfson and Lewis have "Ten Principles of Integral Training." Many of these principles are nuanced restatements of Ferris' ideas, but original elements include the "metaphor of service," [347] the idea of "trainers...[as] mentors---fellow servants," the need for both "trainers and trainees [to] assume responsibility for learning outcomes," the "unique design" of each trainee which will be developed in "community," and the standard of the success of the school being the faithfulness and effectiveness of her graduates."[348]

There are many lists of content standards for missionary training schools; a few representative samples will suffice to establish a general consensus. In a companion volume to Ferris' work, called *Preparing to Serve: Training for Cross-Cultural Mission*. Dr. David Harley suggests that curriculum should include "Biblical studies," "Doctrine," "Mission Studies," and "Pastoral Studies."[349] Brant calls for "[s]olidly biblical but contextually relevant theology," "[c]ontextualized missiology that works in the majority world" and "[p]ractical skills that the emerging missions movement is going to need to sustain itself financially as well as contribute to the felt needs of the people they serve.[350] Tiénou gets more detailed as he expresses his advice that "curriculum...must be expanded to include, among other disciplines, African history, sociology, urban studies, political thought, African philosophy, Islamics, and African literature."[351] He also suggests the need for "[t]heological grounding," the fostering of "spiritual fervor and credibility,"[352] "serious reflect[ion] on suffering in the African experience," and "rediscover[ing] the dignity of poverty."[353]

Brynjolfson and Lewis do not include a list of topics to be covered; rather, they guide readers through the process of developing their own list. They do, however, provide a helpful "Training Profile of a Cross-Cultural Church Planter,"[354] which paints a picture of a successful graduate of a missionary training school. Missionary trainers can work backward from this profile, which contains eleven categories, including things like "spiritual maturity," "cultural sensitivity," and "evangelism and discipleship,"[355] to develop curriculum which will facilitate their students' resemblance of the biblically-based profile at graduation and beyond.

Indeed, emphasis on character, spiritual maturity, and personal development have been mentioned in passing by several authors as imperative for Two-Thirds World missionary education, as a corrective of the Enlightenment-influenced Western over-emphasis on head-knowledge. In a discussion of adequate pre-field training, contributors to the book *Too Valuable to Lose* explicitly explain the need for this personal spiritual development aspect of missionary education:

> The whole thrust of missionary training is to ensure that missionary candidates are being conformed to the image of Christ....All training should therefore be focused primarily on the development of our 'being,' anticipating that 'doing' and 'knowing' will facilitate that development. We recommend that special attention in training be given to development of character, having the right attitudes, maintaining daily relationship and walk with Christ; emphasizing holiness of life; understanding what call and commitment really mean...[and being prepared for] spiritual warfare.[356]

These topics, though not as academic as others that have been previously mentioned, are necessary and vital to include in any missionary training curriculum in order to produce a fully-formed, effective, equipped messenger of the Gospel who is adequately prepared to cross barriers for the glory of God among the nations.

In summary, the above-referenced authors agree that there is great need for theological and missiological education (the two go hand-in-hand and are not truly separate) for the burgeoning Two-Thirds World missions force. They argue that training must be contextual and applied if it is to be effective. Western imports will not suffice – African training must be developed for Africans who are preparing to bring a contextualized Gospel to the nations. The only way that they will be able to avoid making the same mistakes of those missionaries who imposed their own culture along with the Gospel will be if they are taught in a way that sensitizes them to their own culture and teaches them to understand the culture of others, allowing them to smoothly cross all kinds of barriers smoothly. A particular aspect of Western educational importation that should be rejected out of hand is theory divorced from practice. Rather, effective missionary training should never separate theology from life – the two should be intertwined, and theology should be brought to bear on the current issues facing Ethiopia and facing the nations that she will reach with the Gospel. Missionary training should be contextualized and applied, and should include Biblical/Theological/Ministry Studies, Intercultural Studies, personal and spiritual life development, and practical skill acquisition.

The above-mentioned literature has come together to create a solid foundation for my research by confirming the fact that barrier-crossing ministry training for Majority World Christians is crucial, and making several suggestions for what should be included in this training. All has not yet been said on this topic, however. In this study, the focus will be more limited compared to most of the extant literature, in terms of the type of training that are being analyzed. Most of what is written seems directed at training Two-Thirds World Christians to be pastors and ministry workers in their own context. We will to focus specifically on the sending of majority world Christians to be barrier-crossing missionaries to other Two-Thirds World countries and the classes and learning experiences which are or could be offered in training schools that would be helpful toward that goal. Second, the focus will be specifically on Ethiopia, a place that the extant literature mentions in passing at best. Rather than speaking in generalities about Africa – which is certainly helpful, but also not sufficient – we will narrow our focus to one country in order to develop some specific contextual, relevant, and practical suggestions for moving forward with greater effectiveness in training believers from this nation to make a unique contribution to the fulfillment of the Great Commission.

Evaluative research will be done in order "to provide useful information based on values for decision making."[357] Evaluative studies of this kind in the area of education are crucial, because "educational research is needed in each community, with each generation and as developmental change occurs to keep the curriculum relevant and effective."[358] Because Ethiopia's recent history has been so tumultuous and rapidly changing, resulting in the explosive growth of the Church, it seems appropriate to consider whether the education that is available now has caught up with the booming growth and resultant needs of the Ethiopian Church.

Research Methodology

Case study research will be done, first through interviews with Ethiopians and knowledgeable non-Ethiopians, and then through a survey of missiological training schools. This two pronged approach will enable the practical evaluation of what is currently being done to prepare and send missionaries in Ethiopia, what challenges Ethiopia faces as she seeks to become a major missionary sending nation, what is being done in other African countries in terms of missionary training, and how Ethiopia can integrate some of these ideas, as well as ideas from the representative Ethiopian training programs, into expansion and establishment of many more missionary training schools.

When conducting the survey, we will employ the criteria established in the precedent research when, looking for the following when evaluating training programs:

- Contextualization
- Application
- Biblical/Theological/Ministry Studies
- Intercultural Studies
- Personal/Spiritual Life Development
- Practical Skill Acquisition

We will examine the interview results in order to identify consistent answers to the questions which would indicate key findings and could lead to relevant recommendations when combined with the survey information. When interview answers are widely varied, conversely, this will indicate to me the need for further study on the particular topic covered by the question.

Survey of Missiological Preparation Currently Available in Ethiopia

The results of the survey were eye-opening, helpful, and offered a mixture of encouragement and sobering reality-check in terms of the state of the preparation of Ethiopians as cross-cultural ministry workers. Much progress was noted, and much potential for growth was revealed.

Progress

There has been heartening progress in the availability of missionary training in the relatively brief history of the Evangelical Church in Ethiopia. Several questions of my survey were geared toward assessing this progress, specifically gauging how barrier-crossing topics are being taught and incorporated into Christian education, and what pathways called individuals would be instructed to take in order to become missionaries.

How Leaders are Preparing Ethiopian Students for Missions

After being asked a question regarding the importance of the Great Commission in their ministries as teachers and mentors, respondents were asked to give specific ways in which they use their teaching to prepare their students or disciples for crossing barriers.

The responses to this question varied widely, but each type of strategy for equipping others for fulfilling the Great Commission is worth mentioning. Five respondents spoke of using case studies – stories of what God is doing in the world through His people – to open students' eyes to the need for and power of the Gospel worldwide. Real-life examples of God's people living out God's missionary call on their lives makes the possibility of becoming a barrier-crossing missionary more concrete and attainable for students, for they can follow the missionaries' example as the missionaries follow the example of Christ (1 Cor. 11:1). Up-to-date reports of the spread of the Gospel and the frontiers that are still unreached also can be used of God to stir the hearts of the students to become His witnesses so that the ends of the earth might finally know His Name.

Four respondents spoke of how they show their students the Biblical foundation for mission in order to motivate their students to fulfill the Great Commission. If God commanded that his disciples take the Gospel to every nation, Ethiopia is not exempted – she has a responsibility to pass on the Good News that was brought to her so many years ago. The Biblical mandate for missions, say these respondents, is the core of any robust barrier-crossing strategy or initiative.

Four votes also were cast for cross-cultural skills training as a crucial way to prepare disciples to fulfill the Great Commission. Because of Ethiopia's isolated history, several respondents feel that in order to be effective, Ethiopian missionaries should have thorough training on how to differentiate Ethiopian culture from "Jesus culture." If they know the difference and their ministry reflects this knowledge, they will avoid shaping converts into Ethiopian Christian clones and inadvertently following in the misguided footsteps of too many nationalistic European and American Christian missionaries.

Short-term missions were also suggested by three respondents as a way to equip students to fulfill the Great Commission. The exposure that the students receive on these journeys is incalculably more impactful than any lecture would be. If used as a vision trip of sorts, these experiences could be a powerful recruitment tool for long-term missionaries. It should be noted that many reports from student organizations which regularly incorporate short term mission trips into their yearly schedule indicate that these trips are not merely spiritual vacations – as unfortunately many supposed missions trips turn out to be – but are used greatly by God to bring many into His kingdom and are treated by those involved as intensive ministry. There is a seriousness and purposefulness and maturity about these Ethiopian-initiated trips that is lacking in many Western-initiated ones.

Three respondents shared that they work on their students attitudes in order to prepare them to be effective as they seek to fulfill the Great Commission. If someone brings a wonderful message but has a terrible attitude, it is likely that their ministry will be dampened. In order to avoid this, one respondent shares that he works with his students until they "love people from every culture and race." Another administrator and professor shared that "more than any other thing" he teaches his students "when they go for cross-cultural missions to go first as learners [then] teachers." This learner's attitude earns the missionary an opportunity to teach after trust and mutual "respect" has been established.

Other strategies for equipping disciples to carry out the Great Commission were less commonly mentioned but equally helpful. Two respondents work to fit their disciples' professional degrees into relevant ministry roles. Two mentioned that they keep the concept of 2 Timothy 2:2 in mind when discipling – they teach their disciples to disciple others so that the chain of the Great Commission keeps going indefinitely. A pioneer in online ministry shared that he recruits people to be online missionaries – an opportunity that allows anyone to cross cultural barriers without ever leaving their country, their city, or even their home! Lastly, one person emphasized what is perhaps so foundational that others did not even think to mention it: prayer is essential not only in order to fulfilling the Great Commission, but also in order to equip others to fulfill it.

Next Steps for Ethiopian Called as a Missionary

When asked what next steps they would advise for an Ethiopian friend who wanted to be a missionary, the majority of respondents mentioned that the friend should seek to be sent – that is, that he or she should share the vision with his or her church and community and raise prayer and financial support. The next most common answer is that he should study culture his own and that which he is trying to reach – in order to cross cultural barriers effectively. Broader but related to this is the suggestion that he should get training – in Bible, theology, missions, and other helpful topics.

Six respondents would ask questions in order to dig deeper with the friend in exploring his call – they would ask questions like where they felt called to, how long they had felt this way, etc. Related to this, five respondents would advise him to pray about his calling in order to receive God's direction and leading in his next steps. Three had the practical suggestion that he should learn to communicate well and a simple and effective way to share the Gospel. As already mentioned by some respondents, three people suggested that he go and visit the people group that he thought God was calling him to in order to confirm his specific calling, to find out more about the people group, and to better prepare for his long-term barrier-crossing assignment.

Other less popular but still thought-provoking pieces of advice include: learn English in order to be able to function well internationally and remove a language barrier, interact with the stories of other missionaries, whether in person or through biographies, pray for the people you are called to serve, make connections with churches in the area where you are going to serve, and get training in medical treatment and other practical skills.

What an Ethiopian Should Know as a Missionary

When asked what things an Ethiopian missionary should know before going to another culture with the Gospel, a vast majority of respondents emphasized that an Ethiopian missionary should have cultural barrier-crossing skills and should understand the culture of the group which they will serve. This will be key in building relationships and earning trust. As a subset of this, but mentioned separately,

Ethiopian missionaries should understand the worldview and beliefs of the group which they will serve. This worldview contains the ideas and philosophies that undergird the culture, and one cannot truly understand the culture without understanding it.

Practically speaking, four respondents said that an Ethiopian missionary should know the language of a group they will serve. Though not absolutely necessary – the missionary could learn the language by immersion after arriving – already being conversant will obviously remove a barrier, facilitating relationship building and opportunities for Gospel witness more quickly.

On a different note, three respondents said that Ethiopian missionaries – and all missionaries – should know that they will face challenges. A missionary assignment is not a bed of roses; rather, loneliness, rejection, deprivation, lack of fruit, and many other hardships may come along with the joys of missionary life. It would be helpful for a missionary to be aware of the coming challenges so that he will not be caught off-guard and begin to doubt God or become discouraged.

Two respondents suggested that an Ethiopian missionary should research the state of the church in the area where they are going. Even if there is no existing church in the specific city or region to which he are going, he should become informed if there are any individual Christians living in isolation or if there are churches in neighboring cities or regions. These existing Christians will be valuable partners for the missionary and will help him greatly by allowing him to live in community and not as a lone ranger.

Two respondents also reiterated the need for the Ethiopian missionary to go first as a learner. Nothing will go further, they say, in establishing trust and building relationships than respecting others, listening to their ideas, and learning from them. By listening, the missionary can discern entrance points for the Gospel as good news, and will have greater effectiveness when he earns a hearing after a time.

Other things that an Ethiopian cross-cultural missionary should know include: evangelism and apologetics, a trade or profession which can act as an entry into a community, the educational background of the people to which he is going, the reality of spiritual warfare, the fact that they should not compare themselves to other missionaries and ministry workers, the fact that they can accept and love people who are different, and how to deal with insider movements.

Potential for Growth

Along with encouraging progress markers, the survey respondents mentioned several areas of missionary preparation in Ethiopia that still have much potential for growth.

What Ethiopian Missionaries Still Need to Learn

When administrators, professors, and leaders were asked where their students and disciples needed more training, many mentioned training in barrier-crossing cultural skills. This, according to several respondents, is a particular need in Ethiopia, since the country has been culturally homogenous and isolated from outside influences for so many centuries. Though there are many positive things about having such a strong sense of national identity, cross-cultural training is very necessary to ensure that nationalism does not become unhealthy and unbalanced. Also, because Ethiopians have little experience with interacting with those who are different than them, training is necessary to ensure that they are able to build relationships and not put up unnecessary cultural barriers between themselves and those to whom they are called to go.

When culture is mentioned, language is never far behind! Four respondents shared that they believed that language is a weak area of current missionary training. It would be helpful to Ethiopian missionaries to learn the language of the people they are called to before they leave for their assignment, and it is often necessary for the Ethiopian missionary to know English, as it is the lingua franca of the world.

Three respondents are concerned that more training in the "authentic Christian life" and more "discipleship" is needed for those who want to be missionaries. The reality of huge numbers of Ethiopians coming to the Lord has meant that the ratio of younger believers to older, more mature ones is unbalanced, issuing in more demand than supply of in-depth discipleship. There are many initiatives in order to meet this ever-growing need for teaching and training, but it will continue to be an issue into the foreseeable future.

Three respondents also shared that they believe that more emphasis should be given to "the big picture of global missions." This would help all Christian students, whether or not they become long-term missionaries, to understand the multifaceted roles that the people of the Body of Christ have in fulfilling the Great Commission.

Though their answer was not an exact match to the question, two respondents shared that specific "mentoring and monitoring" during missionaries' time on the field is something that is needed yet lacking in Ethiopia today. While this is not something that students and disciples need to learn per se, it is nevertheless an interesting insight into a problem to be addressed: lack of oversight of existing missionaries. Perhaps these two answers could be reworded to answer the question at hand by stating that students and disciples should learn what proper missionary care looks like.

Obstacles to Major Missionary Sending

The heart of the survey addressed the paradoxical growth of the Church in Ethiopia without a resultant surge of missionaries. Why are these spiritually strong, vibrantly faithful servants of Christ not being shot like arrows into the most spiritually dark areas of the globe? What barriers are holding the Body of Christ in Ethiopia back from fulfilling her Great Commission calling on a large-scale basis?

The respondents had many theories to share, the most common of which was unawareness of the need and lack of vision for the cause of global evangelization. The average person sitting in church on a Sunday is simply not cognizant of the fact that millions have not yet heard the Gospel of Christ.

This lack of vision among Christians can be traced, according to five respondents, to the lack of teaching from church leaders on the subject of missions. Missions education is not a common priority among Ethiopian churches, and many leaders do not have not caught the vision for missions themselves, and so therefore cannot help impart it to the other church members.

Language was also cited as a significant barrier which prevents Ethiopians from being more involved in fulfilling the Great Commission cross-culturally. Though the struggle for English fluency experienced by many Ethiopians is due to a good thing – the fact that Ethiopia was never colonized – it nevertheless has made international travel more daunting for Ethiopians. Since English is the global language, it is almost essential to speak if living as an expat in another country and working with a global missionary team. Add to this the need to likely learn yet another language of the people to whom the missionary is going, and the whole road to missionary service can begin to seem too challenging and arduous.

Perhaps one of the most insidious of the reasons why Ethiopia is not yet a major missionary sending nation is that, according to four respondents, she suffers from a receiving mentality. Perhaps due to historical paternalism or perhaps due to widespread poverty, this mental barrier of being characterized by *lack* and *need* permeates much of the Body of Christ in Ethiopia today. It is assumed that mission initiatives and the money to fund them must come from outside.

Intertwined with the problem of the receiving mentality is the problem of money. The Ethiopian Church as a whole on the global scale does not have much of it. This can become defining to the church, a death knell of sure ineffectiveness, and a cry for help. Money is a delicate issue, for the lack of it is onerous, but receiving it in wrong manner or receiving too much of it can end up hurting more than it helps. Money – the lack of it, and the reception of it from the outside – forms a complex and thorny challenge for Ethiopian-initiated missions.

Ways Forward Toward Major Missionary Sending

The respondents were bursting with thought-provoking insights and wonderful ideas when asked, "What needs to happen for Ethiopia to become a major missionary sending nation in the future?" It was encouraging to see the amount of consensus on several of the answers, indicating ideas whose time has come.

The most popular answer was the general idea that the Ethiopian Church should become more missions-minded. While broad in scope, individual respondents had specific steps which the Church should take in order to achieve this goal. All eight who voiced this opinion agreed that missions should be a primary focus of the Church, and that this focus should be duly reflected both in its teaching and allocation of resources.

The need for mission sending groups was also keenly felt, in order to provide a channel through which Ethiopians who are called to be missionaries could pass with minimal logistical hassles. Indigenous Ethiopian sending groups are currently few and far between. An increase in such groups could be very helpful in helping Ethiopians to navigate and eliminate barriers to their missionary service so that they can be effective in fulfilling the Great Commission.

Related to this, more missionary training schools and missionary training programs within other schools were recognized as a need. The missionaries who would be sent by the missions-minded church through the mission sending agency must first be trained by a mission sending school or program, so these first three suggestions are really quite intertwined. Beyond specialized education for missionary candidates, four respondents also noted the need for intensive education and discipleship for all members of the Ethiopian Church so that all of them could become aware of God's global plan and play their part for His

CHAPTER SIX

Preparing Ethiopians for Barrier-Crossing Ministry: Survey of Missionary Preparation in Ethiopia and in Other African Countries

Much Great Commission good is happening in institutions of higher religious education in Ethiopia (and in Africa at large). Missionaries are being equipped and sent out. As we have seen in the last chapter, however, there is still much *more* Great Commission good that could be done so that Ethiopia could become a major missionary sending nation in the near future.

In order to avoid studying the topic of missionary preparation in a theoretical and abstract fashion, it will be helpful to survey three Ethiopian schools and three schools from other countries in Africa, evaluating them in terms of the globally agreed upon necessary components for adequate and effective barrier-crossing missionary training: contextualization of the curriculum, focus on application of what is learned, inclusion of Biblical/Theological/Ministry Studies, inclusion of Intercultural Studies, personal/spiritual life development, and training in practical skills.

Survey and Analysis of Ethiopian Schools

Shiloh Bible College Ethiopia (SBCE) – Certificate in Missionary Outreach (9 months)

Located in the city of Hawassa, SBCE is an interdenominational Bible college which "was found[ed] in 1994 in collaboration with Shiloh Bible College [in] Oakland, California."[359] It offers a certificate in missionary outreach specifically contextualized to prepare missionaries to work in an African Muslim context. It should be noted that this school is working in conjunction with Rift Valley Vision, which is "a new mission society...in Southern Ethiopia...[whose] goal is to train missionaries, plant churches, and see healthy productive communities" which is seeing many conversions among Muslims.[360]

Contextualization

The training is given in Amharic – the national language of Ethiopia – making it more accessible to Ethiopians who are hoping to work cross-culturally within the country. The majority of the thirty-three unreached people groups within Ethiopia are Muslim, so even without fluency in Arabic or English, graduates of this program will have enormous opportunities to share the Gospel in a contextualized way. The leaders of SBCE state that "as an Ethiopian Bible College, we seek to be aware of the needs of our continent and to equip students in particular context. The Ethiopian context in which we are located provides the basic concrete situation within which we do theology, while also providing strong motivation for cross-cultural missions and ministry." Graduates are expected to "have a good understanding of Islamic teaching and culture relevant to the area in which they will be ministering,"[361] and should "understand the principles of...contextualization of the gospel." The writers of the program description make a point to mention that included in every lecture or learning experience is an explanation of "the relevance of the teaching, course or experience for Islamic outreach."[362] The program is a tight six months of training, so each lesson is expertly tailored to pertain directly and practically to the context in which the missionaries will work – no frills, no extras.

Application

According to their philosophy of education, SBCE affirms that "our experience of truth must also integrate thought and life. Therefore, we...seek to draw our students into the learning process so that thought and life [are] integrated in their experiences."[363] Toward this end, the six months of classroom training is broken into two halves by a three-month outreach stint known as "field work" in "an Islamic area."[364] The last three months, after the field work segment, are specifically designed to allow students "to interact around what they have learned in their field experience and to learn from one another." Even during the months of classroom training, "the students gather for prayer and devotion together at which time they practice leading prayer, worship, preaching, communion, and receive instruction in personal prayer and devotional time."[365]

Biblical/Theological/Ministry Studies

The program description lists "The scripture through the guidance of the Holy Spirit" as "the final authority for life and practice." Listed as the number one program goal is: "Have a good biblical foundation in sound biblical doctrine and teaching especially as relates to issues and controversies related to Islamic evangelization."[366] Doctrinal classes, as well as Romans/Galatians and Luke/Acts, are taught during the six-month classroom training.[367]

Intercultural Studies/Missiology

The leaders of Shiloh desire their graduates "Have a good understanding of Islamic teaching and culture relevant to the area in which they will be ministering," and to be "well prepared to do evangelistic work among Muslims."[368] Toward this end, several classes are offered, including Islamic Culture and Teaching, Christian-Islamic Controversy, Muslim Evangelism, Mission Outreach Strategies and Church Planting in Muslim Areas, and Cross-Cultural Ministry.[369] After taking these classes, it is hoped that students will "understand the principles of cross-cultural ministry and contextualization of the gospel."[370]

Personal/Spiritual Life Development

As previously mentioned, students gather together for prayer, worship, and mutual edification each day while attending SBCE. By the time they graduate, they are expected to, "Understand and be prepared to practice the principles of servant leadership in a missionary context" by demonstrating "Christian character reflecting the fruit of the Spirit."[371]

Practical Skill Acquisition

Two classes are offered that are geared toward developing practical skills that will benefit the graduates of the Certificate in Missionary Outreach program: Christian Leadership Principles for Missionaries and Marketplace Missions (which teaches missionaries how to run a small business while on the field).[372]

Ethiopian Kaleheywet School of Missions (EKSM) – Diploma in Missions (2 year)

Located first in Durame and then in satellite form in eight other Ethiopian cities, "EKSM [has] graduated 218 missionaries," from a 2-year diploma program since 2001, 90% of whom are "in the field" within Ethiopia as well as in places as diverse as "South Sudan, China, Pakistan,

North Kenya, Chad, Malawi, and Cambodia."³⁷³ EKSM is the denominational mission school of the Kaleheywet Church. Prospective students must have completed Bible school in order to enroll. It should be noted that Dr. Steven Hardy, who "works with the Overseas Council and has been assessing Bible Schools and seminaries all over the world" picked this very school when asked to recommend a paradigm for duplication for missionary education in Africa.³⁷⁴ This is no small praise!

Contextualization

EKSM states that its "primary focus" is "Islamic and ATR (African Traditional Religion) people groups,"³⁷⁵ indicating a contextual understanding of the religion of Ethiopia and her neighbors – the countries to which Ethiopians are likely to go as missionaries. Their strategy to train effective "cross-cultural missionaries and church planters" is to utilize "carefully designed contextual curriculum."³⁷⁶ Specific classes deal with how to preach to ATR, Muslim, and Ethiopian Orthodox Tewahedo Church (EOTC) hearers.³⁷⁷ Courses such as Contextualized Evangelism and Church Planting Among Muslims and Contextualization: Gospel and Culture are also offered. Indeed, "Contextualization and mission work" is listed as one of eight major modules which make up the entirety of the program.³⁷⁸

Application

A motto of EKSM is "Classroom Instruction—KNOW, Character and Spiritual Development – BE, and Field practicum – DO."³⁷⁹ These elements work together in the training in order to produce contemporary, dedicated and effective missionaries that are reaching the unreached people groups and least evangelised parts of Ethiopia and beyond.

Biblical Studies/Theological/Ministry Studies

Students at EKSM study the Old and New Testaments as well as Doctrine, Hermeneutics, and Exegesis. They also are prepared for ministry through classes like Developing Church Leaders, Church Growth Principles, Theology of Church Function, and Follow-Up and Discipleship.[380]

Intercultural Studies/Missiology

Understandably, this School of Missions is particularly strong in this area. As they state at the beginning of their program description:

> It is a fact that an evangelist who is going to be sent for cross-cultural mission work needs cross-cultural training, as well as theological knowledge and practical experience, so that he/she will be effective in the ministry. The Ethiopian Kaleheywet Church analyzed that for national, as well as international missions, the church needs many workers who are trained in the field of cross-cultural missions.[381]

Because the courses in this area are so numerous, they have simply been listed in bulleted form here:[382]

- Church Planting Movements
- Understanding Islam
- Historical Models of Evangelism Among Muslims
- Contemporary Models of Evangelism Among Muslims

- Contextualized Evangelism and Church Planting Among Muslims
- Philosophy and Phenomenology of Islam
- Apologetics For Muslims
- Church Planting Movements Among Muslims
- Cultural Anthropology
- Cross-Cultural Communication
- Ethnographic Research
- Communication with Oral Learner
- Intercultural Leadership
- Ethnographic Research
- Religious Ethnography
- Sociological Research
- Structured Field Language Learning
- Cross-Cultural Social Dynamics
- Applied Theology Among MBB
- Biblical Foundations of Missions
- Understanding the EOC
- Cults
- Contextualization of the Gospel and Culture
- Biblical Theology of Missions
- Kingdom of God and Mission
- History of Missions
- Missiological Survey of Acts
- Missions in the Local Church
- Applied Missiological Ecclesiology
- Cultural Entry, Adaptation, and Interaction Skills
- Preaching to ATR, Muslim, and EOTC Audiences

Personal/Spiritual Life Development

EKSM offers several courses aimed at the spiritual, "BE" aspect of the missionary candidate's life: Spiritual Formation, Commitment and Discipleship, Spiritual Disciplines, Hearing God, Spiritual Warfare and Deliverance, Standing Strong in the Storms, and Life in the Spirit. Also offered are courses that deal with the communal aspect of the Christian – and specifically missionary – life: Team Building, Team in Missions, Issues in Missionary Living, Interpersonal Communication, Interpersonal Conflict Management, Conflict Transformation, and Marriage and Family Development.[383]

Practical Skill Acquisition

EKSM offers some practical courses in order to boost the effectiveness of their missionary graduates: English, Language Acquisition, Study Skills, Sports, Personal Maintenance, Health Maintenance, Administration, Literacy, and Animal Husbandry.[384]

Evangelical Theological College (ETC) – B.Th. with Missions major (4 year)

Located in Addis Ababa, ETC has been in existence since 1983 and is one of the largest Protestant theological schools in Ethiopia.[385] Students can major in Missions while studying for a Bachelor of Theology (B.Th.) degree. According to ETC's catalog: "This major is designed for those who will be involved in cross cultural evangelism and church planting in Ethiopia and beyond."[386]

Contextualization

On top of the typical biblical and theological courses expected in a theology degree program, a required Understanding Islam course is wise in the context in which most Ethiopian missionaries will find themselves (either within Ethiopia, in the bordering Muslim nations, or in the Arab World). Potential electives also include contextual classes such as African Church History, Ethiopian Church History, and The Response of the Church to HIV-AIDS in Ethiopia.[387]

Application

ETC's philosophy of application is clear, saying that "spiritual truth learned apart from personal application dulls the student to the power of the Spirit of God and the relevance of the Word of God," ETC's goal is "that classroom, chapel, and other sessions be relevant to building the student's personal walk with the Lord." "Head...hands...heart"[388] are mentioned in the school's purpose statement, indicating its stance that cognitive knowledge alone is insufficient ETC expects its students to participate in "in-service training," which is guided and evaluated ministry within their churches even during their four years of study as well as a capstone internship near the end of their program.[389]

Biblical/Theological/Ministry Studies

"Biblical Focus" is one of ETC's stated distinctives: "In all programmes of the ETC the Word of God is central" and has "authority over all areas of life."[390] The leadership desires "that students have a working knowledge of the content of the Bible and an in-depth understanding of passages especially crucial to their ministries." Several electives – Homiletics, Principles and Methods of Teaching, Small Group Ministry, and Worship and Music in the Church – teach essential ministry skills.[391]

Intercultural/Missiological Studies

As an essential component of missions studies, Intercultural Studies is present in the required courses – Cross-Cultural Communication, Advanced Evangelism, Understanding Islam, and Church Planting and Growth – and is also featured prominently in the elective courses offered: Linguistics, Islam in the Horn of Africa, Theology of Mission, Understanding the Ethiopian Orthodox Church, Cults and False Teachings, African Traditional Religions, and World Religions.[392]

Personal/Spiritual Life Development

One of ETC's stated goals is "Building Christian Character." (5) To this end, the "faculty will be involved in the lives of and ministries of the students outside the classroom," and the school will seek to help students "pursue a lifetime of maturing into the likeness of Jesus Christ."[393]

Practical Skill Acquisition

Christian Home teaches students about "marriage and family" from God's perspective.[394]

Survey and Analysis of Schools in Other African Countries

In order to decide upon which schools in other African nations to feature in this paper, I consulted Brynjolfson and Lewis' chapter entitled "Program Descriptions," which "describe[s] innovative, strategic, and best practices from our global missionary movement."[395] I have included all of the African schools profiled except Logos Mission School in South Africa, whose goal of primarily training students from other nations does not fit with the educational possibilities we are exploring in this paper.

Focus Team Leadership Training (FTLT) Missional Leadership Training School (MLTS) – (11 month training)

Located in Pretoria, South Africa, The FTLT MLTS is "a high impact, high intensity, fulltime training program that runs for 11 months."[396] It has been in existence since 2003.[397]

Contextualization

The FTLT MLTS was founded to address the need for younger leaders with a missional focus and understanding – this training is itself is a contextualized offering to meet a perceived need.

Application

The "bush phase" of the training is a two to three week survival trek through the wilderness to teach and test practical skills that missionaries will need in more remote areas. Once a week, students of FTLT MLTS do "Inner-city exposure outreaches" to share the love of Christ with the hurting. Many students also go to Botswana on an outreach and all students do a "three month outreach at the end of the year" as an internship of sorts."[398]

Biblical/Theological/Ministry Studies

FTLT MLTS students study Discipleship and also take an Overview of Theology course.[399]

Intercultural Studies/Missiology

This is understandably an important element of the training at FTLT MLTS, both in formal and informal learning. Students take classes in Cultural Intelligence and Anthropology, Introduction to Missions, and Folk Religion, and they get exposure to different cultures through their various outreaches throughout the course of the year.[400] They also state: "We purposely go out of our way to have an international staff. This is essential to give the students a practical, first hand, cross-cultural experience."[401]

Personal/Spiritual Life Development

FTLT MLTS students study Discipleship, Spiritual Gifts, Spiritual Authority, Leadership Principles, and Perseverance in Ministry. Mentoring is also a key aspect of the training, and "strong emphasis is placed on the spiritual, character, personal and leadership development of every student."[402] Specifically, the leadership of this school desires that their graduates "will impact their sphere of influence through a focused lifestyle, working with others in a team, expressing Godly character and continuing to develop themselves and those around them into better leaders."[403] Teamwork is emphasized in the daily lives, ministry, and training of students.[404]

Practical Skill Acquisition

Practical training is one of the hallmarks of FTLT MLTS. Students also take a wide variety of hands-on courses designed to make them effective as missionaries: Biblical Entrepreneurship, Finances, Basic Cooking, Introduction to Computers & the Internet, Research and Writing, Sports Ministry, Children's Ministry, Creative Arts, Oral Communication (Story Telling), Community Health and Development, and Farming God's Way.[405]

FTLT MLTS students are given rigorous physical training to prepare them for their "bush phase" as well as for the often "harsh realities" of life as a missionary in a remote location. During the bush phase, students get good at "sleeping in tents, [dealing with] limited water, food preparation on an open fire, navigation and emergency evacuation." They also "learn how to read a map, use a compass, how to communicate via two-way radios, survival first aid, and general camping and hiking guidelines."[406] During the course of the formal training, students also learn tools for sharing the Gospel such as dance and drama, and also learn how to take care of vehicles.[407]

Nigeria Evangelical Missionary Institute (NEMI)

Begun in 1986, NEMI is "committed to cross-cultural training of prospective missionaries for frontier missions." They seek to empower the Nigerian Evangelical Missions Association by providing training for those that NEMA wishes to send. Most students are sent to NEMI by their NEMA-affiliated mission agencies, and many end up going to what are called the 5015 nations (the "34 intervening countries between Nigeria and Israel"). Once those missionaries are sent, they have the option of returning to NEMI for refresher courses at any time.[408]

Contextualization

NEMI seeks to "provide practical cross-cultural missionary training to all called of God to serve among the unreached tribes and peoples of the world," but they do have a contextualized focus on the "Vision 5015 nations," namely "Northern Nigeria, North Africa, Arabian Peninsula, Horn of Africa and Jerusalem Neighborhood," and their training reflects these destinations. Contextualization is also taught as a class.[409]

Application

According to their blog, "NEMI's training is not geared toward giving paper qualifications to students, but toward making them effective field missionaries." Leaders at NEMI are interested in "train[ing] the whole person," incorporating a three-part curriculum which emphasizes "knowledge, character, and skills." NEMI students regularly take part in leading prayer and preaching at chapel, and their capstone experience is four months of fieldwork with an ethnographic research component,[410] and on Saturdays, NEMI students go out into the community to share the Gospel.[411] All that was theoretical in the classroom becomes practical during these times.

Biblical Studies/Theological/Ministry Studies

NEMI students are required to have completed Bible College elsewhere, but they do study Demons, Witchcraft, and Spiritual Warfare, as well as Church Planting while at NEMI.[412]

Intercultural Studies/Missiology

NEMI students certainly major in this area, studying broad topics like Global Mission Trends and Models, Perspectives on the World Christian Movement, Cultural Anthropology, and Contextualization. They then get more specific by studying Diaspora Missiology, Islam and World Religions, and ATR and Cults. Ethnographic Research is also taught in order to prepare students for their culminating fieldwork project.[413]

Personal/Spiritual Life Development

NEMI students participate in "regular corporate prayer, worship, and fasting" with each other, and they also study Discipleship, Interpersonal Relationship Skills, Personal Edification for the Missionary, and Stress Management.[414]

Practical Skill Acquisition

Some practical classes are taught at NEMI, including Tentmaking/Vocational Ministry and Linguistics and Bible Translation.[415] Students are also required to cook for themselves and their roommates, developing both cooking stills and teamwork.[416]

Ghana Evangelical Missionary Institute – Certificate in Missions (2 year) and Diploma in Missions (3 year)

Known as "Ghana's first truly indigenous missionary training institution,"[417] GEMI is located in Accra and was founded in 1993.[418] It is a ministry of Africa Christian

Mission,[419] and is associated with the nationwide Ghana Evangelical Missions Association (GEMA).[420]

Contextualization

Faculty are international and seek to give students "a culturally contextualized and balanced training diet." Rather than believing that diversity kills contextualization, "An operating assumption [of GEMI] is that vivid interaction between two different contexts (that of the student and foreign lecturer) provides a clearer picture of the study in question."[421]

In order to help their faculty to achieve this balance, and because "GEMI places much emphasis on the practicality of lectures...[they urge] lecturers to use practical illustrations as much as possible to help students deepen their understanding of the course being taught."[422] Foreign professors are even specially oriented so that they can achieve the contextualized balance for which GEMI is looking.[423] GEMI tries when possible to incorporate "local traditional training methods that will help students develop skills and form attitudes leading to genuine character growth based on the students' worldview."[424]

Application

GEMI does not seek "only to train the head, but also the heart and the hands for service. The emphasis is not only on academics but also on spiritual and practical aspects of ministry."[425] Brynjolfson and Lewis' description of their educational philosophy is worth quoting at length:

> Classroom lectures are presented in such a way that students see the urgent need for application, rather than learning theories for informative purposes

only. The class assignments and examinations require answers with practical illustrations from student rather than merely reproducing what is written in the textbooks. Students are encouraged to go beyond informative scholarship to transformative scholarship. By so doing, the field work is not seen as tourism, but rather where God proves Himself as dependable, reliable, and faithful.[426]

Biblical/Theological/Ministry Studies

Students who apply to GEMI are expected to have "previous Bible school education."[427]

Intercultural Studies/Missiology

I was not able to find a copy of courses offered in the area of Intercultural Studies at GEMI, though it is assumed that there are many.

Personal/Spiritual Life Development

See "Application."

Practical Skill Acquisition

GEMI places great emphasis upon the field work required by its students: "Learning through field work implies demonstration of acquired theories. There is undoubtedly a mutual relationship between practical cross-cultural ministry missions work." The students' "skills" are "strengthened" by learning in the classroom, and their learning is "sharpened" by doing field work, for: ""The field work is a confirmation of the reality of what is taught in the classroom."[428]

Recommendations Based on Interviews and Survey

Given the strides that Ethiopian evangelicals have taken toward greater involvement in fulfilling the Great Commission, what steps can be taken to encourage Ethiopia's further development into a major missionary sending nation?

Recommendations for Ethiopian Missionary Training

Contextualization for Empowerment

The first recommendation is the most tentative. The receiving mentality of many in the Ethiopian Church is one of the things the survey respondents noted when considering why the otherwise vibrant Ethiopian Church is not a major missionary sender. Perhaps one of the reasons for this is the lack of contextualization of training literature and lectures. This theory is supported by the strong emphasis of GEMI on orienting their foreign faculty in such a way that courses were taught in a Ghanaian way and in concert with the Ghanaian worldview. This healthy self-respect is admirable: rather than simply accept whatever the foreigners (read: Westerners) wanted to give in the way they wanted to give it, the leaders of GEMI respectfully required foreign teachers to see the world through their students' eyes before they got permission to teach. If Ethiopian schools gave a similar cultural orientation to their foreign faculty and also to visiting professors, we would see less of a receiving mentality and more of a self-reflective "blessed to be a blessing" (Gen 12:3) type of outlook.

Production of Amharic Language Literature on Missions-Related Topics

Related to this needed shift from receiving mentality to giving mentality, Amharic language literature is needed. If Ethiopians are mostly required to read in a foreign language if they want to study deeply about biblical, theological, or ministry related issues, they will inevitably be tempted to see themselves as dependent upon another culture's scholarship. Feelings of dependence are lethal to local initiative, so it can be implied that lack of mother-tongue resources on Christian topics is partially to blame for the relative lack of missionaries from Ethiopia's dynamic church. Ethiopian missionary training schools should be on the forefront of the effort to produce more Amharic-medium literature and teaching on biblical, theological, missiological, and ministry-related topics. These resources can delve deep into contextualized issues facing the Ethiopian Church – including the struggle to send missionaries – from an informed, emic perspective.

Expanded Intensive Language Training

Paradoxically, though the previous recommendations lean toward increased contextualization and indigenization of training, the fact remains that English is the lingua franca of the globe and is a key to success for expatriates working in international teams. Though two of the three Ethiopian schools reviewed in this study offered at least one English course, it is recommended that the intensity and variety of these classes be increased, as the language barrier was mentioned as one of the main things holding Ethiopians back from becoming cross-cultural missionaries.

In addition to English, it would be helpful for Ethiopian missionary training schools to offer courses in other common languages in Africa and the Arab World, such as Swahili and Arabic. This would give many missionary candidates a chance to have a leg up at least on the trade language of the nations to which they are going and would thus minimize their culture shock and maximize their effectiveness in their early days on the field.

Increased Focus on Ethnographic Research

Ethnographic research may be a key component which would enhance the effectiveness of Ethiopian missionary candidates. A program such as NEMI's field work plus ethnographic paper assignment would be ideal and would allow the student to have first-hand missionary experience while still reflecting upon and intentionally applying principles and strategies which they learned in the classroom in order to better understand the group among whom they are living.

Once Ethiopian missionaries start being sent in large numbers, there will be a need for refresher courses such as GEMI offers. The same missionary schools which initially trained the Ethiopian missionaries could offer periodic courses designed to review, enhance, and deepen the knowledge base of the active missionaries, giving them fresh inspiration for their current ministries and helping to prevent fatigue and burnout.

Training on Self-Care for Missionaries

Related to the issue of fatigue and burnout is training for the missionary on how to care for him or herself while on the field. This is an often overlooked area in many institutions around the world, and it would behoove Ethiopian schools to incorporate classes such as the

Personal Edification for the Missionary and Stress Management offered at NEMI. This would directly meet the need spoken of by one of the interviewees when he said, "I [still] need training on how to deal with stress and depression and culture shock."

Vocational Training

Vocational skills and tentmaking strategies are currently included in the curriculum of the Ethiopian schools which were reviewed, but it would be helpful for this area to be enhanced in coming years, as lack of funds is a major factor holding many Ethiopians back from fulfilling the call that God has placed on their lives. Much more creative thinking is needed in this area, but a concrete step in the right direction would be offering specific classes which train missionary candidates in marketable skills like hairdressing, cooking, carpentry, welding, farming, and language teaching.

Training in Survival Skills

Survival skills are an area that should be covered in missionary training in Ethiopia. Many of the fields to which Ethiopian missionaries will go are rugged and remote, and the missionaries who hail from the major cities in Ethiopia will not necessarily be equipped to handle the living conditions they will face. Ethiopian schools can borrow from FTLT MLTS in order to prepare their students to survive even in difficult conditions.

Recommendations for Removing Barriers and Increasing Systemic Support for Major Missionary Involvement:

Missionary sending schools do not exist in a vacuum. In order to operate, they must have missionary candidates pursuing education. In order for those missionary candidates to pursue missionary education, they need to have received a call to missions, usually from someone within the Church. Thus, missionary sending schools cannot exist without the support of the Church. Though relationships between the Church and Christians schools in general has often been strained, it is necessary for both to be connected if we are to be effective in reaching the nations with the Gospel of Christ. In order to thrive, Ethiopian missionary sending schools must have systemic support from churches and other Christian organizations within Ethiopian.

Mobilization of Churches to Become Missions-Minded

As the majority of survey participants stated, one of the main things that is holding Ethiopia back from becoming a major missionary-sending nation is lack of vision for missions within the churches. Churches must be mobilized for missions through being informed about the need and the commands of God on this subject. They must be asked to participate and given specific ways to be involved.

One of the ways that the churches in Ethiopia can be involved in the Great Commission is by sending missionaries. The most common answer to the question of what to do next if one has a call to be a missionary was some variation on this theme: "Be sent by a Church." Sending means being intimately connected through prayer and usually finances to a person who is called of God to go to preach the Gospel in a dark place across cultural barriers. NEMI requires students to have the support of their home churches before enrolling in school. This is wise; GEMI leaders showed the problem of allowing the opposite when they said that "One of the 'greatest challenge[s] that the school faces' is how do graduates relate to their churches after their graduation from GEMI, as most have had only minor support from their churches during their studies?" Ethiopia should note the difference between the results of these two policies and choose to nurture in every way possible the missionary candidate's relationship with their home church family.

Establishment of an Ethiopian Evangelical Missions Association

NEMI missionary candidates are also usually sent by the Nigeria Evangelical Missionary Association (NEMA) – a country-wide association of missions organizations, sending agencies, and churches for the purpose of fulfilling the Great Commission in a unified way. I would like to suggest blatant borrowing of this concept to form the Ethiopian Evangelical Missionary Association (EEMA), which would bring all Ethiopian missionary efforts under one umbrella and would avoid duplication and "redundancy."

Recruitment of Missionaries from Strategic Demographics

Ethiopia should also be wise about recruiting missionaries from strategic and hitherto largely untapped sources. As one of the interviewees mentioned, the Ethiopian university students who have gone on short-term missions have been extremely effective, but these same students are becoming graduates who are not challenged to take up the missionary calling in a long-term way. The challenge to enter full-time ministry after graduation is certainly put before them by campus and church leaders, but it is rare that they are specifically challenged to pray about whether God would have them be long-term missionaries. There are potentially hundreds of missionaries who could be called through intentional challenging of Ethiopian former short-term mission trip alumni to consider long-term missions.

Another strategic group of people who have largely not been tapped for potential long-term missionaries is the large Ethiopian Diaspora community which is spread out all over the globe. NEMI has a class called Diaspora Missiology. It would be helpful for Ethiopia to begin thinking about how to activate the Ethiopian Diaspora as missionaries in the countries they go to instead of merely being immigrants. By waking up the Diaspora to their great responsibility and opportunity, even countries that are supposedly closed to the Gospel – like Saudi Arabia, Oman, and Turkey – could be reached by their significant population of Ethiopian guests.

Conclusion

In this chapter and the previous one, we have endeavored to examine what progress has been made in preparing Ethiopian evangelicals to work cross-culturally to fulfill the Great Commission as well as what potential for growth still remains. This was accomplished first by explaining the need for Christian education – particularly missionary education – for the booming church in the Global South. If the massive numbers of people coming to the Lord are not intentionally discipled, empowered, and equipped to pass on the Good News, then the flood of conversions will slow and this promising movement will not reach its full potential. Ethiopia is a country with a particularly unique potential to be a robust witness to many formerly unreached people groups, but she also faces several obstacles on the road to becoming a major missionary sending nation. I explored some of the reasons behind her potential: refined faith due to persecution, effectiveness of student ministry among unreached people groups within the borders of Ethiopia, and strategic location on the border of the 10/40 Window with open doors to many countries which are closed or hostile to Westerners. If any or all of these suggestions – based on the interviews and survey discussed – are implemented, I believe that Ethiopia will be moving in the right direction toward fulfilling her unique potential to become a major missionary sending nation in the near future.

Many questions and ideas worthy of further study were brought up in the research of the topic of missionary preparation and sending in Ethiopia. First, which are more effective and helpful in the Ethiopian context: denominational or non-denominational missionary training schools?

Second, would it be helpful for people entering missionary training school in Ethiopia to be expected to have previous Bible school training, as two out of the three other African schools which I evaluated required?

Third, what is the stance of the Evangelical Churches Fellowship of Ethiopia (ECFE) – the umbrella organization which nearly every Ethiopian evangelical denomination has joined – on missionary training and sending? Is there any united effort to systematically adopt unreached people groups within Ethiopia or outside the country by assigning them to be "adopted" by a particular missionary training school or denomination? Might there be the possibility to start EEMA under the auspices of ECFE?

Fourth, what is the extent of the contextualization of curriculum used in Ethiopian missionary training schools? How can the Westernization of theological education be minimized and the natural non-Western orientation of the students be cultivated to prepare them as contextualized missionaries to other non-Western groups?

Fifth, how can the needed funds for missions be generated by the Ethiopian Church? What can be done to educate Ethiopian believers on God's command to give toward the work of His Kingdom? How can Ethiopians use their professions in order to partially or totally support themselves financially in their missionary work?

CHAPTER SEVEN

Ethiopian Immigrants as Cross-Cultural Missionaries: Activating the Diaspora for Great Commission Impact[2]

Introduction

There have been many voices in recent years calling American Christians to evangelize the internationals who immigrate to their countries, and such teaching is good and right. However, it seems to be assumed in conversations about "reaching out to internationals" that all of them are unsaved. Though many immigrants do indeed come from countries or people groups which are minimally evangelized or even unreached, acknowledgement and appreciation of Christian immigrants is needed in order to come to a more nuanced understanding of the international community in America. Indeed, believing immigrants may be the American church's greatest asset in crossing the barriers preventing them from effectively reaching the world on their doorstep.

In the process of doing MA thesis research on barrier-crossing missiological education in the Ethiopian church, the great potential of immigrants – in this case, Ethiopian immigrants – as a powerful force for tremendous missiological good first became evident to me.[429] The Ethiopian Diaspora is widespread, with Washington DC

---

[2] This chapter is an adapted version of an article originally published as follows: Jessica A. Udall, "The Ethiopian Diaspora: Ethiopian Immigrants as Cross-Cultural Missionaries; Activating the Diaspora for Great Commission Impact," in *Diaspora Missiology: Reflections on Reaching the Scattered Peoples of the World*, vol. 23 of *Evangelical Missiological Society Series*, eds. Michael Pocock and Enoch Wan (Pasadena, CA: William Carey Library, 2015).

being nearly the largest Ethiopian city in the world, second only to Addis Ababa, Ethiopia's capital.[430] Ethiopians also have significant presence in Canada, Sweden, Saudi Arabia, and many other countries.[431]

This chapter examines the great potential of the millions of Ethiopians in the Diaspora to participate in the Great Commission by realizing their responsibility and opportunity to cross barriers to reach other immigrants in their countries of residence with the Gospel of Christ. Practical steps are suggested for how this – or any – immigrant community can begin moving toward increasingly powerful missionary impact wherever they may live.

The length of this chapter necessitates several limitations to make the topic sufficiently narrow. My focus will be on Ethiopians as a potential missions force in the United States, as most of my interviewees are Ethiopians with experience living in this country. I will also focus exclusively on those immigrants who live and work in communities which are mostly made up of other internationals. I am well aware of the many Ethiopians who have been in America for some time and hold prestigious jobs in academia, medicine, or law, and who generally live surrounded by Americans. These immigrants certainly have great potential to take part in the Great Commission as well, but their level of acclimation to American culture will likely make it easier for them to get sufficient training in evangelism, missions, or cross-cultural issues if they so desire. Suggestions for further research are listed at the end of the chapter to facilitate the further exploration of this multifaceted topic.

Potential

Evangelical Christians made up approximately 19.6% of the population of Ethiopia as of 2010.[432] Getting reliable figures on any aspect of the Ethiopian Diaspora living in America is difficult as population estimates vary wildly depending on the source. The Migration Policy Institute reports 201,000 Ethiopian immigrants living in the United States as of 2012,[433] while more popular estimates say there are well above 200,000 living in the Washington DC area alone.[434] Calculating a simple extrapolated ratio, suffice it to say that there are many thousands of Evangelicals among the Ethiopian Diaspora who have the potential to be invaluable allies to the American church in barrier-crossing Great Commission work among non-Christian immigrants.

In my thesis research, I asserted that the cultural proximity of Ethiopian missionaries – and, it could be extrapolated, all Majority World missionaries – to other non-Western cultures means there are less barriers for them to cross, which makes them more natural and possibly more effective messengers of the Gospel to these other cultures. Cultural proximity is the number one reason, in my opinion, why the Diaspora reaching the Diaspora is an idea whose time has come.

The Ethiopian Diaspora is in a particularly advantageous position to begin cross-cultural ministry as compared to their counterparts still living in Ethiopia because they have already overcome the barriers that hold most potential Majority World missionaries back. There are several hurdles facing Ethiopians residing in Ethiopia who desire to do cross-cultural ministry, including difficulty of obtaining visas and lack of world language fluency. Ethiopians in the Diaspora, however, have already obtained a visa and are likely already ensconced in a diverse community – often living in a large apartment complex with immigrants and refugees from various other cultures and working in a similar environment. Though not all immigrants are well-versed in the language of the host culture, it will be easier for them to learn in the host culture than it would have been in Ethiopia, so this is yet another way that the Diaspora are a step ahead in terms of getting started in cross-cultural ministry.

Diaspora Ethiopians also have a staying power as cross-cultural missionaries living in the West that they might not have in a more "closed" country, but they will likely be surrounded by people from these "closed" countries where they live and work. They will have access to these people who are from countries which are hostile to the Gospel and to Gospel workers, yet they will likely not get in legal trouble for their witness. They are generally not choosing to come to the West in order to reach other immigrants – which, practically speaking, could mean that they could also choose *not* to do this when the going gets hard – rather, the West is where they will likely remain, and they generally are not going to leave their immigrant communities. This staying power is an asset. For these reasons and more, the opportunity for the Diaspora to reach the Diaspora is too good to miss.

There are many encouraging signs of Ethiopians taking up the Great Commission mantel and intentionally reaching out to those who are different than them with the love of Christ. They are proving to be invaluable assets to the cause of Christ in some of the most difficult places on earth to be a believer. According to a missionary mobilizer: "So far [Ethiopians] have sent [missionaries] to India, Pakistan, China, Zambia, South Sudan, Chad, and Malawi." Additionally, an Ethiopian couple has begun a ministry which intentionally seeks to strengthen Diaspora churches in reaching out to their communities with the love of Christ.

Diaspora Ethiopians will often "use ceremonial events" for Gospel good by sharing the Gospel with unsaved attendees at weddings, funerals, and holiday celebrations. They will also sometimes have special conferences with guest speakers and will invite their friends and neighbors to come and hear the message. These conferences often involve intense prayer, deliverance, and healings – God often uses these demonstrations of His truth and power to convert some who visit. Some Ethiopians are active in sharing their faith in their cross-cultural workplaces as well.

An example of Ethiopian Diaspora church (EDC) which has been successful in cross-cultural witness is Dallas Ethiopian Bible Church in Garland, TX, which is active in cultivating connections and sharing the Gospel with other cultural groups despite its ethnic distinctness. Another notable Diaspora Ethiopian who was mentioned by an interviewee is Daniel Tassew, who runs International Revival Ministries (IRM) and is based in the United States but is actively preaching the Gospel to various cultural groups.

Challenges

In my thesis, I asked several questions regarding what holds Ethiopian back from being the major missionary sending nation which God desires her to be. When asked, "In what area do you feel your students/disciples need more training [in order to be effective barrier-crossing missionaries]?" respondents answered that training in cross-cultural skills was the area which needed the most work. Unfortunately, crossing cultures and living in the West did not change the response by the second round of respondents whom I interviewed on the topic of Diaspora Missiology. Many of these also cited lack of cross-cultural training as a major thing holding Ethiopians back from being effective witnesses for Christ to people who are different from them. How could this be so for people who are already living cross-culturally?

The answer lies in the tight-knit and comfortable nature of the Ethiopian Diaspora community. Ethiopians have "a highly defined background and culture" which is dear to them, and they tend to hang on to their ethnic identity even tighter when they are strangers in a strange land. This is of course true of any immigrants, but Ethiopia as a never-colonized society with tendencies toward isolationism could be classed as an extremely "high context" people group, meaning that their attachment to their way of life and culture is perhaps stronger than that of other groups to theirs.

There are many aspects of this love for the motherland that are admirable and allow Ethiopians to have a sense of home and belonging even in a foreign country. There are also some potentially negative manifestations of this mindset, however; manifestations which erect unnecessary barriers between Ethiopians and those from other ethnic groups. First, sometimes pride in one's own culture leads to looking down on and avoiding other cultures. No contact means no converts, so this is a mentality which must be fought against if Ethiopian Evangelicals are to be effective in crossing cultural barriers with the Gospel. Second, in the name of non-compromise with the world (a commendable and biblical value), Ethiopian immigrants can sometimes erect intentional barriers in order to guard themselves from the rest of society, fearing the contamination that comes from mixing with unbelievers of any culture. Again, lack of contact with nonbelievers makes it impossible to share the Gospel and leads to unfruitfulness and stagnation.

This lack of contact often begins a vicious cycle: because of the limited interaction they have with unbelievers of other cultures, Ethiopians are often not well-versed in worldviews that are uncommon in Ethiopia like "new age thought, atheism, and Eastern religions" (though they usually are well aware of the nuances separating Ethiopian Orthodox and Protestant thought). Because of this lack of exposure, many Ethiopians feel insecure in starting evangelistic conversations because of concerns that they will not be able to adequately understand their conversation partner's religious beliefs (or lack thereof). Fear of failure leads to further withdrawal, which leads to deeper fear, and the great potential of Ethiopians as bold barrier-cultural evangelists is not realized.

A practical concern is that barrier-crossing mission is not a priority for the Ethiopian Diaspora because other aspects of life are so pressing. Many Ethiopian immigrants are not financially secure, but being in the West gives them a chance for bettering their situation and that of their family. Most are also supporting relatives back home in Ethiopia, so the pressure is great to work harder and longer and more profitably each day. It is easy to become myopic in focusing on the American Dream, on getting ahead, and on advancing up the ladder of success. The bigger picture of God's plan and purpose in bringing Ethiopians to their country of residence "for such a time as this" (Esther 4:14) is often lost in the helter-skelter rush of everyday life in the fast lane of Western culture. Though one interviewee commented that "every migrant is a potential missionary," few realize that potential. Distraction is the name of the game.

There is also an insidious stereotype which seems to exist among believers from many non-Western societies, including Ethiopia, that Westerners are the only ones who cross cultures with the Gospel. Cross-cultural ministry is not thought of as a feasible option or even as a possibility for non-Westerners because of historical precedent as well as lack of publicity in both Western and non-Western circles regarding Majority World missionaries. This may be partially due to a short-circuited discipleship process initiated by Western missionaries when they brought the Gospel to non-Western areas without instilling in their non-Western disciples the need to pass on the Gospel to "all nations" according to Jesus' Great Commission (Matthew 28:18-20). This stereotype must be aggressively combated and non-Western believers empowered with the knowledge that they have the responsibility and the privilege to cross barriers with the Gospel of Christ.

Lack of unity is also cited as a problem hindering Ethiopians from sharing cross-culturally. Because of division which exists even between people of the same culture, it is hard to contemplate uniting with people of a different culture. Church politics steals time and energy away from outreach, and inward focus becomes necessary in order to just keep the congregation stable. This is a challenge in every church, but particularly in immigrant churches due to the added stressors of living in a foreign land and having few choices when searching for a culturally appropriate church to call home.

Where there is great potential, great challenges also crop up, like weeds among a planted field. The presence of barriers standing in the way of the Ethiopian Diaspora reaching other peoples of the Diaspora with the Gospel could be a cause for discouragement, but these challenges are not insurmountable. Rather, they are opportunities for the worldwide Church – particularly the Ethiopian Church in the Diaspora – to rise up and overcome and to reaching the potential for which God has created her: reaching the nations around her with the Gospel of Christ.

Suggestions

Polling the interviewees with the question: "What do you recommend for the Habesha Diaspora's evangelistic impact to be maximized?" produced ten insightful suggestions, many of which have application beyond the Ethiopian community to the Christian Diaspora at large. I will categorize these suggestions and add a few subpoints of my own in order to begin a brainstorm regarding how Christians in the Diaspora can remove any barriers hindering them and move towards increased Great Commission fruitfulness. It is my hope that this brainstorming will continue well after this conference and that these words will lead to actions and to new brothers and sisters in Christ from every ethnicity entering the Kingdom of God.

Realizing the Bigger Purpose

An Ethiopian seminary leader with experience in the West suggests that Ethiopians in the Diaspora "need to realize that they are [in another country] for a bigger purpose than to fulfill their economic needs…They need to be missions minded…to…say that '[T]he Lord has brought me here to preach the gospel for others.'" Despite the fact that several respondents shared that those in the Diaspora feel inferior or incapable since they are in an unfamiliar setting, the same leader goes on to say: "There is a lot that the Ethiopian Diaspora can give…[based on their] previous Christian experience back home." Being empowered by these realizations that they are both called and equipped by God will be a key to increasing Great Commission effectiveness among the Ethiopian Diaspora.

Church Leaders Catching the Vision

The importance of leadership cannot be overstated in any plan to change. Twenty-five percent of the interviewees responded with some version of this statement, underscoring its importance. If leaders of a church are inspired by the great worth of the Good News they believe, the great need of the world around them, and the great responsibility they have to preach that Good News to all nations, then it is likely that their congregations will catch the same vision.

Of course, this inspiration of leaders is easy to talk about in vague terms, but it is more complicated when articulating a concrete plan of action. A practical suggestion for enabling this inspiration might be through the Perspectives courses or seminars.[435] Advertisement for this program and others like it could be intentionally extended to leaders of Diaspora churches in the hopes that their participation would awaken them – as it tends to do for people from all cultures – to the reality of the unreached world and the commands of Jesus to reach the unreached. As a side note, the Perspectives course has recently been offered in Ethiopia and was very well-received, which gives me confidence that this suggestion is culturally appropriate and not too oriented towards a Western audience.

Praying for the Nations

This suggestion is so simple, particularly to the Ethiopian community which is already very strong in prayer, but a specific focus of praying for the salvation of the nations will likely be a new concept to EDCs. This suggestion is without doubt the most important key to maximizing the Great Commission impact of any community, and I believe it should be the first one implemented in a church after the church leader has caught the vision for reaching the unreached. It is not a new suggestion, for, as an Ethiopian seminary student studying in the United States remarked: "The apostles and the church fathers throughout history used prayer as a primary tool in the evangelistic ministry of the church as it proactively encountered various cultures."[436] Taking a cue from the early church and all the other generations that have gone before her, the EDC cannot but succeed in fulfilling the Great Commission with prayer as the bedrock of her barrier-crossing efforts.

Training Members

Leaders who love God and love people cannot reach the nations alone. Leading their people in prayer is essential, but they must also inspire and equip their followers to go and work in the harvest field. An Ethiopian pastor of an EDC shared: "If we dedicate ourselves to teach and train believers to be true disciple[s] of Jesus Christ [rather] than being just member[s] of the church and source[s] of income; we would impact so many people with the message of the Gospel." In terms of content, an Ethiopian studying for his MA in the West added some specific suggestions such as "teachings and trainings on [cross-cultural] mission and evangelism" and "personal and group

[B]ible studies" that promote "deeper understanding of the [B]ible." It is hoped that the deeper people go in studying the Bible, the more they will understand God's heart for the nations and their responsibility to share the Good News with them.

Collaborating With Other Churches

Two respondents suggested that Ethiopian Diaspora churches should consider collaborating with other churches – both Western churches as well as other EDCs and non-Ethiopian Diaspora churches – to increase effectiveness through partnership and sharing of information. It is possible that some Western churches have valuable experience in reaching out to diverse communities that they could share with the EDC. Other EDCs could understand the unique challenges as well as increase the man-power and geographical reach of an EDC, creating a network of connected churches with a common Great Commission purpose. Non-Ethiopian Diaspora churches could give valuable information to an EDC about the cultures they are trying to reach and could also be a safe place to begin practicing cross-cultural communication in a gracious atmosphere with brothers and sisters in Christ.

Opening Up to Other Cultures

This suggestion goes against the normal human tendency to stay within one's comfort zone and with people who seem familiar. This tendency is exacerbated by unfamiliar surroundings that come with immigration, which is why most large American cities have a Chinatown and a Little Italy. "Little Addis" is a phenomenon that is growing as more and more Ethiopian immigrants settle near one another and form their own enclaves. In Washington DC, for example: "There are so many restaurants, shops and businesses catering to Ethiopians that the community has its own 1,000-page telephone book."[437]

As discussed above, there is nothing inherently wrong with enjoying one's own people, food, products, and customs, but in order to be effective as cross-cultural witnesses, the EDC must guard against the inward gaze and ethnocentrism that sometimes results from love of country. Compelled by the love of Christ, they must intentionally move out of their comfortable cultural enclaves to seek out friendships with people who are different from them.

Becoming friends across cultural barriers brings with it many requirements, particularly for the Christian who is called to be "all things to all people" (1 Corinthians 9:22 ESV). Learning different cultures, different customs, and even different languages may be involved (or working to become proficient in the language of the host culture in order to communicate in a second language for both parties). It will require social interactions that are sometimes uncomfortable or awkward, and it will require the delicate art of being in the world but not of it, which has historically been difficult for Ethiopian Evangelicals, according to the majority of respondents. Once this opening up of the community has happened, however – fueled by love of Christ and desire to obey him regardless of discomfort – I believe that Ethiopians will be extremely effective in befriending other immigrants because of their warmth, sense of humor, and love of conversation.

Evangelizing as a Lifestyle

According to an Ethiopian who has studied in Europe and the United States, Ethiopians are good at using special occasions – like weddings, funerals, or holiday celebrations – for intentional evangelism. He suggests, however, that Ethiopians in the Diaspora "use [that] boldness" to "address other immigrants or natives on [a] day to day basis instead of occasional[ly]." Indeed, this suggestion would benefit people from any culture: evangelizing "as you go" (Matthew 28:19 International Standard Version) in daily life rather than viewing evangelism as an event-oriented activity. A pastor of an EDC sees this suggestion as being intertwined with training church members: "If we have well educated, informed and trained disciples [presumably in the necessity of daily-life evangelism], we can evangelize other immigrants at work, in school and in different social places."

Using Technology

Ethiopians love technology – as much or perhaps more than any other culture I have interacted with. There are great initiatives, such as "Habesha Student,"[438] which uses websites and social media to share the Gospel within Ethiopia and beyond her borders. There is still room for many other initiatives of this kind, however, and also for individuals to simply be intentional with using various forms of media to share the Gospel. Some examples of this might be posting religious material on social media websites, hosting neighbors or friends to watch the Jesus Film, or giving the Jesus Film to other immigrants to watch in their own language (Jesus Films in numerous languages are available to order very affordably on their website).[439]

Equipping the Younger Generation

One of the largest issues facing any Diaspora church is how to relate to its younger members who are often second generation immigrants and who have a bicultural identity. According to an Ethiopian pastor residing in Ethiopia who regularly preaches in EDCs, it is imperative that they "work on equipping young generation spiritually but free them to integrate culturally." Ethiopian-American young people have the potential to be a powerful mission force to reach other bicultural young people; they will understand the unique life experience of one another like few others can. Younger children also can be used by God to break the ice in new cross-cultural friendships between immigrant families, since they give the parents common ground and a reason to laugh together.

Striving for Unity

This suggestion rings true for any church in any culture, but particularly for the Diaspora church. People whose only similarity may be their country of birth are thrown together and often have no choice as to which congregation to join if they wish to worship in their native language.

Conflicts which might have been swept under the rug in Ethiopia because a discontented family could quietly move to a congregation down the road are not so easily solved in another country, where the next EDC might be hours away. All congregants are under the multiple stressors that come from trying to live and work and raise a family in a cross-cultural environment. The situation makes tension likely, but not inevitable. Ethiopians have a strong and vibrant faith in God and, as an Ethiopian full-time minister living cross-culturally says, they should "trust God for the impossible." The exhortation to the Diaspora in Peter's day echoes down to present day EDCs: "Above all, keep loving one another earnestly, since love covers over a multitude of sins" (1 Peter 4:8).

Conclusion

This chapter has only scratched the surface in terms of examining the great potential of Christian immigrants to be the most effective way to reach the Diaspora in any given country. Ethiopian immigrants, as we have seen, are in a prime position to be used by God as cross-cultural missionaries in the new places in which they live, having already overcome many of the barriers that face Ethiopians who want to be cross-cultural missionaries but who still live in Ethiopia. The challenges that have been mentioned are real but are no match for the Spirit of God and the intentional efforts of His people in the EDC. The suggestions given by my twelve interviewees provide a way forward, making change possible by providing concrete steps toward change.

These few pages cannot contain all the research that needs to be done. A Western missiologist with extensive experience in Ethiopia responded to my interview questions by commenting that Diaspora reaching Diaspora is a "huge topic" with "a vast amount of research that could and should be done." I have included three ways in which I hope this research will be deepened and expanded in the future.

Other Christian Diaspora Groups

There are numerous ethnic groups which have a significant Diaspora presence in the West, and many of these groups have significant Christian populations. Similar studies should be carried out researching each group and asking its members to consider what is being done and what could be done by their group to reach other Diaspora groups around them. This self-reflection might well lead to increased Great Commission impact by the groups studied, so the value of this potential further research is high.

Diaspora Reaching Diaspora in the Muslim World

The challenges and suggestions for the Diaspora reaching the Diaspora in the Muslim World will likely be quite different than those for the Diaspora in the West, but they are equally deserving of attention and study. Immigrants may be the best hope of reaching the unreached in currently closed countries, because they have already jumped through the legal hoops associated with living and working in the countries without incident. They have a legitimate reason to be in the closed country and can be used to share the love of Christ with neighbors, coworkers, and all others they come into contact with in their already established daily routines. Further probing the best practices in these areas via case studies would be helpful so as to give an inspirational template to others in similar situations.

Contextualized Training for Diaspora Churches

The Perspectives on the World Christian Movement program and other programs and books like it are excellent and will be helpful in the short-run to raise awareness among Diaspora churches and to train them for cross-cultural ministry, but they are not ideal. Eventually, contextualized training materials should be developed specifically to train Ethiopians and other non-Westerners, approaching missions from their worldview and customized to address the issues that are important to them. Producing this kind of literature in Amharic and other heart-languages of Diaspora peoples should be the ultimate goal.

Part IV:

Crossing Geographical Barriers for the Great Commission

CHAPTER EIGHT

Connected Ethiopians Connecting the Lost to Christ: Harnessing Internet Technology to Cross Barriers for the Great Commission

The rate of internet usage growth has been astoundingly rapid worldwide, jumping from approximately 394 million internet users in 2000 to well over 2.9 billion in 2014.[440] The continent of Africa has seen the fastest rate of recent growth, with a 3,606.7% increase in internet usage from 2000 to 2012.[441] Ethiopia is well-behind many other African nations in terms of internet usage, but the government is investing 10% of its GDP in internet and communications technology in order to adequately supply the strong and ever-increasing demand of its people.[442]

If there is any doubt that technology is powerful and culture-changing, one has only to look at news stories showing social media to be the catalysts for recent uprisings across the Arab World.[443] Social media is used to organize everything from flash mobs to protests to charitable initiatives. Within the palm of one's hand lies limitless possibility for connection and creation. Indeed, "mobile devices [as the primary way that most people around the world access the internet] are no longer phones; they are a person's link to the world" and to new ideas.[444]

Can this power of connection and creation be harnessed for transformational Gospel change? Many Christians around the world are realizing that "[t]he Internet has become a twenty-first-century Roman road" as well as "a worldwide marketplace, a theater, front porch and backyard fence, and an office watercooler." Because it is connected to nearly every aspect of modern day life and interwoven into relationships, the internet – particularly social media – can serve Christians as "an electronic train terminal connecting all the various parts of your evangelism strategy and providing the crucial means for people to respond directly to the gospel message."[445]

To people who have woken up to their responsibility as God's ambassadors "every interpersonal exchange can be seen as an opportunity to participate in the ending of suffering and an opportunity to encourage fullness of life": and in this day and age, these interpersonal exchanges often happen most authentically online.[446]

As Christians with a passion for reaching the lost, we must be willing to go wherever people are. Since people, particularly young people, are going online in droves, that is where we must go, too![447] In the present day, "the primary missional challenge of the church will be to incarnate the gospel in a Google world."[448]

Unfortunately, "the church has yet to fully embrace this internet revolution – especially regarding evangelism on the Web." Leonard Sweet even goes to far to say that many in the modern church suffer from "technophobia."[449] There are many reasons – varying by culture – for this reticence to use technology to spread the Gospel. We will discuss some specifically Ethiopian reasons in a subsequent section.

There are certainly drawbacks to internet evangelism in that some aspects of interpersonal connection are lacking. However, there is also a unique "sense of being able to ask and discuss with someone online things you would perhaps find hard or impossible to talk through face-to-face." In other words, the anonymity of the internet encourages honesty and willingness to talk about uncomfortable subjects like sin and conversion. There are pros and cons to internet evangelism just as there are pros and cons in any evangelistic strategy, be it going door to door or inviting neighbors to an Easter service. Though it is of course ideal for any relationship to eventually have a face-to-face component, the internet is a particularly effective place to find new friends and begin conversations casually because it is a low-pressure environment.[450]

As mentioned above, there are a growing number of Christians who are "beginning to recognize the immense potential for harvest that exists through the World Wide Web." These early adopters are starting exciting initiatives which are reaching people all over the world, including places where the possibility of in-person Gospel witness is rare or non-existent.

One of these early adopters is Miheret Tilahun, the Director for Digital Strategies for Southern and Eastern Africa with Great Commission Ministries Ethiopia (a branch of Cru). Miheret studied IT at university, worked for an Ethiopian Telecom company for a season, and then transitioned into his current ministry role.

"I'm always amazed at the questions people are asking online," says Tilahun. In light of this fact, his motivation for doing online evangelism is simple: "When the people we are trying to reach for Christ are most open on the internet, we need to put missionaries there to share Christ with them."[451] After all, when people have a question in this day and age, "they go to GOOGLE to get an answer for their questions," so online missionaries must be ready to provide answers when people have "questions about Life and God."[452]

Miheret has noticed that those in the older generations feel hesitant to evangelize online because technology is not a part of their daily lives and access to it is sometimes limited. Internet connectivity and availability is increasing at an incredible rate in Ethiopia, however, so increasing usage even among older church leaders is likely only a matter of time.

On the other hand, Ethiopian young people "spend [much] of their time on the internet," and are adept at using it, but they simply have "never heard of the potential or sharing Christ with their friend using online [methods]."

They have not rejected technology as a means for sharing the Gospel – instead, they have never even *considered* using it as an evangelistic tool.

The tide is turning, however, among university students and those that disciple them. Miheret is getting more and more "requests...to train students of different campuses to use Everystudent.com as an outreach strategy."[453] His methods of training are practical – not only exposing students to the reasons why they should reach out online but actually walking them through various ways to share their faith using technology and encouraging them to engage in supervised practice using their own social networks. For example, one group of fifteen recent trainees spent two hours taking "the initiative to share the gospel with their unbeliever Facebook friends through:

- chatting and having gospel conversation;
- posting articles from evangelistic websites like http://www.habeshastudent.com;
- sharing Bible verse pictures

"Within that short period of time, those 15 students were able to talk about Jesus to 50 of their unbeliever friends on Facebook. And five of them showed interest for future offline discussions."[454] Days and weeks of similar activity have been scheduled periodically with good participation and results.

Miheret mentioned three prongs of current online ministry being carried out by Ethiopians. First, online missionaries participate in "email based evangelism websites" such as www.habeshastudent.com and www.everystudent.com, "where [they] accept requests and respond to needs" and questions related to articles about spiritual things. Second, Ethiopians such as the students in training mentioned above carry out "Facebook Evangelism Campaigns" by reaching out to friends with spiritual content, starting various Facebook pages and chatting with interested people using that social media platform. Third,

Ethiopians operate a telephone line associated with a specific Facebook page in order "to respond to calls and emails to [the] prayer line."

The Ethiopian Church using technology to share the Gospel in Ethiopia and beyond is an idea whose time has come, but there must be more early adopters participating in this type of ministry and working to raise awareness before the strategy will become mainstream. Miheret suggests three ways that "someone who is planning to work with churches or starting digital strategies to minister among Ethiopians" could get started with groundbreaking efforts. First, they could be involved in "local content production" such as "articles on different topics" as well as "videos and other resources" in the heart languages of Ethiopians. Second, they could be involved in "training and capacity building among young leaders" who likely will spearhead any large-scale movement in Ethiopian internet evangelism. Third, they could be part of the effort to "[resource] churches" with a "model digital strategy" for equipping their members to do internet evangelism which could in turn be reproduced in other Ethiopian churches.

For an individual Ethiopian who wants to get personally involved with online evangelism, Miheret also has a few suggestions of places to explore for inspiration: websites like and www.indigitous.org have myriad ideas and free training on how any person can get involved in fulfilling the Great Commission online which require only an internet connection and a social media account. The Jesus Film Media App is also a wonderful resource which has free access to "Jesus Film clips and other short films" which a person "can use for personal evangelism" on their mobile phone or computer.

Part V:

Crossing Other Barriers for the Great Commission

CHAPTER NINE

Current Methods of Ethiopian Involvement in the Great Commission[3]

"God is a missionary God"[455] who preached the global Gospel to Abraham, saying: "'All nations will be blessed through you'" (Gal 3:8). The Father sent His Son, Jesus Christ, to this world to proclaim the Good News (Mark 1:14-15). The Lord Jesus, after he finished his earthly ministry, gave the responsibility of sharing and proclaiming the Gospel to His Church so that others might hear the Good News. He said to his disciples "Peace be with you! As the Father has sent me, I am also sending you" (John 20:21). Jesus has sent the Church. Thus, the main purpose of the ministry of the Church is mission, that is, proclamation of the Good News across cultural barriers, as can be seen in Jesus' last command:

> "All authority in heaven and on earth has been given to me. Therefore, go and make disciples of all nations, baptizing them in the name of the Father and of the Son and of the Holy Spirit, and teaching them to obey everything I have commanded you. And surely I am with you always, to the very end of the age" (Matt 28:18-20 NIV).

From these passages and others, it is clear that this Great Commission is our primary responsibility on this earth, but how can we be effective in carrying out this vital mandate? The following three chapters will discuss various facets of

---

[3] Chapters nine through eleven are adapted from the following: Nahom Tegene Yefru, "Missiological Models for Multi-Ethnic Ethiopian Evangelical Churches in Light of the Antioch Church's Perspectives" (master's thesis, Presbyterian College and Theological Seminary, 2012).

the answer to this question. This chapter will focus on how the Ethiopian Church is already carrying out the missionary mandate. In the following chapter, some challenges facing the Ethiopian Church's mission efforts – particularly lack of unity – will be examined. In the next chapter, the Church at Antioch will be analyzed as an inspiration and model for the Ethiopian Church – particularly on the matter of unity amidst diversity – as it moves forward toward greater effectiveness in mission.

Ethiopian Evangelical churches have implemented various methods of evangelistic mission. Most of these methods will likely be familiar to the reader because they are practiced worldwide, but it is helpful to investigate what each method looks like in the Ethiopian context in order to evaluate and promote Great Commission effectiveness.

Mass Evangelism

Mass evangelism is the preaching of the Good News publicly in an outdoor setting or in a very large gathering. Mass evangelism can be seen in the New Testament in several instances. For example, after Peter preached on the day of Pentecost to the crowd in Jerusalem, three thousand people were added to the church, and in the following days that number grew to five thousand (Acts 2:41; 4:4).

The churches in Ethiopia often use this evangelistic method by conducting conferences and special programs such as open-air meetings using stadiums and public halls as meeting places. Though this method has its weaknesses, churches are seeing many people responding to the Gospel proclaimed in this way. When they conduct such kinds of evangelistic gatherings, there are often power encounters such as healings, the casting out of demons and praying effectively for those who have different kinds of problems. This is the main method of evangelism in the Ethiopian evangelical church today, and many people are being set free and transformed through it. When individuals who have come to hear the Gospel in a mass meeting still have doubts or questions, further encouragement by an evangelistic team member through personal contact and counseling has often brought them to the place of response.

This method of evangelism helps Ethiopian churches to be influential because when they conduct mass evangelism, they are creating an awareness of their presence in the minds of the community, even those of other religious groups. With this method, churches in Ethiopia are showing progress and expanding, and as a result, the Christian population is growing in the country.

One-to-one Evangelism

The second method that the churches in Ethiopia are using to reach the lost is one-to-one evangelism, otherwise known as personal evangelism. In one-to-one evangelism, Ethiopian churches are sharing the Gospel with people who are around them, such as people on the street and in marketplaces. In one-to-one evangelism, individual Christians are directly involved in presenting the Gospel to those who have not heard it. In the New Testament, following the persecution in Jerusalem, the disciples scattered themselves and evangelized using this method throughout the land (Acts 8:1-4).

Much of the Ethiopian church's growth has taken place through the personal relationships of the church members with family, friends, and co-workers. Though many lament that this evangelistic spirit is declining in the present day, members of the churches generally continue to be active in sharing the Gospel with their neighbors. In most cases, after almost every church service, in Ethiopian churches, there are people who give their lives to Christ. This happens due to the church members actively engaging the world and committing their way to the Lord. In addition, most churches have *Yemissekerenet Budin* (Evangelism Teams). Church members evangelize their community by sending these teams into the streets around the church area and far from the church to share the Gospel with individuals or groups. In addition, along with this kind of evangelistic endeavor, churches conduct special evangelistic services for members to invite their unbelieving friends to attend.

Looking at the Bible where Andrew shares his faith with his brother, the first thing that he did was to find his brother Simon and tell him, "'We have found the Messiah.' . . . And he brought him to Jesus (John 1:41-42). Philip found Nathanael and told him, 'We have found the one Moses wrote about in the Law. . . . Come and see'" (John 1:45-46). The present author of this chapter encountered Jesus and embraced the gospel through such a method and became a bridge to his family who also became followers of Christ.

Friendship Evangelism

Friendship evangelism is similar to one-to-one evangelism, but there is a slight difference between the two. Friendship evangelism means the purposeful approaching of a person whom one did not know before to make him or her a friend then to share the Gospel so that he or she can become a follower of Jesus. In universities around the country, there are several Christian student fellowships (such as EvaSUE and Great Commission Ministry Ethiopia) which encourage their students to do evangelistic outreach to other students on their campuses using this method. After the Christian students befriend someone, they invite them to the student Bible study group, and many of those invited end up coming to Christ.

Literature Evangelism

Literature evangelism is another of the evangelistic methods which Ethiopian churches and parachurch organizations are employing to effectively spread the Gospel. Tracts, Bibles, booklets, newspapers and passages of Scripture are translated into people's native languages and churches distribute these materials in order to reach the community with the Good News about Christ.

This method helps to spread the Gospel and it can be particularly helpful for those who fear sharing their faith to others since this method lets the printed materials start the conversation. Literature evangelism is also helpful to reach those areas whose doors are closed to the Good News by quietly introducing Gospel literature materials translated into their language so that they can be read privately.

Holistic Approach

The holistic approach is an evangelistic method in which the church involves the community by offering social services in the name of Jesus Christ. Many of these services are offered through a program called Compassion Project: through this ministry Ethiopian churches are serving the community by providing food and clothes, and by helping underprivileged students to pursue their education. Compassion Project serves all members of the community, whether Muslim, Orthodox or Evangelical.

This kind of holistic approach is an avenue for the churches to address human needs as they spread the Gospel in the community. Anyone who benefits from the ministry – especially students – is asked to attend Sunday school and other church activities. In this way, the churches share the Gospel with the students and their families. Through this ministry, many students have become Christians and their lives have been changed. Many of them have joined universities and have become upright, responsible citizens, and some of them have become ministers of the Gospel. Some churches are also serving the community by providing elementary and secondary education. Because the schools have compulsory chapel worship services, many students become Christians after hearing the Gospel explained day by day. In regards to the holistic method, the Ethiopian Evangelical Church Mekane Yesus (EECMY) and Ethiopian Kale Heywet Church (EKHC) are leading the way.

In addition, most churches are participating in helping HIV/AIDS patients both within and outside of the church, as well as children those who have lost their parents because of AIDS. In these programs, many children and families are being helped by the churches through counseling, home visits and material support. Some churches also have clinic which they are using to serve the community by giving health education and treatment. Many of the members of the community benefit from these ministries and some of them give their lives to the Lord Jesus Christ as a result of their interaction with Christian workers.

Church Planting

Church planting is the most successful way of spreading the Gospel all over Ethiopia because when the church is present in a particular community, it brings influence and becomes a testimony of the Lord Jesus Christ. For example, the Ethiopian Full Gospel Believers' Church (EFGBC) has gotten its tremendous growth through the intentionality of many of its professional church members. Whenever these church members relocate from one place to another because of their job, they begin sharing their faith with others and inviting them to come to fellowships in their homes, effectively starting house churches. Occasionally, the evangelists from their old churches visit them to teach and encourage the new believers in their faith. Through time, these small fellowships grow into established local churches, and then they expand and plant other local churches in the surrounding areas.

Many men of God sacrificially went far from their homes for the purpose of planting churches, traveling on the backs of animals and on foot for long distances to spread the Gospel all over the country. Especially in the Southern and Western parts of the country, there are many Christians who actively travel and preach the Gospel to expand the Kingdom of God. As the history of the church shows, though the Ethiopian Kale Heywet Church was founded by a Western mission agency (SIM), it expanded throughout the country through the local churches' evangelists.

Audio-visual Evangelism

Religious broadcasting has played an integral role in radio and television from the inception of both media.[456] In Ethiopia, radio and television do an excellent job of 0reaching a large percentage of the community. Audio-visual evangelism has a very long history in Ethiopia; in fact, the Lutheran Church had a radio station in the country many years ago called "Radio Voice of the Gospel (RVOG)."[457] Unfortunately, the Communist regime took control of this radio station when the regime governed Ethiopia and the churches went underground, but Kenyan radio stations broadcast several evangelistic programs in the Ethiopian language even during this time. These radio stations played a vital role in spreading the Gospel in the country and in encouraging the persecuted believers in those days. Though it is currently still illegal to have private radio or TV stations in Ethiopia, there are still several international stations which transmit religious programs to Ethiopian audiences. These stations are still playing an important role in continuing to spread the Good News and encouraging the Church in Ethiopia.

Great Commission Ministry Ethiopia (GCME) has given particular attention to audio-visual evangelism for years. One of their methods is using the Jesus Film to expose people to the Gospel. According to their website:

> The Jesus Film has been translated in about 25 languages of Ethiopia so far. It has been a powerful evangelistic tool to reach many through the country. Many people got the chance to hear the clear presentation of the Gospel of Jesus Christ, in their own language as a result of this, quite a number of new churches have been planted.[458]

Vocational Evangelism

This method is one which is used by people within the Ethiopian Church who are active in sharing their faith at work and/or using their careers as platforms to bring the Gospel to the unreached. An example of a group which uses this method is Christian Medical Doctors and Dentists Fellowship – Ethiopia (CMDDF), which is engaged in serving the community by providing free medical treatment for those who are in prison or who cannot afford medical care. Whenever a team of medical or dental professionals provide services, they are clearly affiliated with local churches and local evangelists and pastors are part of the team. Ethiopian Interior Mission (EIM) is another organization which evangelizes the community by providing health education to schools and communities.

Evaluation of the Methods

Each method for mission discussed above which the Ethiopian Church is employing has its own strengths and weaknesses. Indeed, ultimately, the method itself does not matter as much as the commitment to use it well. Ideally, a combination of methods should be used so as to reach various groups in various ways. Literature and audio-visual evangelism methods are very helpful to spread the Gospel in areas that have closed their doors for the Gospel. Today there are Bibles in various formats such as audio CDs, DVDs and online, all of which facilitate the sharing of God's Word even across barriers like hostile borders. Satellite TV also has a great impact when used as a tool for evangelistic ministry. Literature evangelism is also valuable where there is a lack of trained witnesses or in conjunction with other efforts. The possibility of a full explanation of the message through literature makes it very valuable for those who will read the material.

Mass evangelism is an effective method when there has been significant preparation through the guidance of the Holy Spirit. The church spends a lot of money and other resources to conduct programs like this, so if their efforts are not well-organized, they will not be cost-effective. Prayerfulness, careful planning and organization, and strong commitment from church members is necessary. Unfortunately, churches in Ethiopia are sometimes conducting large programs just for the sake of having programs or because they are trying to compete with other churches.

The personal or one-to-one evangelism methods have the advantage of being direct and customized, with the possibility of meeting the individuals where they are and answering their particular questions. This method also has the potential to reach those who would never go to a church meeting to hear the Gospel. The disadvantage of this method is that the preparation of individual Christians is often limited and the message is not able to be made clear in the time available.

Holistic and vocational methods are effective where poor or needy people are present. Through showing them the love of Christ through service, many people come to Him for salvation.

Friendship evangelism is a good method especially in schools and work places because members of the churches spend most of their time with their fellow students or colleagues. In addition, most people who came to Christ with this method endure in their faith and become strong Christians because the one who shared Christ with them also follows up with them closely.

For any church, including the Ethiopian Church, to be effective in mission, their methods for mission must be strategically evaluated, and, if necessary, revised. This chapter has been a preliminary attempt to do just that. Though the message is unchanged, the ways of presenting it should change in order to fit with the immediate context. Ethiopian churches should consider the various methods available to them to share the Good News and should seek to utilize these methods in ways that are both biblically sound and contextually relevant.

CHAPTER TEN

Barriers to Great Commission Effectiveness Among the Ethiopian Mission Force

The previous chapter makes it clear that the Ethiopian Church is active in carrying out the Great Commission by sharing the Gospel using various methods. This should be commended and celebrated, especially as we look back on the impressive surge of the Evangelical Church both during and after the era of Communism (1974-1991). The author's investigation of evangelistic methods in Ethiopia also made him aware of several troublesome barriers, however, which hinder the Ethiopian Church from being as effective in mission as it could be.

In John 16:33, Jesus tells his disciples: "I have told you these things, so that in me you may have peace. In this world, you will have trouble. But take heart! I have overcome the world" (NIV). Indeed, the early Church did have many troubles, both internally and externally. These troubles could have easily affected their unity and the work of the mission to some extent. However, through the help and power of the Holy Spirit, the early Christians were able to face these challenges squarely. They kept the Church and the work of the Church moving, as they continued working to remove the barriers which hindered them and to continue on the expansion of the Kingdom of God by propagating the Gospel.

The challenges and troubles have not gone away in the modern age. Though the type of hardships differ from one culture or church to another, we know that having troubles is a universal experience for the universal Church of Jesus Christ. As part of the universal Church, Ethiopian Evangelical churches face several internal and external barriers as they engage in mission. The author brings these barriers up in order to encourage his countrymen and brothers and sisters in Christ to face them courageously so as to overcome them for the sake of God's Name and his glory among the nations.

Internal Barriers

Economic and Financial Management

Economic problems are one of the internal barriers of the Ethiopian Church. Though Ethiopia is blessed with numerous natural and human resources, its citizens do not significantly benefit from them due to the corruption, greed and laziness which affect many both inside and outside the church and also due to the problem of natural phenomena. Most of the Ethiopian population lives in rural areas and their basic income for daily living and survival largely depends on agriculture and farm produce in a land that is subject to frequent drought.

The other factor that makes the economy weak is the country's political instability. When the country was ruled by the Communist regime for seventeen years, the Ethiopian economy was also adversely affected and become the poorest country in the world. Even after Communism fell, it has remained among the poorest nations. Unfortunately, in Ethiopia, like in many other African nations, the government changing from time to time has greatly affected the economy of the country. The Church faces money problems whether facing lack or abundance: on the one hand, if churches do not have enough money, they are faced with challenges that may hinder them from doing missions. On the other hand, if they have money and are not using it properly, it destroys the effectiveness of the churches' ministries as a whole.

The power of the Holy Spirit and the call of God are important issues in doing mission. However, money also has its own impact on doing mission. As we can see in

Scripture, the first century church needed money to spread the Gospel of Jesus Christ and also to care for its own needy. The believers also were dedicated to give what they had to the church so that the Good News could reach the whole world. Acts 4:34-35 says: "There were no needy persons among them. For from time to time those who owned lands or houses sold them, brought the money from the sales and put it at the apostles' feet, and it was distributed to anyone as he had need" (NIV). Their dedication helped the church to continue in its ministry and to have influence on the community.

For the churches in Ethiopia – particularly those in the rural area – lack of money is a big barrier that hinders most of them from moving forward in mission. Most of the churches are struggling even to pay salaries for their own ministers; in fact, most ministers' salaries by themselves are not enough to sustain a family. These days, the number of those who serve full time in the church in Ethiopia is on the decline. The main reason for this is that the ministers in churches are not paid as they ought to be, and as a result, most are struggling financially. Many people in the churches, including full-time ministers, become more focused on their day-to-day life rather than on mission. Unfortunately, some ministers leave serving in the church and look for another job to feed their family. In the face of this financial challenge, the mentality of some is to expect money from outside the country to fix their problems, and to wait to begin missionary work until it arrives. As a result, the church's barrier-crossing mission is delayed or is never carried out. If this financial problem is solved in a sustainable way, however, the ministers will do tremendous work toward the expansion of the Kingdom of God.

Along with the economic challenge, churches in Ethiopia have a lack of skilled workers who can handle the church administration. For instance, most churches do not have strong financial systems which are transparent to all.

In the country, most churches do not have strong office structures which can help the ministries of the churches function easily. This is due to the fact that the churches do not have the manpower or trained personnel in that specific area or field; and even if they want to have skilled people, the church does not have enough money to employ them. Also, some churches view administrative systems as if they are secular and therefore not spiritual. Because of these two things, most Ethiopian churches have financial management problems.

Priority Confusion

Priority confusion in resource allocation is one of the challenges in Ethiopian churches. The churches cannot do all things at the same time and with the same urgency; rather, they must identify which things come first, second and so on. This clarity leads to effectiveness in ministry. Too often, Ethiopian churches become muddled in the daily grind of activity after activity, lacking vision because priorities have not been clearly established. *Mission* should be the dominant and controlling passion and priority of the Church. The Church exists primarily for the sake of its mission in the world. If this is true, then the Ethiopian churches need to focus intentionally on furthering the Gospel. All resources and every aspect of the life of a church should contribute towards mission in some way. Giving mission the priority in this way does not mean that other ministries are unimportant. However, clear priorities help to define the number one goal and to understand what is important in terms of that goal, making other things secondary and yet important as they relate to the ultimate goal. Proclamation must remain the Church's priority in this world, that the Name of Jesus would be known among the nations. The Great Commission is what the Church is sent into the world to accomplish, as seen in Matthew

28:18-19 and numerous other verses. The Lausanne Covenant says: "In the Church's mission of sacrificial service evangelism is primary. World evangelization requires the whole Church to take the whole Gospel to the whole world."[459] The churches in Ethiopia must also give priority to evangelism. Unfortunately, some churches spend money on musical instruments rather than on paying a salary of one minister or missionary. To be sure, the church has several responsibilities, but it should set mission as the greatest priority among its responsibilities so that churches can become effective in obeying the Lord's command to cross cultural barriers and make disciples of all nations.

Lack of Discipleship

A lack of discipleship programs is another challenging issue in the churches in Ethiopia. Praise God, people are being saved in almost every service of the churches, but because of lack of discipleship, too many return back to the world or become lukewarm or nominal "Christians."

Ethiopian churches are not adequately fulfilling their responsibility of discipling the new believers who are coming to the faith. Too many churches are overly focused on weekly programs and conferences to the neglect of deep discipleship. Some churches are more concerned about church buildings than about discipling their members. One of the reasons for this undervaluing of discipleship becomes evident when one realizes that the number of pastors and evangelists in the churches have received little or no discipleship training themselves. Thus, even if new believers continue to be added to the churches, they are not deeply rooted in the teachings of the Bible.

To understand this unhealthy cycle, it is helpful to understand recent Ethiopian history. During the *Derg* Communist regime, the churches in Ethiopia were underground, but as soon as the Communism fell, the churches got freedom to worship openly in public. Afterwards, great floods of new converts came to Christ like a wild fire. The churches at that time were not prepared to handle that situation. Many of the sound teachers, pastors and theologians were either imprisoned or killed. While the churches were underground, there was lack of teaching and training because people legitimately feared to even meet together with other believers openly. Unfortunately, when the churches got freedom of worship when Communism fell, everyone was so overjoyed about the freedom of worship that they did not think about working for more than this. As the result, many church members engage in church ministry and even some leaders hold high positions in the church without having been discipled themselves.[460]

Even though most churches have a teaching ministry program, it is often not well organized and certainly not sufficient. Usually, churches give teaching to their brand new converts but after that initial introduction of basic Christian teachings, they do not continue training and discipling members deeply in the ensuing years. This absence of long-term spiritual training causes lots of problems in all the churches' ministries as well as in the spirituality of the members.

To complicate matters further, when Ethiopians do receive discipleship training, it is often not contextually relevant. Ethiopian churches usually use translated foreign discipleship materials when they begin a discipleship program. The writer believes that in all areas of their ministries churches need to develop their own contextual materials with a relevant and pointed message to the people of God in their specific culture. Thus alongside discipleship, the churches have a challenge to contextualize their teachings. Contextual discipleship is a crucial ministry on which the Ethiopian Evangelical churches should focus in order to continue growing and to have a sustainable

Great Commission impact on society both within Ethiopia and beyond.

Leadership Problems

Churches today are growing in number in Africa as a whole, and Ethiopia is no exception. However, the question now is, are there enough leaders who can lead and teach the new converts in these churches so that they become mature in their faith in Christ? This is closely related to the discipleship problem examined above. Paul advises Timothy, his disciple, on how to disciple others as a leader: "You then, my son, be strong in the grace that is in Christ Jesus. And the things you have heard me say in the presence of many witnesses entrust to reliable men who will also be qualified to teach others" (2 Tim 2:1-2). The concern of Paul was to have responsible leaders, those who would receive the responsibility of passing on truth to the next generation. He was concerned that their training be of good quality so that they would be "qualified to teach others" (2 Tim 2:2).

In all his missionary journeys, Paul gathered believers together as soon as he found them, training and appointing leaders for the newly established church. In his book on mission, Roger Greenway explains, "The apostle Paul is often regarded as a church planter, and rightly so. However, he not only started new churches, but also spent a great deal of time and effort *training local leaders.*"[461] As a missionary, Paul understood that all too soon he would have to leave the new churches and go to other places. Thus, he did not leave them without local leaders who were trained and who could take responsibility. In Acts 20, Paul wanted the believers to remember clearly how he had planted and organized the church in their city, and to challenge them for the last time to carry out their responsibilities loyally as leaders of God's people.[462]

According to the research of Leaders Equipped for Transformation (LET) Ministry in Ethiopian Evangelical churches, 58% of church leaders are working part time, 52% of the leaders have one year or less in training, and 92% of this training is not related to the dynamics of church leadership. There is a 4% rate of annual church growth in Ethiopia. This shows that the number of trained church leaders is not keeping pace with the rate of church growth.[463]

The Ethiopian churches have made a great effort to overcome their limitations and challenges to spread the Gospel of Jesus Christ. There are some commendable initiatives to develop leaders currently underway. However, the leadership gap is wide and remains a very big and serious challenge to mission and to all other ministries of the Ethiopian Church.

External Barriers

Besides the internal challenges Ethiopian churches face, they also must grapple with external barriers that hinder them in implementing the call of God to proclaim the Gospel to the nations. Though there are number of external challenges facing the churches, the writer will focus on only a few.

Religious Conflicts

In this 21st century, religious conflict instigated by religious fundamentalists and extremists has grown as never before. Ethiopia has historically been known as a country that has different religions that have coexisted together for long time with mutual respect for each other. Recently, however, the country is experiencing some clashes and conflicts among its three primary religions. Though the government does not officially sanction any form of religious persecution, dangerous religious conflict can and does break out in the country without warning, with Evangelicals very often being the target of both Coptic Orthodox and Muslim persecution. This reality of persecution is one of a major challenge to mission for Ethiopian Evangelical Churches. It is difficult and risky to reach the unreached people groups in Ethiopia because the majority of these groups are staunchly Muslim or Coptic Orthodox. Certainly believers must be willing to follow in the steps of the apostles and gladly die for the sake of the Gospel, but in the modern day people often forget the fact that "everyone who wants to live a godly life in Christ Jesus will be persecuted" (1 Tim 3:12). Any Ethiopian missionary must be reminded to soberly count the cost of taking the Good News to the unreached, as their lives may be at risk.

Ethnic Conflicts

Currently, ethnic conflicts have become a huge barrier not only for Evangelical churches' mission work but also for the progress of Ethiopia at large. In the previous years in Ethiopia, there were a few conflicts between some tribes because of border and land issues from time to time. However, in recent years conflicts between ethnic groups are increasing steadily.

These days in Ethiopian churches, it is normal to seeing ethnic-based congregations in both the rural areas and the urban centers of the country. This trend is also very evident outside of Ethiopia, with Ethiopians in the Diaspora. Surely, having ethnic-based churches is not a problem in and of itself, but the way the system is being run and implemented is not upholding the unity of believers. Miriam Adeney exposes the potential negative effects of over-focusing on ethnicity:

> Sometimes ethnicity is turned into an idol. Like other idols of modern society—money, sex, and power, for example—ethnicity is not bad in itself. When we exalt it as though it were the highest good, however, ethnicity becomes evil. Racism, feuds, wars, and "ethnic cleansing" results. When ethnicity becomes an idol, it must be confronted and judged.[464]

African Theologian Samuel Waje Kunhiyop defines ethnicity as follows:

> Ethnicity is characteristics of a group of people, whether a few thousand or several million, who "share a persisting sense of common interest and identity that is based on some combination of shared historical experience and valued cultural traits." It is associated with shared culture, language, religion, social customs, physical appearance and geographic origins, and affects whom people turn to for security and protection.[465]

Ethnicity is accepted and even celebrated by God, and we too can celebrate and enjoy diversity. Yet we must always be aware and stay rooted in our greater unity as brothers and sisters in Christ. Charles Van Engen explains: "God recognizes and values cultural and ethnic diversity. Yet, within the particularity of ethnicity God loves all peoples and invites all to faith in Jesus Christ, each in their own special cultural and ethnic make-up."[466] Over-emphasis on diversity has become a killer of unity in the Ethiopian Evangelical Church in recent times. This lack of unity in the Church necessarily leads to lack of unity in mission as well. And where there is no unity, there is little effectiveness.

These are some of the barriers of Ethiopian Evangelical churches as they are engaged in mission of the Church: reaching the unreached for Christ. These challenges are not brought up to merely criticize or lament, but rather to begin a dialogue with the intent of transformation. Only in recognizing the barriers that we face will we be able to overcome them for the glory of God and the good of the nations.

CHAPTER ELEVEN

The Antioch Model and Its Great Commission Implications for the Ethiopian Church

In this chapter, we will discuss the Antioch Church as an example and model for multi-ethnic Ethiopian Evangelical churches as they seek to fulfill their missionary mandate in these present times. The writer will adapt Robert E. Thomas' "Antioch model" from the book *Mission in Acts: Ancient Narratives in Contemporary Context*, combining his insights with those from other sources to create a relevant application for the Ethiopian context.

Robert Garrett, in his describes the city of Antioch as follows:

> A special chemistry occurred in Antioch of Syria. The city was a cosmopolitan center at the crossroads of ancient trade routes. Accustomed to the jostling marketplaces full of people from many nations and exotic places, the society was a natural place for the church to first embrace a truly cross-cultural message and to build a multiethnic fellowship (Acts 11:20.21). Without doubt, the Gentiles who heard the Gospel in Antioch heard a message that did not sound foreign or Jewish to them; but it sounded relevant to their own situation in life.[467]

Antioch was a melting pot of Western and Eastern cultures: Greek and Roman traditions mingled with Semitic, Arabic and Persian influence. Antioch had everything to offer. It had political prestige. Under Roman rule, it was the third city of the Empire to be declared a provincial capital city of Syria. Antioch had dark side, however, as it was known for its immorality. Tourists came to see dancing girls. Corruption was rampant among politicians and business figures. Yet, Luke wrote nothing about Antioch's wickedness in the book of Acts. Instead, he told only of the great spiritual events that took place there, providing a wonderful biblical model of mission. At Antioch, the Gospel was preached to the Gentiles for the first time. Furthermore, it was the Antioch Church which commissioned and sent out some of the first missionaries to the Gentiles. Later on, it became a mother church of the Gentile churches. It was also the Apostle Paul's home church.[468]

For all these reasons, Antioch played a significant role in New Testament mission. It was destined by God to become the key to evangelizing the western Mediterranean area. This congregation "was noteworthy as a multi-ethnic, evangelistic, well-taught and outstandingly generous company of the Lord's people."[469] According to Stephen B. Bevans and Roger P. Schroeder: "Antioch was where the complete breakthrough to an open mission to the Gentiles took place, where Jewish and Gentile converts live side by side."[470] These authors go on to explain several ways in which what happened in the church at Antioch was radical and special:

> [The] first hint is that the Gospel is presented in the terms of the "Lord Jesus" (11:20). Whereas in all previous proclamations . . . the significance of Jesus had been expressed by the use of the Jewish title the "Messiah" (translated in Greek literally as *Christos*). . . .Second indication of the significance of this passage is that, where when news reached Jerusalem, the community there sent a trusted representative—Barnabas who like some of the Antioch evangelists was himself a Hellenist from Cyprus (4:36)—to investigate the situation....the third and final sign in the text that the developments at Antioch were a breakthrough for the community's growing consciousness of itself as church"

is the statement in verse 26 that "it was in Antioch that the disciples were called Christians for the first time."[471]

The Bible tells us how the Antioch church was founded in Acts 11:19-23:

> Now those who had been scattered by the persecution in connection with Stephen traveled as far as Phoenicia, Cyprus and Antioch, telling the message only to Jews. Some of them, however, men from Cyprus and Cyrene, went to Antioch and began to speak to Greeks also, telling them the good news about the Lord Jesus. The Lord's hand was with them, and a great number of people believed and turned to the Lord. News of this reached the ears of the church at Jerusalem, and they sent Barnabas to Antioch. When he arrived and saw the evidence of the grace of God, he was glad and encouraged them all to remain true to the Lord with all their hearts.

Those who were persecuted because of Stephen's death scattered all over the surrounding areas and preached the Gospel, and, as the result, the Antioch church came to being. From the ministry of Paul in Antioch, we can draw a helpful model for missiological ministry work. We see a faithful, missional and Holy Spirit inspired life in the Antioch Church. Using this church as a model in several key aspects could be relevant and helpful for the current Ethiopian Evangelical church context.

Aspects of the Model for Mission

1. Strong Spiritual Life of Congregation

The first characteristic of the Antioch Church model is the church members' devotion to the Lord. In the Antioch Church, a strong spiritual life was very evident (Acts 13:3).

Their prayer and fasting life and commitment to the Lord's service is exemplary (Acts 13:1-3).

Prayer is the act through which a Christian communicates and talks with God. It is the act of making a respectful petition to God. Fasting is the Biblical way of humbling oneself (Ps 35). Prayer and fasting have always been ways to minister to the Lord (e.g. Luke 2:36-38). We should keep in mind that Jesus, the Son of God, regularly withdrew to a quiet place to commune with the Father in prayer and fasting, and the New Testament Church was marked by these disciplines as well.

The Bible often refers to Jesus' prayer life. According to Matthew 4:1-2 (NIV): "Then Jesus was led by the Spirit into the desert to be tempted by the devil. After fasting forty days and forty nights, he was hungry." Jesus, in the desert, after fasting for forty days and nights, defeated the devil's temptation. Luke also reveals to us how important prayer was in the life of Jesus and the disciples throughout his Gospel (see 5:16; 9:28-29; 18:1; 22:39-40).

It can be considered a fact that all the great men of God (as shown in the Scriptures) have been men of prayer. Notable examples include Moses, David, Elijah, and Paul. However, most believers have also felt the poverty of their prayer life. Even the disciples, realizing their insufficiency, asked the Lord Jesus to teach them how to pray (Luke 11:1).

The Bible shows us the danger of neglecting prayer in Joshua 9:13-15. Joshua and the elders of Israelite missed the will of God because they did not ask God before they made a covenant with the people of Gibeon. Joshua and the Israelites received the people of Gibeon without inquiring the will of God and made a covenant with them. Later, they found that the people of Gibeon had deceived them. Though the people of Gibeon were one of the nations that should perish, the Israelite had to let them live because of the mistake. In contrast, the Antioch Church was characterized by prayer and fasting, seeking God's will and direction. As the result, they paid attention to the Holy Spirit and identified the will of God: to send out Barnabas and Paul as missionaries from among them.

Thomas identified some widely applicable points the Antioch Church's mission:

> Note the...components of the church's response to the Spirit's call to mission (13:3). First, the members fasted. This was not their weekly custom. In fact, fasting is rarely mentioned in Acts (only in 13:3 and 14:23), and never in the letter of Paul. Clearly this call required a solemn preparation for decision-making and action. Second, they prayed. Earnestly they sought for divine guidance. They desire the commission about to be given to Soul and Barnabas.[472]

As a result of their vibrant spiritual life, evidenced by waiting on the Lord through prayer and fasting, the Antioch Church's influence and growth were tremendous.

2. Evangelism By Lay Leadership

Antioch gives a model of evangelism done by lay leadership. At first, the Jewish believers witnessed only to Jews (11:9), who were a large and dynamic community of an estimated twenty-two thousand persons at the time. However, the witnesses also included Greek-speaking Jewish Christians from Cyprus and Cyrene. They crossed a cultural bridge as they shared the good news with Gentiles. Luke's contrast of Hellenists with Jews suggests that the former had adopted the Greek language and culture in that cosmopolitan city.[473]

In Acts 11:20, we read that unnamed Christians in Antioch began "proclaiming the Lord Jesus." Some later writers named Peter as the founder of the church there. This is significant because later churches vied to name an apostle as their founder, but Luke does not name a founder. Acts 8:1 says, "...all except the apostles were scattered." In the first Jerusalem persecution, we see that lay people held a significant role in evangelism. The first Christian martyr was Stephen—a layman—not Peter, James, or John. When the Antioch Church began to grow, the apostles sent Barnabas, a layman, to investigate. The Antioch church was founded, led, and multiplied by laypeople.[474]

E. Stanly Jones reflects on Thomas' Antioch model in the following words:

> Hitherto, the center of gravity has been on the minister; now the center of gravity has to be shifted to the laity. We ministers, missionaries, and evangelists are never going to win the world. We are too few to do it and if we could do it it would not be good, for it would take away from the laity that spiritual growth and development which comes through sharing one's faith.[475]

Another remarkable feature of the Antioch church was its ability to successfully cross what has been called "the most fundamental division in the Roman Empire—that between rural people and city dwellers."[476] Among all the other marks of the Antioch model, this one is the most remarkable, for, as the believers scattered from the city to the more rural areas, "The Lord's hand was with them, and a great number of people believed and turned to the Lord" (Acts 11:21).

3. Every Member a Minister

The third aspect of the Antioch model is the concept of "Every Member a Minister."[477] Thomas mentions that news of the Antioch revival reached Jerusalem and the Jerusalem Church sent Barnabas to Antioch to investigate. Luke describes him as "a good man, full of the Holy Spirit and of faith" (Acts 11:24 NIV). Earlier, he had been introduced as a Levite, a native of Cyprus, and a generous giver (Acts 4:36). Barnabas had the complete trust of the Twelve. The apostles sent him to Antioch and he rejoiced with what he saw there. It should be noted that Barnabas "exhorted them all to remain faithful to the Lord with steadfast devotion" (Acts 11:23 NRS). He did not only gather the leaders for a revival conference. Rather, he addressed *all* of the members of the church. As the result, the Antioch Church grew like wildfire because every Christian was invested in the church and had a ministry to do.[478]

Leaders are certainly needed in the church and should be appointed, but for the sake of the expansion of God's Kingdom, *all* members should be involved and mobilized for ministry. Paul's metaphor of the church as a human body is a perfect representation to show that every member should be an active participant in the church:

> The body is a unit, though it is made up of many parts; and though all its parts are many, they form one body. So it is with Christ. For we were all baptized by one Spirit into one body—whether Jews or Greeks, slave or free—and we were all given the one Spirit to drink. Now the body is not made up of one part but of many.... But in fact God has arranged the parts in the body, every one of them, just as he wanted them to be. If they were all one part, where would the body be? As it is, there are many parts, but one body. The eye cannot say to the hand, "I don't need you!" And the head cannot say to the feet, "I don't need you!" (1Cor. 12:12-21, NIV).

Paul emphasizes the essence of having all members operate as a single entity for the health of the church. When each member of the church, as the eye or the ear, is active in the body, then the body can work and function properly for the good of all. In the church, leaders are not the only ones to do ministry; instead, all members also should be included in ministry. For this to be true of a church, it takes the initiative and willingness of the main leaders. The Bible says, "Now the body is not made up of one part but of many" (12:14), because the whole body cannot be a single part, or it would not be a functioning body. God distributes gifts to all members in the body so that every member can contribute its own part and benefit all the other parts, enabling the body to function and do good things. This model is seen clearly in the Antioch Church — every member was active in the ministry.

4. Discipleship and Follow Up

A fourth aspect of the Antioch Church model is "Caring for New Believers." Barnabas knew that he needed to do more than urge the believers at Antioch to be good Christians. So he recruited the best trainer he knew—Saul of Tarsus (11:25). What followed was more than a weekend retreat for new Christians or even a four-week new members' class. We read that Saul and Barnabas met with the church "for an entire year" and taught "a great many people" (11:26). [479]

Discipling new converts is the Christian mandate that Jesus gave to His Church. In Matthew 28:18-20 (NIV), Jesus says to His disciples:

> All authority in heaven and on earth has been given to me. Therefore go and make disciples of all nations, baptizing them in the name of the Father and of the Son and of the Holy Spirit, and teaching them to obey everything I have commanded you. And surely I am with you always, to the very end of the age.

This is the command from the Lord: that in every generation, the church should carry out the ministry of discipleship to all the nations. Jesus Himself was devoted to discipling His followers, especially the Twelve: "Now when he saw the crowds, he went up on a mountainside and sat down. His disciples came to him, and he began to teach them" (Matt 5:1-2 NIV).

As all four Gospels present Him, Jesus' ministry focuses on discipling. Kent Hunter points out: "One of the key aspects to God's strategy for winning the world is to disciple the few to win the many....[Jesus] gathered twelve disciples from among the common people of His area, and He spent three years teaching them....He trained them, not only in theory, but also in practice....Jesus spent a lot of time teaching doctrine. The truth of God's will is the foundation for discipleship....God's plan for healthy and comprehensive church growth involve the fact that disciples should be trained to know and do." [480]

In his book, *Making Kingdom Disciples: A New Framework*, Charles H. Dunahoo writes about the importance of discipling believers:

> The importance of those words [Mt. 28:18-20] cannot be overstated. They express God's revealed will of for his church until he returns at the consummation of all things. The church's mission is to make disciples by evangelizing and educating the believers. In return, the believers are to be transformed into the likeness of Christ, demonstrated by a life of Christlike service within the Kingdom of God.[481]

Thus, evangelism and discipleship are the supreme responsibility of the Church, and the understanding of this is clearly seen in the Church at Antioch. Though Christian witness was the initial priority, instruction became a necessary part of the church's life. Those who came out of non-Jewish traditions needed a solid foundation in faith if they were to become disciples. Paul had time to develop his strategy of mission to Gentiles in Antioch. Antioch became the center of mission activities for the next twelve to fourteen years which Paul spent "in the regions of Syria and Cilicia" (Gal. 1:21).[482]

Follow-up is a crucial element of discipleship and is modeled by the Antioch Church. Acts 15:36 says, "Sometime later Paul said to Barnabas, 'Let us go back and visit the brothers in all the towns where we preached the word of the Lord and see how they are doing.'" The original purpose of the second missionary journey — though it also opened vast new areas to the Gospel along the way — was to revisit the churches that were already planted so that they might be strengthened in the faith.

Paul does not only follow up with the churches by visiting them; he also writes letters to them so that he could strengthen their faith in the Lord even from a distance. In his book, *Church Planting Approach in Mission*, Ponraj S. Devasahayam states:

> Spiritual nurture is also called follow-up, after-care and post-baptismal teaching. It includes both Bible teaching and pastoral care. Proper Spiritual nurture is vital for an effective church planting ministry. The process of church planting starts with baptism and is completed by effective spiritual nurture. Spiritual nurture is part of the discipleship process and is commanded in the Great Commission (Matt. 28:20). A missionary should make every effort in their post-baptismal care for new believers to grow in their spiritual life. He should aim at making now believers responsible and reproducing members of the church.[483]

Evangelism and discipleship (including follow-up) go together. The Church of Antioch fulfilled Jesus' vision — preaching to, converting, baptizing, and discipling sinners to be a part of the local church.

5. Unity in Diversity

The fifth aspect of the Antioch model is their unity regardless of their background. Luke mentions that "it was in Antioch that the disciples were first called 'Christians'" (Acts 11:26). Thomas referred to this aspect as "Overcoming Racial and Ethnic Barriers."[484] He explains:

> Luke recorded in Acts 11:19 the results of the Jerusalem persecution. Disciples of Jesus were scattered as far as Phoenicia, Cyprus, and Antioch. But as they fled, they witnessed only to Jews. Thus the breakthrough to a more inclusive church came at Antioch. Christians from Cyprus and Cyrene began to tell the good news to Gentiles. The Spirit could not be walled up in homogeneous Christianity. Picture the table fellowship of the Antioch ministry team (13:1). Barnabas, a Cypriot landowner and Levite was there. Next to him sat Simeon "who was called Niger"—meaning "black," possibly from Africa. Next sat Lucius of Cyrene who was also from Africa. Together with Lucius sat Manaen—an aristocrat from the court of the ruler, Herod. Paul, that fiery intellectual from Tarsus, completed the table fellowship.[485]

This was a multicultural team on mission, a dynamic example of God's heart for all nations. While these leaders were from different races, nations and cultures, they were one in Christ; in fact, they were celebrating their unity in diversity. Unity is very important for God's children. In his book *The Purpose Driven Life*, Rick Warren writes: "When we place our faith in Christ, other believers become our brothers and sisters, and the church becomes our spiritual family. The family of God includes all believers in the past, the present, and the future."[486] Thomas comments on the uniqueness of the Antioch church's unity, saying:

> "You are not your own…. For you were bought with a price," Paul wrote (1 Cor. 6:19-20). Later he called the Corinthian Christians "slaves of Christ" (1 Cor. 7:21-14). Could he first have used those words in his Antioch ministry? I believe so. Later, Paul must have longed to

return to the Antioch model of Christian unity. The church in Corinth had no such unity. We read that divisions sprang up. Members claimed that their first loyalty was to Paul, or Apollos, or Peter (1 Cor. 1:10-17). Was this an early form of denominationalism? Certainly it was an early fracture of Christian unity.[487]

Christians from all over the world, redeemed by the blood of Jesus Christ, are the members of the family of God. Receptivity to the Gospel of Jesus Christ and faith in Him are the only criteria for membership into this family of God. In his book titled *The Church and its Mission: A Shattering Critique from the Third World*, Orlando E. Costas wrote:

> [The church] is a multitude of men and women from all walks of life, without distinction of race, nationality, economic an education background. It is a community gathered from every tribe, tongue, and nation. It is a people called out of darkness in to God's marvelous light through the Holy Spirit, as a result of God's revealed and redeeming grace in Jesus, to be God's own people, Christ's own body, and the temple of the Holy Spirit in the concrete situations of their everyday life.[488]

The concept that each part of the body, or system, doing its work is vital to the health and growth of the church is revisited. The Antioch Church was able to picture perfectly the family of God that represents the unification of all the parts of the body. In spite of their different backgrounds, the barriers that had once separated them had been destroyed in Christ, and they were now worshiping God together. The Antioch Church became the mother of many Gentile churches which followed her same model throughout the surrounding area.

6. Balanced Leadership

Thomas' sixth aspect of the Antioch model is "Balanced Leadership."[489] He explains:

> In Antioch there were both "prophets and teachers" (13:1), as well as members ready for action. Luke, in his account of Pentecost, included the conviction that Christian prophecy is a possibility for every Christian (2:17-18, 38). Nevertheless, there emerged persons with special gifts to interpret the purpose of God for particular situations. Prophets were gifted to speak God's truth. In cosmopolitan Antioch they spoke both to fulfill christens and to inquirers. It took sensitivity and courage to speak God's truth in love. Those from Jewish backgrounds must have heard the Gospel differently from those of Gentiles background. But there were also teachers. Their task was to deepen the understandings of new believers. Later Paul would write, perhaps out of his earlier Antioch experience: "Speaking the truth in love, we must grow up in every way ... into Christ" (Eph. 4:15). Earlier in Acts, Luke presented persons who could be both prophets and teachers.... Therefore, it is not surprising that Luke did not try to designate certain Antioch leaders as prophets and others as teachers.[490]

In each aspect of human organization, leadership is a key. It is commonly accepted that "Leadership is influence." Since leadership is influence, the leaders of the church must give attention to the following: (1) how to influence, (2) what to influence, (3) where to influence, and (4) whom to influence.[491] Thus, leadership is essential for the church so that it can grow and fulfill the Great Commission. In the Antioch Church, we see that the church is blessed by different types of church leaders: prophets, pastors, teachers and apostles. In his article, "A Missional Church Model," Robert Lionel Elkington wrote:

In Acts 13:1-3, the next phase of the ministry of Paul and Barnabas emerged at a certain phase of that church's life. In Acts 11, the church was birthed and Barnabas is sent to teach and minister, and in the process, then calls Paul to assist him in doing this. By the time the reader comes upon Acts 13, 2 years later, there is a multiplicity of leadership within the Antioch church, leadership that has grown through the spiritual ministry of Paul and Barnabas. Ephesians 4:7-16 highlights the equipping role of the teaching and shepherding leadership within a local church. Acts 13:1-3 exemplifies the principles laid out in Ephesians 4:7-16.[492]

As Elkington points out, the model that we find in Antioch became the model for other churches founded in Paul and Barnabas' cross-cultural ministries. Further, the Antioch model is very important for churches today. Though Thomas mentions more aspects of the Antioch model, the writer has chosen to focus on the six aspects that are most applicable in his context. Thus, in the next section, the writer will apply these aspects of the Antioch model to the context of the Ethiopian Evangelical Church.

Application to the Ethiopian Context

In a previous chapter, the writer examined the challenges of the Ethiopian Church in mission, including lack of leadership, lack of discipleship and lack of unity. The Ethiopian Evangelical churches need to reexamine their missiological models and methods according to the present situation of the country. The writer believes that the Antioch model could be applicable and helpful to today's Ethiopian Evangelical Church situation, helping her to become more effective in sharing and spreading the Good News to the nations within Ethiopia and beyond.

The Antioch model will help the church to see the importance of missional leaders, the crucial nature of long-term discipleship, and the necessity of unity in diversity. If the Antioch model is to be implemented in the Ethiopian Evangelical Church, several groups must catch the vision and take their share of responsibility. The writer will discuss specific suggestions for how church leaders, the Evangelical Churches Fellowship of Ethiopia (ECFE), parachurch ministries, and theological colleges and seminaries can join hands in an effort to make this biblical model a reality in Ethiopia and beyond.

1. The Role of Church Leaders in Implementing the Antioch Model

When applying the missiological model of Antioch to the context of Ethiopia, the role of church leaders is paramount. Christ gave leaders to His Church so that the believers could be equipped and grow in their faith. Paul wrote to the church in Ephesians 4:11-14:

> It was he who gave some to be apostles, some to be prophets, some to be evangelists, and some to be pastors and teachers, to prepare God's people for works of service, so that the body of Christ may be built up until we all reach unity in the faith and in the knowledge of the Son of God and become mature, attaining to the whole measure of the fullness of Christ. Then we will no longer be infants, tossed back and forth by the waves, and blown here and there by every wind of teaching and by the cunning and craftiness of men in their deceitful scheming.

As Paul stated, the role of the leaders in the Church is to equip the saints for the works of the ministry. Leaders have a great responsibility to equip and mobilize God's people for the works to which they are called. The Antioch Church was led well and in a way that helped people to grow. The Ethiopian churches, and indeed all churches, also need leaders like this – prophets, evangelists, pastors and teachers. When the churches have balanced leadership, pastors lead, evangelists proclaim the Good News, prophets encourage God's people and teachers teach the truth. If leadership is balanced, the church will become healthy and God's people will mature in the faith. Furthermore, leaders serve the church in many other ways. Churches without leaders are like sheep without a shepherd. Qualified leaders provide direction, teach, disciple, and help the church to achieve their vision, promote the saints' growth into maturity, train future leaders and live exemplary lives. (Acts 20:25-31; 1Tim 1:3; 3:4-5; 5:17; 6:20). Their role is advisory and supervisory, not imbued with lordly authority of command and conformity. All members of the church, both leaders and laymen, submit to the Lord, and then to one another in the Lord.

Therefore, leaders should mobilize the members towards God's plan and develop lay leaders for the service of the Lord. Paul, in Romans 1:11-12 (NIV), says, "I long to see you so that I may impart to you some spiritual gift to make you strong—that is, that you and I may be mutually encouraged by each other's faith." Paul's longing to see them was not only to share spiritual gifts, but he gave room for mutual encouragement because individuals alone do not accomplish ministry — rather, effective ministry is done in community. Thus, in the Ethiopian churches, lay leadership should play a great part to expand the Kingdom and build the community. For this to be so, the leaders of the church have a responsibility to develop emergent leaders. The author agrees with the suggestion of C. Peter Wagner about the essential nature of the pastors or leaders mobilizing lay leaders for the growth of the church. He suggested a few important points where he discussed the vital signs of a growing church:

> If the first vital sign of a growing church is a pastor who is using his gifts to lead his church in to growth, the second is a well-mobilized laity. One cannot function apart from the other any more than blood circulation and respiration can function apart from each other in the human body....Pastors of growing churches, whether they be large or small, know how to motivate their laypeople, how to create structures which permit them to be active and productive and how to guide them into meaningful avenues of Christians service.[493]

The writer also believes that if the leaders fulfill their responsibility – mobilize the laity and involve all the members of the church in ministry – the problems that the churches are now facing, such as the lack of leadership and discipleship will be addressed. In the process of discipling members and developing leaders, the emphasis should be the youth. Since they are the next generation of leaders, the churches should by all means involve them in all of their ministries. In addition, much emphasis should be placed on them because they are the asset of the churches and they can play a great role in the expansion of God's Kingdom and building of the community.

However, as the author mentioned in chapter three, there are not enough leaders in the Ethiopian Church, and the lack of leadership is a challenge for the Ethiopian Church. Since leaders are key in the church, the churches in Ethiopia should develop leaders at every level to overcome the challenge. For this particular reason, the Antioch Church is a good example for the contemporary Ethiopian church. The Antioch church was effective in doing mission, discipling the members, and speaking the truth in their context. Why? Because the church had effective multicultural leadership which led the church towards growth into involvement in God's mission.

Discipling the youth today provides leaders for the Church and the world tomorrow. If the churches were committed and engaged in discipling today's youth, they will be able to win the leadership of tomorrow's world for the glory of God, for the young generation of today will be the pillars of the church and the world leaders of tomorrow. Lesslie Newbigin argues, "The full participation of the members of the body in its activity does not happen without leadership. The business of leadership is precisely to enable, encourage, and sustain the activity of all members. To set 'participation' and 'leadership' against each other is absurd."[494] Consequently, the churches in Ethiopia should involve all members of the church community, especially the youth.

In addressing the ethnic and religious conflicts which Ethiopian churches are now experiencing, the churches can challenge the status quo with biblical teaching. Having an ethnic-based church is not a problem but it should work to keep the unity of the whole body of the church. In fact, the problem of ethnicity does not only occur in Ethiopian churches, but is also prominent in other African countries. Barje S. Maigadi, quoting from Elmer A. Martens, discusses the nature of "the one Family of God" and ethnic relations,

> The faith community, while a "particular," [by origin] is now definitely not an ethnic particular. Its leadership is not chosen ethnically. The ministry of the community, both by its composition and its leadership, [extends beyond] all ethnic definitions, even though it owes its life to an ethnically-oriented origin.[495]

In addition, he also quoted from Allen Mawhinney:

> There is no racial, religious, or sociologically division today, which is stronger, more bitter or more dangerous than the division of Jew and Gentile in New Testament times....that the problem of divisive ethnicity in the

church is one of the reasons Paul in his epistles emphasizes the theme of adoption.[496]

Sometimes even the leaders of the early church fell back into ethnocentrism. The apostle Paul confronted Peter on this issue:

> When Peter came to Antioch, I opposed him to his face, because he was clearly in the wrong. Before certain men came from James, he used to eat with the Gentiles. But when they arrived, he began to draw back and separate himself from the Gentiles because he was afraid of those who belonged to the circumcision group. The other Jews joined him in his hypocrisy, so that by their hypocrisy even Barnabas was led astray (Gal 2:11-13 NIV).

Barje S. Maigadi explains the above-mentioned passage as follows:

> Paul saw Peter's act as a form of hypocrisy. Peter's action influenced others Christians, even Barnabas whose name means "Son of Encouragement" (Acts 4:36). The localization of God by divisive ethnicity is a contagious disease that can infect even the most highly placed leaders in the churches. It has to be denounced publicly or else it can even [end] in genocide as in Rwanda.[497]

It took the whole assembly of apostles to work together in order to resolve the problem that arose in Acts 6:1-4. Maigadi concludes:

> The destruction of divisive ethnicity may require leaders full of the Spirit and wisdom to be examples of what it means to be members of God's family. The church knew that the localization of God would destroy its relationship with God and one another tarnish its public image as well as negate its fulfillment of the mission of God.[498]

Furthermore, the issue of ethnicity in Africa is very sensitive. Thus, the leaders of the church in Ethiopia should be able to teach their members, and only leaders who are full of Spirit and wisdom to tackle the issue should be chosen. While the church members have different ethnic backgrounds, they can still celebrate their unity in the one family of God because of Christ's barrier-destroying work. Actually, unity in the church does not mean uniformity. People have different cultures and backgrounds, thus the church in Ethiopia should celebrate their diversity while keeping the unity of the church. Maigadi explains what it means to be one family of God while having a multi-ethnic background:

> Since the scope of the one family of God is universal and multi-ethnic, and since its nature is God-centered, do members of the one family of God have to abandon their natural ethnicity totally in order to avoid divisive ethnicity?... does being a child of God mean committing what Ralph D. Winter calls cultural suicide"? Some people think that to become a child of God means rejection of one's ethnicity. Not so. The natural ethnicity of members of the one family of God is perfected by its fundamental character of Christianity which is *agape,* bestowed by the Holy Spirit (Romans 5:5). Lamin Sanneh elegantly and rightly says: "It is difficult to receive the Jesus of place and time through the vessels and arteries of his own ethnic mother's blood and milk and not celebrate ethnic diversity in all its concreteness and rich variety." He further states that it is in the celebration of ethnic diversity that unity of purpose in the church is accomplished.[499]

God loves to see unity in the midst of our diversity; in fact, God is the one who gave different languages and cultures with the command for people to fill the earth. "God blessed them and said to them, 'Be fruitful and increase in number; fill the earth and subdue it. Rule over the fish of the sea and the birds of the air and over every living creature that moves on the ground'" (Gen. 1:28). However, when the people refused to scatter and fill the earth, God confused their languages (Genesis 11:4, 9). Charles Van Engen also affirms the particularity and diversity of humankind:

> Three times in the first eleven chapters of Genesis we are told that God is the creator and judge of all peoples. All people are created in Adam and Eve; all people descend from Noah; all people have their languages confused and are then spread out over the entire earth after the Babel episode. In each case, there is a recognition of the particularity and difference of various peoples–as is signaled by the inclusion of the Table of Nations in Genesis 10–yet in each case this multiplicity of peoples are collectively and unitedly said to be the object of God's concern. Thus it is no accident that Jesus, the Messiah of Israel, would use Isaiah's language in speaking of Herod's Temple as "a house of prayer for all the nations" (Isa. 56:7; Mk. 11:17). The complementarity of universality and particularity is very strong in Jesus' ministry. At one point Jesus sends his disciples "to the lost sheep of the house of Israel" (Matt. 10:6). Yet this is the same Jesus and the same Gospel of Matthew that will strongly emphasize that the disciples are to meet him in the cosmopolitan, multi-cultural setting of Galilee. There he will say, "All authority is given to me in heaven and on earth, go therefore and disciple *ta ethne*–the nations (Matt. 28:18-19). Paul emphasized this complementarity. Even in the oft-cited universal passages like Galatians 3:28 ("There is neither Jew nor Greek, slave nor free, male nor female....") and Colossians 3:11 ("Here there is no Greek or Jew, circumcised or uncircumcised, barbarian, Scythian, slave or free....") the cultural distinctives are not erased. The particularity of ethnicity, sexuality, and socio-economics is not ignored. Rather, in the midst of such specific

forms of homogeneity, there is a universality of union (not uniformity of culture)–a universality of oneness in Jesus Christ: "you are all one in Christ Jesus." (Gal. 3:28); "but Christ is all, and in all" (Col. 3:11). As I read Scripture, I see God affirming cultural distinctives. I see Babel as judgment, yes, but also as grace. The beauty of resplendent creativity shines forth in the wonderful multiplication of families, tribes, tongues and peoples of humanity. Rather than destroy humanity (which in the Noahic covenant God had promised not to do), God chooses to confuse the languages. This confusion, although an act of judgment, mercifully preserves all humanity in its cultural and ethnic distinctives, differences so significant that we are given a Table of Nations to enumerate the civilizations known to the compilers of the Pentateuch. These differences are so significant that when the Holy Spirit comes at Pentecost one of the first extraordinary acts of the Holy Spirit is to enable people of many different languages to hear the proclamation of the Gospel in their own language. Yet these distinctive features of multiple cultures are not allowed to divide humanity's relation to YHWH, nor to support the concept of a national or ethnic plurality of gods. There is one God, creator and sustainer of all peoples. Oneness in plurality, plurality in oneness: particular universality, universal particularity.[500]

Therefore, leaders in the churches should also be qualified in their leadership ability, not by their material or worldly status, but based on biblical qualifications. Further, they have a responsibility to teach biblical truth to the congregation about their new identity in Christ (2 Cor 5:17-18). As Paul rebuked Peter and dealt with ethnic problems, the church of Jesus Christ should never give support to any act of discrimination against others, because divisive ethnicity is a sin. Though it is sensitive to talk about the issue of ethnicity in Ethiopia and in Africa as a whole, the

Church of Jesus Christ in Ethiopia should denounce divisive ethnicity publicly because it is equal to the sin of idolatry.

Furthermore, in regards to today's tension, we are tending to forget our differences on one hand while on the other hand, we are constantly reminded of them. In other words, some go to one extreme, trying to eliminate diversity, while others go to the other extreme, trying to magnify diversity. Both are wrong, and we should strike a balance between them. Thus, anywhere the problem of ethnic conflict rises, the prayers of the saints are needed. Prayer can destroy all sorts of evil forces, such as ethnic conflict. Maigadi observes that when the church in Antioch prayed and fasted, the Holy Spirit commanded the church to set apart Barnabas and Paul for Him, for the work to which He had called them to do (Acts 13:2). When divisive ethnicity begins to invade the life of any Christian community, it is a signal that the community is losing touch with God. Therefore, there is a need for Ethiopian churches to seriously call for prayer, fasting and repentance to overcome this giant barrier called "ethnic conflict."

In conclusion, without the Holy Spirit, all efforts to fulfill the Great Commission are in vain. Donald A. McGavran affirms:

> Since there can be no effective mission to reconcile men to God without the Holy Spirit, it follows that His leadership must be sought and His empowering presence must be in evident manifestation if there is to be any success is carrying out the Church's mission.[501]

God's purpose for the diversity of people's languages, cultures, and nations is the unity in their dependence on Him. Unity and diversity are joined to show God's glory. The Psalmist praises and thanks the Lord for His creation: "How many are your works, O LORD? In wisdom you made them all; the earth is full of your creatures" (Ps 104:24). God loves diversity, and without diversity, unity does not hold any significance. In fact, in uniformity, there is no unity.

Thus, the Ethiopian Evangelical Church leaders – while they are discipling God's people, developing leaders and expanding the Kingdom of God – should to continue worship the Lord as one family of God celebrating their unity in diversity. They also should teach the Christian community about the biblical truth of their identity in Christ in order to live together in God's love. As McGavran confirmed, "The biblical teaching is plain that in Christ two peoples become one. Christian Jews and Gentiles become one people of God, parts of the one body of Christ. But the one body is complex."[502] People's oneness in Christ does not erase their cultural uniqueness.

2. The Role of Evangelical Churches Fellowship of Ethiopia (ECFE) in Implementing the Antioch Model

The establishment of the Evangelical Churches Fellowship of Ethiopia (ECFE) is described in their own words:

> The history of the Fellowship in Ethiopia goes back to the early 1970s. Some evangelical through inter-church prayer meetings attempted to bring all churches together in 1970-72.The most significant event considered by many church leaders as the cornerstone for the initiation of the Fellowship of was evangelical churches union conference in 1977. The communist regime that came into power in 1974 banned all evangelical practices. This political reality then forced the evangelical church institutions to accept and work towards the establishment of the Fellowship as a necessity of survival. This strong belief in the establishment of an umbrella association was not only concentrated in head

offices of the churches, but also to a wide extent to the local churches all over the country. Suffering together for the sake of righteousness and we are living testimony to the crucified Lord. These conditions led to the establishment of an umbrella organization in 1976 by 9 evangelical churches. The vision of ECFE is to see "*Churches United* (italics mine) in Christ and *Equipped* (italics mine) in Fulfilling the Great Commission in Ethiopia and beyond." Its mission is "Equip members to fulfill the goal of the Great Commission through capacity building, advocacy and peace building." The core values that are upheld during its operation are Unity, Holiness, Serving the Whole Person, Integrity and Transparency, Good Governance, Peace and Justice, Responsiveness and Servanthood.[503]

The ECFE should be challenged to move forward towards its mission and vision: to see the churches in Ethiopia united with responsible, well-equipped members and effective leadership. This Fellowship has a great opportunity to bring churches to strong unity and integration for the fulfillment of the Great Commission.

Among Ethiopian Evangelical churches, many splits have occurred for various reasons – some because of administration problems and self-interest, some because they wanted their own ethnic-based churches. As a result, much destruction has been experienced in the unity of the churches as well as in the lives of the believers. For example, some churches in Ethiopia faced severe challenges of divisions, which took more than a decade to resolve; in fact, the issue was treated by the intervention of the Ethiopian government's court. In all these problems, the ECFE tried its best to make peace between the squabbling groups. At the current time, it seemed as though the problems were resolved but there are still some divisions among the churches; some pastors and ministers left their churches because of disagreements and planted other churches, which is not the way to preserve unity. Thus, the Fellowship has a lot to do in order to keep the unity of the churches and to bring true reconciliation between them so that the Gospel can spread without hindrance. Paul instructs the Corinthian Church:

> If any of you has a dispute with another, dare he take it before the ungodly for judgment instead of before the saints? Do you not know that the saints will judge the world? And if you are to judge the world, are you not competent to judge trivial cases? Do you not know that we will judge angels? How much more the things of this life! Therefore, if you have disputes about such matters, appoint as judges even men of little account in the church! I say this to shame you. Is it possible that there is nobody among you wise enough to judge a dispute between believers? But instead, one brother goes to law against another—and this in front of unbelievers! The very fact that you have lawsuits among you means you have been completely defeated already. Why not rather be wronged? Why not rather be cheated? Instead, you yourselves cheat and do wrong, and you do this to your brothers (1Cor 6:1-8 NIV).

The believers in Corinth were acting like ungodly people in their treatment of each other so Paul explains that if mediation is necessary, they should find Christians who are able to do so within the Church rather than allowing Christian brothers and sisters to oppose each other in secular litigation. They should be ashamed of the way they were acting. In addition, Paul senses that the very existence of legal cases among the Corinthians shows a hateful attitude and spiritual failure. Instead of being involved in all these disputes and cheating their fellow Christians, they should be willing to suffer wrong; in fact, this is a basic Christian principle.

Therefore, the ECFE should first develop its organizational structure of human and material resources in order to have larger positive influence on the churches; in turn, the local church leaders also should work with the Fellowship for the healthy growth of all believers and God's Kingdom. No individual or one local church is sufficient to do all things, thus we have to stay in partnership with one another. The churches need to work together to finish the task – preaching the Gospel to all of creation as Jesus commanded His disciples: "Go into all the world and preach the good news to all creation" (Mark 16:15).

Let us rise up as the Ethiopian Evangelical Church and participate in finishing the task – the Great Commission – as we celebrate our unity in diversity. We have biblical principles and a pattern of life laid out for us in Scripture; thus, let us follow and implement the lessons learned from the model of the Antioch Church in order to address our problems and overcome our challenges. We are not called to follow the secular worldview; rather, the Lord called us to be the salt and light of the world (Matt 5:13-16) as we follow Him as His Body on earth.

In addition, the ECFE should include young and influential leaders so that its vision could be fulfilled. In the history of the Ethiopian Evangelical churches, young people have had a great role in the expansion of the Gospel; in fact, university and high school students planted some of the churches. Let us give attention to the youth because they are the next generation and the leaders of tomorrow for the church and for the nation. Thus, let us strive to make them responsible church members by involving them in leadership in order to have a positive influence in the Christian community and the country as a whole. Today, there are many youth inside the churches; if the churches mobilize and involve them in leadership, the ministries of the churches will see positive changes in their midst. This is also the role of ECFE, because it represents the majority of the churches in the country.

The ECFE can also play a great role in mobilizing different church leaders and preparing a reconciliation program to deal with issues which arise between churches and ethnic groups. The ECFE, in spite of its limitations, is playing a very good role in bringing the new-planted churches and the mainline churches together and creating a door for discussion towards unity and partnership among all churches. This is the time for partnership, not division; we have to continue doing mission together to expand the Kingdom of God.

3. The Role of Parachurch Ministries in Implementing the Antioch Model

In Ethiopia, there are a number of different parachurch organizations. Some of these are professional gatherings or associations of believers who are in the same field. There are also non-denominational Evangelical organizations which work together for the purposes of evangelism, humanitarian aid, charitable services, and outreach activities, whose aim is to lead people to Christ and to plant churches.

The Lausanne Covenant calls churches and parachurch organizations to pray earnestly for the salvation of unreached people, especially since two-thirds of the world population is unreached. Therefore, to finish the task of world evangelization, the partnership and synergy of all Christian organizations working together is necessary.[504] In this regard, the role of parachurch organizations is crucial, because involving professionals in this ministry means reaching the community. Parachurch organizations have a vast and diverse influence on society because they can influence their co-workers for good.

At this time, these parachurch organizations are doing several holistic ministries which are a context in which to share the Gospel. Because parachurch organizations have these effective ways of reaching the community, their work should be integrated with local churches to achieve even greater effectiveness. For instance, the Evangelical Students' and Graduates' Union of Ethiopia (EvaSUE) currently ministers in 118 college and university Christian students' fellowships around the country. These fellowships are made up of approximately 45,000 Christian students. The organization focuses on the evangelism, discipleship and leadership development of the students.[505] EvaSUE has the platform to reach emerging leaders both for churches and for the country; thus, it should do more to address the nation's contemporary problems by preparing Bible studies which are directly related to those issues dealing with ethnic conflicts, co-existing with people of other faiths, and handling religious conflicts.

Furthermore, other parachurch organizations also have big roles in solving various problems, for instance, by providing financial help to the church's ministers and local missionaries, developing leaders, and addressing the community through providing assistance. They can also play a role in mobilizing the Christian Diaspora to help the mission in the country. There are many ministers of the Gospel and missionaries who are dedicated to spreading the Good News, but they need financial help. In all parachurch programs, they have to integrate and associate their ministries with local churches to obtain big results. They can fill in the gaps which the local churches struggle to address. Parachurch organizations help the churches by taking the Gospel even to resistant places via media, medical mission and charity work.

4. The Role of Theological Colleges and Seminaries

Theological colleges and seminaries can be very helpful in addressing problems in the Ethiopian Evangelical Church. Education is very important in the development of leaders and building the country. The development and growth that we are seeing throughout the world today came about because of education. Thus, educational institutes have a great part and role, for good or for bad, to influence the community and to form worldview.

To be more effective and successful, theological seminaries and colleges should evaluate and adjust their curriculum according to the current context and needs. The curriculum of the schools should be evaluated and revised according to missional objectives, building a bridge between schools and churches so that they can work together to fulfill the Great Commission. Maigadi argues,

> It seems theological institutions in Africa are yet to incorporate the modeling approach in training church leaders. Many African theologians have advocated the need to contextualize theological training in Africa so that those trained will have relevant tools to address issues that affect the life of the church such as divisive ethnicity.[506]

Furthermore, because of the way theological education is viewed, there is sometimes a lack of spiritual concern in theological training. "The dichotomy between the roles of theological institutions and that of the church has created such a gap that there is little theological reflection between the two."[507] In light of this, Maigadi suggests:

> Theological institutions in Africa need to view themselves as instruments in the hands of God for equipping men and women to become agents of change in the church and society. The type of students theological institutions produce will determine the type of leadership style the graduates will employ in their various ministries in the church.[508]

Therefore, the primary role of theological institutions should not be imparting knowledge merely for the purpose of academic excellence. Rather, they should be training places where servant leaders train and make a difference in the church and community, maintaining a biblical perspective even during ethnic and religious conflicts. Further, they should be places where men and women of God prepare themselves for ministry within the local church.

Conclusion

In any given task, especially group work, unity is not optional but is needed to fulfill the group's purpose in an effective way and in the limited time. The Biblical teachings also give us lessons on the importance of unity because the Church is the Body of Christ who carries the message of peace and love to this fallen world. In fact, the Church of Christ is where unity and love should be found. The teachings of Jesus also focused on the unity and love of His disciples (John 15:12; 17:23). Unity and oneness are consistent themes in apostle Paul's teaching, as seen in the epistles of Ephesians, Galatians, and Colossians.

The Christian Mission has faced barriers throughout the church history. The challenges are not any different for the contemporary Ethiopian church as they try to spread the Gospel of Jesus Christ. Ethiopia has faced a great difficulty throughout its history, such as economic and political strife and increasing ethnic and religious conflicts. However, for every challenge and problem there is an answer from the Lord who sent His Church to the world.

This chapter suggests using the Antioch model for the present challenges to effective mission within the Ethiopian Church, applying it to our cross-cultural mission both inside and outside the country. The Antioch model can help Ethiopian churches and other churches worldwide as they try to contextualize and fit the model to their context.

Applying the Antioch model will certainly not be an easy task, because the problems are very challenging and sensitive and solving them will require our extra effort and willingness. Nevertheless, even if the problems are very difficult and even when we face barriers in our attempts to fulfill the Great Commission, Jesus Christ – who sent His Church to the world – never leaves us (Matt 28:20). He said, "I have told you these things, so that in me you may have peace. In this world, you will have trouble. However, take heart! I have overcome the world" (John 16:33 NIV).

Jesus' promises and grace are always with us and give us strength and courage in order to continue fulfill our mandate despite any challenges. In fact, none of us are capable by ourselves, as it is written: "Not that we are competent in ourselves to claim anything for ourselves, but our competence comes from God. He has made us competent as ministers of a new covenant..." (2 Cor 3:5-6 NIV). God is our strength, giving us power in all our challenges; in fact, the Bible says, "Not by might nor by power, but by my Spirit,' says the LORD Almighty" (Zech 4:6 NIV).

Today Ethiopians are living in a multicultural context and multi-ethnic communities. As members of the family of God, we need to work together to bring meaningful change to the world through the Gospel of Jesus Christ. We need work together because we are mutually interdependent, since "in Christ we who are many form one body, and each member belongs to all the others" (Rom 12:5 NIV).

As a Christian community, we are called to live in love, sharing with and caring for one another. Today, the Ethiopian Church needs unity in mission even more than before, because the country needs so much reconciliation, collaboration, development, respect and trust to be restored. One tribal church cannot do mission alone; we need each other to reach the world, counting our new identity in Christ as even more important than our ethnic affiliations.

The Body of Christ in Ethiopia can and should celebrate their unity in diversity as they move in the direction of multi-ethnic congregations. The author's prayer is that the Church in Ethiopia will share and talk about the love of Christ effectively inside the country to every tribe and beyond the borders of Ethiopia, to the numerous Ethiopians in the Diaspora and to the world at large, following the missiological model of the Antioch Church.

CHAPTER TWELVE

Ethiopia's Up and Coming Mission Force: Students and Graduates Crossing Barriers for the Great Commission

Student mission movements have played an extremely important role in the overall history of mission. This role has taken two forms: first, students themselves have been part of harvesting souls during and in between their years in school. Second, graduates who began on a missionary trajectory while completing their education have gone on to make a great impact as well-prepared long-term missionaries throughout the world.

In the 1600's, several Germans studying in Paris caught the vision for God's global glory and they "committed themselves to carry the Gospel to other nations." Notably, one of them was Peter Heiling, who is responsible for "translating the Bible into Amharic in 1634" before "he died as a martyr." The Moravians – one of the best known missionary sending movements in history – had its roots in "The Order of the Grain of the Mustard Seed," a mission prayer group started by Nicolaus Ludwig Von Zinzendorf and some of his classmates that "lasted for 100 years."[509] Around the time of the Second World War, a cohort of friends at Cambridge all "responded to God...during a university mission" in which the call for world evangelization was strong. Most of the group became missionaries, including C.T. Studd who famously went to China and joined the China Inland Mission.[510]

`In American history, "[s]tudents have been in the vanguard of the North American church's missionary outreach, spearheading each of the three eras of missionary advance." Students began America's involvement in foreign mission through the Haystack Prayer Meetings.[511]

This first movement eventually birthed the best known and one of the longest lasting student mission movements was known as the Student Volunteer Movement for Foreign Mission (often abbreviated as SVM) and began in the United States in 1886.[512] Using the slogan "The evangelization of the world in this generation,"[513] the SVM was instrumental in recruiting over "20,000 students to work in foreign missions."[514] At the peak of the movement, it was accurately said "that the student movements had furnished the large majority of all the foreign missionaries in the world."[515] Philosophical pillars of the movement included "[t]he authority of Scripture," "the deity and authority of Christ," "[t]he urgency of missions," "the necessity of individual conversion" and thus "the necessity of evangelism," and "the doctrine of the Holy Spirit."[516] The SVM also "provided volunteers with missions study materials and a bureau of information" to help them prepare for the field. These materials and others like them were also used to train students and lay people to help prepare them for leading their home churches in participating in the Great Commission.[517] One result of this broad awareness of the missionary task was a great increase in giving to missionary causes, thereby allowing more missionaries to work unimpeded in their fields. There were certainly faults in the movement's ethos – including "spiritual imperialism" and "deemphasizing education"[518] The most recent student mission movement in American history has been through the Urbana conferences, which has awakened, challenged, recruited, and equipped thousands of young people for short-term and long-term missionary service through biannual conferences.[519]

The day of students and graduates leading the charge in world mission is not over. Mobilizers must learn from the past both positively and negatively, seeking to carry on all that was holy about previous student mission movements while correcting and reforming all that fell short.

Student Mission in Ethiopia

Modern day Ethiopia has much to draw on in terms of inspiration for student mission. As we have seen, history is rife with examples to follow in this area as well as some pitfalls to avoid. These examples include those listed above as well as some powerful movements from Ethiopia's own not-so-distant past.

In the 1960's, SIM missionaries began "The Youth Center," which quickly became a hub of enthusiastic student involvement and later leadership.[520] This venue gave the students an opportunity to be involved in efforts like "organizing outreach activities, which they were able to use effectively in their own evangelistic enterprises upon graduating from the university."[521] Indeed, one of the founding missionaries shared that many times she was approached by many influential leaders in Ethiopian communities decades later who enthusiastically shared with "her that they 'had found salvation' in the Youth Center"[522] and had held on to the ethos of that place in the years that followed.

Also in the 1960's, the Mekane Yesus Church opened a hostel to Ethiopian students from around the country, letting them stay at unbeatable rates while they received trainings on "evangelism and the systematic study of the Bible" and as they organized "various evangelistic and revival programs."[523] It was an exciting time to be young and there was a "sense of anticipation engendered by being at the forefront of a new youth-led faith movement."[524]

As the Pentecostal movement grew in Ethiopia, it became evident that one of its pillars was "a radical commitment to evangelize the world."[525] Its leaders held a series of conferences to coalesce various groups from around the country and strategize in a unified way. According to participants at the Awasa conference, "those who participated…came away with an invigorated spirit and a sense of anticipation that inspired the young Pentecostals to engage in the aggressive work of evangelism."[526] The evangelistic efforts that flowed out of this conference – summed up in "[t]he Pentecostals' unofficial motto, 'The Gospel for Ethiopia by Ethiopians'"[527] – had "considerable success"[528] and spread the message of the "new birth" far and wide in Ethiopia.[529] The "calling to 'reach out' to one's 'lost' fellows turned converts into bona fide missionaries and preachers,"[530] thus activating not just leaders but lay people in the significant Great Commission work.

In the heady days at the inception of the indigenous Mulu Wongel Church in the late 1960's, its "young believers began to engage in a full-blown process of expanding the gospel 'to all corners of Ethiopia.'" The fact that the church officially funded these missionaries "set a new precedent," as Mulu Wongel was the first Ethiopian "national mission-sending agent independent of any foreign financial assistance."[531]

Currently, Great Commission Ministry Ethiopia and the Evangelical Students' Union of Ethiopia (EvaSUE) work hand in hand on thousands of university and college campuses in Ethiopia to reach and train students to know God and make Him known on their campuses and throughout Ethiopia. Several times a year, both ministries have student mission endeavors which bring teams of students to various cities in Ethiopia to spend several days or weeks serving the local people and sharing the Good News with them.

Campus Ministry Staff Interviews

For the purposes of this chapter, four campus ministry staff were interviewed (two from Great Commission and two from EvaSUE) about how they recruit, train, debrief, and get funds to make these break and summer mission possible for the students they lead.[532]

Recruitment

The initial recruitment pool used by Great Commission staff is each school's Evangelism Team/Action Group. These are the first people to hear about any break or summer mission being planned, but student leaders also make announcements for trips in general student fellowship meetings and "those interested and who have a heart for mission are welcome to sign up to participate." The campus ministry staff seeks to "cast vision and motivate them [the students] for action." An EvaSUE staff member mentioned that EvaSUE staff recruits "students for mission" individually "considering their passion and willingness and through staff/leader's recommendations."

Training

Before leaving for their summer or break mission, Great Commission students go through a "series of materials called New Life Training Curriculum (NLTC) which mainly focuses on basic evangelism and discipleship and also incorporate[s] advanced discipleship methods and movement building principles." EvaSUE brings the students together and trains students on Muslim/Coptic Evangelism, Contextualization, and Evangelism and Prayer followed by intercessory group prayer times.

Debriefing

Each night during Great Commission break and summer mission, the team comes together and "shares their reports on their experiences while out evangelizing." There is a time of praise and prayer, and often a strategy session to address and overcome challenges that have arisen. When the students return home, they "sometimes plan a thanksgiving celebration event and invite all the supporters to attend." They are also "encouraged" by their leaders "to do more wherever they are and might be." After EvaSUE mission, there is a one day "debriefing and thanksgiving program" for the team which includes a "testimony time, games, and refreshments."

Fundraising

Aside from using their own savings, there are a variety of ways that staff and students raise money for break and summer mission. Students sometimes polish shoes, wash cars, or sell "coupons" to family and friends. They are given official letters explaining the mission that they can send to their churches and other contacts. Campus ministry graduates are also encouraged to help fund students, and local churches in the area where the students are traveling to are challenged to "provide accommodation, meals and transport once the students are there with them."

Campus Ministry Student Interviews

Seven students who are or have been involved in break and summer mission also participated in interviews, most bubbling over with positive words regarding their experiences – including a general description of their work, what they learned that has influenced who they are today, whether they had been challenged to consider long-term mission work after graduation, and whether they would indeed consider long-term missionary work in the future.

Description of Work

Students enthusiastically described many facets of mission work they had participated in while on break or summer mission. The daily schedule consisted of prayer first, then ministry, then more prayer and debriefing. Ministry included evangelism in prisons, health centers, and in the open air, counseling women coming out of prostitution, educating church members on key issues like "addiction, pornography, abortion and homosexuality," serving as role models and encouragers to local youth, and, in the case of medical students, providing "free medical service."

What They Learned

Students mentioned personal "reviv[al]," deeper "insight about evangelism," inspiration for future ministry, better understanding of different cultures, increased awareness of the "needs of Ethiopia," growth in "compassion" and "confidence," and realizing that "the small thing I do can make a big difference" as long-term impacts of break and summer mission.

Challenged?

Though students were debriefed after returning from their break or summer mission, only one out of seven indicated that she had been challenged to consider mission work as a long-term calling. Two responses illustrate the fact that this is a missed window of opportunity. First, one student said, "No one has challenged me to be a missionary, I used to have the thought of being a missionary, but currently I don't have any plan of being a missionary." Second, another student lamented that "all these things are in my heart but I am always sad about that

[that no one challenged her to consider doing mission work long-term after graduation]. She continued: "I wish I [would] have [had] a mentor [in considering this option]" but "no" there was "no one."

Future Long-Term Mission Work?

The final interview question asked what the students thought about the possibility of being a long-term missionary (regardless of whether someone had challenged them to consider this before or not). There were a variety of responses. Two students said they do not plan to be missionaries but one nuanced his response by saying that he wants "mission to be my life whether I am working or learning." Another student answered: "Yes, I think I will be a missionary one day though I don't know when and where." Another student replied that he also wants to be a missionary and "for this reason I need [a] mission school" in order to prepare. Yet another student is currently pursuing non-profit work in an area different from what she studied in school. She plans to continue to work with "street children and orphans" as her mission field. Another student exclaimed, "If God opens the door of being [a] long-term missionary" there is "no...great[er] work than this." He went on to say "I [was] really happy when I read this message [which asked him to answer the above research questions]. I was asking God to show me his long term plan for me...this week. I don't know why this happen[ed] but I believe God has something to teach me from this message."

Beyond Student Mission

It is evident that both historically as well as in the present day, students are a vital part of missionary activity in Ethiopia. The question must be asked, however: is the full potential of these students being tapped? While much good is happening in terms of students and graduates being part of fulfilling the Great Commission, much more could be done – in some cases following the example of those in the past and in some cases breaking new ground. The following suggestions give some possible ways to harness the power of all Ethiopian students so that they have maximum Great Commission impact both during their years of education as well as after graduation in their adult lives.

Active Recruitment of Students for Long-Term Mission

During and after break and summer missions would be an ideal time for a staff person to bring up the idea of long-term mission involvement with students either in a formal session or an informal one-on-one conversation. Most people sense God's call to mission through the words of a trusted teacher or advisor sharing the heart of God for the nations with them. Staff members should view themselves not just as short-term mission organizers but also long-term missionary recruiters. The debriefing time after a break or summer mission would be a perfect time to provide potential next steps for those who sense God's calling to long-term missionary involvement: books to read, names of training programs, groups to join, etc. This way, the conversation about the reaching the unreached would continue long after the short-term mission experience and would remain as a real and viable option in students' minds as they return to the normal grind of daily life.

Involved Churches

Local bodies of believers have incredible potential to make the mission mandate an important part of their ethos which they pass on to all their members, including students.

"Synergy"[533] between churches and campus ministries would solidify and drive home the teachings of both on all subjects, including the subject of the Great Commission. Churches could also be a place of training, mentorship, and involvement in ministry for those students who desire to be involved in missionary work long-term after graduation. They could be sent by that church and backed by them in prayer, in community, and in finances.

Missionary Training for Students

Students are already in "study mode," so offering a class on mission such as *Perspectives on the World Christian Movement* or something more contextual would give them an opportunity to be exposed to the heart of God for the nations, the needs of the world, and our responsibility as ambassadors during some of their most formative years – the years when they are figuring out what they are going to do with their lives. Having Great Commission information "on the table," so to speak, can be greatly used by God to channel students' spiritual passion into long-term missionary work after graduation.

Missionary Training for Graduates

In the course of discipleship training of students throughout their years of education, future educational opportunities should be discussed. These educational opportunities could be in the students' current field of study or in another area entirely – perhaps that of missionary preparation. Students should graduate from campus ministries clearly knowing their options of pursuing further missiological education. There are some programs like this in Ethiopia already, but they are not yet well-publicized or well-known and there is room for many more missionary training schools to be established in order to meet the need.

International Exposure for Students

Because Ethiopia is a relatively homogenous country (there are not many immigrants from other nations living within her borders), it would be very beneficial for students to be given opportunities to see another part of the world in order to improve cross-cultural awareness and communication as well as to have a more objective understanding of their own culture (both key aspects of missionary preparedness). One of the easiest and most affordable ways for students to travel outside of their countries is to go to events hosted by campus ministries in other countries. Campus ministry staff members can help students sign up to go to international gatherings like the Pamoja Africa Conference or Focus Kenya's Commission Conference.

Using Careers as a Means for Mission

While still in school, students should be challenged to consider becoming involved in long-term missionary work – for some this will mean diverging from their original career path and for some this will mean using their career path as part of their missionary strategy. Both are viable options for Great Commission involvement and should be promoted by campus ministry staff members for students to consider as they pray about their trajectory after graduation.

One of the best strategies for resilience on the mission field is, especially in areas that are unreached and hostile to the Gospel, is to use one's area of expertise as a platform and means of supporting oneself while being a witness for Christ. Perhaps a student studied pharmacy in school – after graduation, he could establish himself with a pharmacy in a place which is unreached. His business gives him a reason to be there, a natural way to connect with people in the community, and staying power because of financial security. His missionary activity could naturally flow out of relationships developed in the community he has quickly become a part of by virtue of becoming a local business owner. Recent graduates who are required to serve as government employees in their profession in the rural areas of Ethiopia should be encouraged to think of this time as missionary service, not forced exile. God can greatly use them in the (often unreached) areas where they are sent.

CHAPTER THIRTEEN

Sustainable Funding for Great Commission Involvement: Next Steps for Ethiopia

As has been demonstrated in previous chapters, Ethiopia has great potential to become a major missionary sending nation, but one of the major obstacles standing in her way is a lack of traction in terms of financial resources. Missiologist Howard Brant says that "creating and maintaining a sustained income stream" is "probably THE greatest challenge of the emerging mission movement."[534]

The prevailing attitude of evangelical Christians in Ethiopia is a longing to do more in terms of ministry than they feel they are able to do, due to their perceived shortage of money. Indeed, Ethiopia is ranked as the second poorest in the world as measured by the Multidimensional Poverty Index (MPI),[535] and is located in a region (sub-Saharan Africa) where the "average per capita income" is "roughly US$1 a day."[536] Ethiopian *birr* is weak in the global economy (21.20 birr equal US$1 as of 2013),[537] and "97% of the government budget is attributed to foreign aid."[538] Many ministry efforts in the country depend partially or entirely on funds from the West, and many Ethiopian ministers hold back on their ministry vision while they wait for a (usually foreign) sponsor.[539] Sadly, only 3% of the Ethiopian evangelical church is considered to be "missions mobilized."[540]

This state of affairs, in my opinion, poses the greatest challenge to Ethiopia as she seeks to move ahead toward becoming a major missionary sender in the near future. I believe the challenge is seen in three types of barriers: spiritual, psychological, and societal. This hindering trifecta will be further discussed in a later section which is specific to

Ethiopia, but first a foundation of the history and philosophy of aid should be laid.

Aid: A Recent Experiment Failing

The classic historical answer to the financial problems of many Majority World countries has been aid in one form or another. When it has been perceived that a country is hurting and cannot do something for itself, other countries (particularly Western ones) have felt that they should step in and do things for the hurting country.

In her incisive work on the failure of aid in Africa, Dambisa Moyo, a Zambian economist, poses the question: "What is it about Africa that holds it back, that seems to render it incapable of joining the rest of the globe in the twenty-first century?" She then makes her strong case: "The answer has its roots in aid."[541] Though the world has poured "more than US$1 trillion in development assistance of the last several decades" into Africa, "the recipients of this aid are...much worse off" than ever before. She concedes that aid given directly to individuals certainly seems to improve their lives at least for the short-term, but she calls this the "micro-macro paradox" that must be understood if aid is to be seen for what it is.[542] While individual families may be temporarily better off by accepting foreign assistance, the effect of aid on a national level and in the long-term is unhelpful and even destructive.

Robertson McQuilkin chimes in on this point, saying, "In the long-term, support breeds resentment, especially if the support is not sustained indefinitely, because it creates a patronizing dependency."[543] "Domination courts dependency," agrees professor Norma Cook Everist, and "dependency begets dependency."[544] Moyo continues, "The notion that aid can alleviate systemic poverty is a myth," but nevertheless, she laments that "Africa is addicted to aid."[545] This "vicious cycle"[546] that is harming Africa must stop, and someone "must have the courage to say no."[547] Africa must recognize that she has "[taken] the wrong road" in previous years, and must do the hard work of turning around to walk toward self-sustainability in the pursuit of an economically brighter tomorrow.[548]

Unfortunately, dependence on aid is no less a reality in the Christian realm. Wealthier churches (usually Western) have historically funded the ministries and outreach efforts of poorer churches (usually in the Majority World), despite the fact that in Scripture, there is "no instance, let alone any command, to give toward the ministry of another church."[549] This has led to many consequences for Majority World Christians and has slowed the outreach that they could be having by keeping them dependent on outside funds and often controlled by outside funders. Brant cautions that "unless this paradigm is challenged and changed...no long lasting change will result....the needed income for the emerging missions movements will only become sustainable as their leaders develop internal systems which generate core funds." The Majority World missions movement "must be powered by local initiatives" if it is to be effective and long-lasting.[550]

Glenn Schwartz, an American missionary who has devoted his life to speaking out and training others on the topic of self-reliance for Majority World churches, states strongly that "unhealthy dependency makes it nearly impossible for churches to send out their own missionaries."[551] Obviously, this should be of huge concern to the global Christian community who collectively want to reach all nations in order to fulfill the Great Commission and usher in the second coming of Christ, but Schwartz is also realistic: he acknowledges that this issue is "emotionally charged"[552] and dependency is "hard to admit."[553]

Robert Reese, a nearly lifelong missionary to Zimbabwe, decries dependence as a "relic of colonialism."[554] Though this is not literally true in Ethiopia – who was never colonized – it begs the question whether Ethiopia has been unknowingly colonized by the Western Church, whom they have allowed to continue holding the purse strings and setting the agenda in many ways and for many years.

Reese calls for a doing away with the "mission station" model of sustaining not only the church but schools, hospitals, etc., because these things are generally not able to exist without outside funds and are not essential to the work of the church.[555] Local ideas and models for ministry and outreach will likely cost less and be more effective. Replacing cumbersome structures with contextual ones will allow Africa to rise up and transform herself by God's grace in a way that is truly indigenous and sustainable.

Sustainability: An Ancient Philosophy Rising

Since the later years of the last century, there has been an increasing chorus of voices decrying the failure of aid and pushing for local sustainability in secular matters as well as in the global Church. This groundswell has recently reached a critical mass to the point that sustainability in mission is considered a movement, but there have been prophetic voices calling for self-reliance – Venn, Nevius, and Allen, among others – throughout the past centuries. Sadly, most of what they said was scorned or ignored until long after their deaths[556] and their names are only recently becoming well-known in missionary circles.

Though buzzwords like "sustainable," "organic," and "grassroots" may make this movement seem like the latest fad, the philosophy behind these ideas is ancient and biblical. Sustainability in mission was strongly employed in the early church and can be seen in the methods of Paul the apostle as well as other early missionaries. Reese shows that though many would call the apostle Paul's missionary strategy "minimalist," he succeeded in "produc[ing] indigenous churches wherever he went."[557] The fact that they did not depend on him or on other churches should recommend his sustainable method very strongly to us.[558] Indeed, "Pauline orthopraxy"[559] is scripturally commanded when Paul says, "Follow my example as I follow the example of Christ."[560]

Melvin Hodges, a classic writer on sustainability in missions, agrees with Reese on the fact that even new church plants should be "self-supporting." He asserts that even a cursory reading of the book of Acts reveals that sustainability was "the Bible plan," for "we find no hint that the churches among the Gentiles were supported by the Jewish congregation."[561] Schwartz calls this biblical self-support and sustainability "self-reliance," which he defines not as independence from God but on refusal to be unhealthily dependent on other people (long-term acceptance of aid being the primary manifestation of unhealthy dependence).[562]

The writers of books on sustainability in Majority World missions agree: they do not believe that people should seek independence for its own sake. Rather, it is a means to an end: true interdependence between equals. As it is now, the terms "interdependence" and "partnership" are loaded with contraindications in practice – the power dynamic is strongly skewed toward the wealthier partner since he is the one holding the purse strings for the both of them. The Majority World must pursue independence first before returning to the global table to take part in interdependence and true partnership.[563] This is the "logical" thing to do.[564] It is also the only way that Majority World churches will make a valuable contribution in missions: if they decide that they have received enough and that it is now time for them to give sacrificially, believing the promise that "What is impossible with men is possible with God (Luke 18:27 NIV).

Benefits of Sustainability

The benefits of sustainability are numerous, but a few are of extreme importance and should be noted. First, sustainable funding promotes local initiative and ownership. When people are left alone with Scripture and asked to brainstorm new and innovative ideas for getting the Word out – rather than copying and pasting tried and true tricks from another time and another place – big things happen. Western missionary efforts have served their purpose and will surely continue to be a valuable part of global evangelization, but those in the Majority World would do well to realize that *their* time has come to be more than just receivers and obedient disciples. They can and should view themselves as givers and disciplers in their own right who use their own resources and own methods for doing ministry. Hodges shares an example which illustrates the possibility and promise of sustainability:

> Some of our congregations in Central America have struggled for ten years to build their chapel. They have begun in a private home, moved into a thatch-roofed hut of their own, and finally after years of sacrifice and labor, have completed their frame or adobe building. Their little chapel means infinitely more to them than if it had been provided by the Mission.[565]

Contrast this picture with the one shared by Glenn Schwartz: a short term team of well-meaning Americans built a church on a mission trip to South America. The mission team spent three weeks on it and "presented it to the local people." Rather than feeling a sense of responsibility and ownership of the church, the local congregation wrote to the mission team a few years later, saying "'The roof on *your* church is leaking. Please come and fix it.'"[566] Because the local people had not planned for, sacrificed for, and been involved in decisions regarding the building of the church, they did not feel a need to show any initiative or have any ownership of it. The psychological power of being part of a solution is a powerful incentive to *keep* people involved in a cause. If the solution is merely handed to them, that incentive for sustained and committed involvement is destroyed.

When Majority World Christians determine to use their own resources, solutions and strategies which are contextual emerge. When sustainability is the goal, Majority World Christians will look at what they have, not at what they lack. Doing what they can with what they have will be the order of the day, and what they can do will be truly spectacular, surprising they themselves as well as the anxiously hovering Westerners from the former non-sustainable era. We must not underestimate the power of what the "global poor" already have in terms of Christian maturity and already are doing in terms of fruitful ministry.[567] The grandeur of the Church of the Global South does not and will not lie in its awe-inspiring pomp or slick showiness, but in its spiritual solidity and organic simplicity, showcasing the idea that "it is not by might, nor by power, but by my Spirit, says the LORD" (Zech 9:6).

The contextual solutions found and implemented by Majority World Christians will also be infinitely reproducible. This means that when a church is planted, that church will easily be able to plant another church without the costly delay of the protracted baton hand-off which has too often been the case between the West and its disciples. In order for infinite reproducibility to become reality, "imported structures" which are remnants from mistakes in Western missionary methodology must be done away with. One of the major perceived difficulties that Majority World missionaries face is the fact that they are financially unable to copy costly Western church structures which have been part of their discipleship experience.[568] A return to contextual simplicity and sustainability will ensure that newly planted churches (as well as more established ones) can reproduce quickly rather than feeling incomplete and focusing their efforts inwardly until they are the owners of a lavish building with high-tech sound equipment and are the administrators of a multi-program empire patterned after Fortune 500 companies.[569]

Lastly, local sustainability removes the ubiquitous anti-Western suspicion which seems to crop up whenever it is remotely possible for it to do so. Satan is using many people's hatred of the West as a stumbling block between people and the Gospel, since the message of Jesus' death and resurrection is so unfortunately associated with Western culture with all its foibles and vices. For the Gospel to spread to the ends of the earth and to reach the unreached in a fruitful way, its messengers must not be viewed as agents or "spies for a foreign power" in the West culture. Unfortunately, "the monthly check" received from the West by many Majority World missionaries "has been used against them" by those who seek to discredit them in any manner possible.[570]

Missionaries who are financially independent from the West will not have complicated questions to answer when asked about their funding and motivations. It is not nearly so suspicious to be supported by one's countrymen or local church than it is to be funded by people on another continent whose government and pop culture seem to be against everything that most unreached people groups hold dear.

Sustainable Funding Case Studies

Now that a philosophy of self-reliance has been established, where should we go from here? It is easy to say that sustainability is a priority, but it is harder to live out this priority in practice. Precedents have been set, habits are comfortable, and maintaining the way things are is relatively easy to do, at least in the short-run. Brant gives a clarion call to move beyond the status quo by a return to the belief that "God has created every culture to be a missionary sending culture" and therefore "God has placed workable systems within each culture that, when redeemed, enable mission to function....If we tap into these indigenous systems that God has already placed in the culture, we will find both the capacity and sustainability that is already there."[571]

Breaking out of the cycle of dependency is hard work, but it can be done, as numerous stories from around the world illustrate. These stories tend to fall into three categories: experiencing spiritual renewal which leads to giving, recovering a biblical understanding of tithing and creative ways to tithe, and redeeming business for kingdom purposes. These correlate respectively with the previously mentioned spiritual, psychological, and societal change that must happen if the Majority World is to gain traction in terms of financial resources to be used for ministry and missions.

Spiritual Renewal

Reese describes spiritual renewal as "the best way out of dependency," because it "depends neither on human ingenuity nor on the current historical movement."[572] He approvingly quotes Richard K. MacMaster and Donald R. Jacobs, who describe the "financially self-reliant" philosophy and practice which was birthed out of the spiritual revival in East Africa in the late 1920's:

> When the "saved ones" felt that God was calling them to do something locally or on a broader scale, they simply announced the need and received the funds from the local fellowships. What they could not afford, they did not undertake. When they commenced huge projects, like the stratified evangelization of an entire town or city, they did so with their own finances.[573]

Schwartz agrees that one of the "way[s] churches become self-reliant" is "through widespread and genuine spiritual renewal."[574] He promotes the concept for all Christians, including those in the Majority World, to live in a state of "perpetual jubilee"[575] as people who "know instinctively that when they have set themselves the goal of doing God's will, all their resources should be dedicated toward that end."[576] He gives readers a reality check when he reminds them: "People who do not know the Lord or have no passion to serve Him are not likely to enjoy the benefits of being self-supporting."

Therefore, "spiritual maturity" needs to be the first goal which must be achieved before any real progress in the area of self-sustainability can be reached.[577]

Prayer must also be a key part of this spiritual renewal[578] because of the "spiritual nature of this battle."[579] Satan himself wants to keep Majority World Christians dependent, because this is one of his most effective tactics in slowing the spread of the Gospel to all peoples. Revival is the only way to increase involvement in missions in any sustainable way, according to Howard Brant, a former missionary to Ethiopia:

> When revival comes people are filled with His Spirit which brings holy boldness – enabling them to take the gospel to Jerusalem, Judea, Samaria and the ends of the earth. Great mission movements have been the direct result of revival movements. A revived church, an informed church and a praying church – very quickly becomes a missional church.[580]

Tithing

The ancient practice of tithing as understood from a Biblical perspective may also help to jumpstart Majority World ministry and outreach. Though not required any longer by law, the Christian's response to the riches of the Gospel and the realization "that God gave [all of my possessions to me] for me to use," should be to say "I will dedicate all of them for His purposes." Indeed, giving is a hallmark of the Christian life, because those who have been transformed by God have a "mindset focused on eternity, and not the moment, [and they] desire to give sacrificially to God's work on the earth."[581]

God's Word is full of extraordinary promises extended to the people of God who give to His work in the world. One of the most well-known is Malachi 3:6-12, a passage in which God is reprimanding his people for their negligence and apathy towards serving Him. In verse 8, He asks them; "'Will a man rob God?' Yet you rob me. But you ask, 'How do we rob you?'

In tithes and offerings." He challenges them lovingly "Test me in this [giving the full tithe]...and see if I will not throw open the floodgates of heaven and pour out so much blessing that you will not have room enough for it." Though these words were spoken to the returned Jewish exiles, God is still the same God today that He was then – indeed, earlier in the same passage, He says: "'I the Lord do not change.'" He still desires and requires His people to give Him what He is due, whether in spiritual matters or financial matters. And He proves in every instance of His people's sacrificial gifts that it is impossible to 'out-give' him. Givers will always receive more blessings than they gave, whether in this life or in the life to come.

The New Testament is consistent with these ideas, telling Christians: "Remember this: Whoever sows sparingly will also reap sparingly, and whoever sows generously will also reap generously." A glorious cycle –seen in the Old Testament and continuing here – is explained: "You will be made rich in every way so that you can be generous on every occasion." We are provided for by God so that we can give to Him and others, and when we give to Him and others, we are provided for by Him. Indeed, tithes and offerings are not a burden but a delightful adventure in watching God provide through and for His people.

Interestingly, 10% of African Christians' income is not even necessary to revolutionize the African church. According to missiologist Dr. David Barrett, "[I]f Christians in Africa gave just 2% of their income they would be able to pay all of their bills [related to running the church and doing outreach]." [582]

Why does this deficit in church and mission funding exist in Africa when Africans are known to be extremely generous people? Schwartz quotes a presentation he saw of African leader Emmanuel Olidapo, answering this very question:

> It isn't that African people don't know how to give. There are hardly more generous people on earth. They give for festivals and many other special occasions. They give to relatives needing education or to unemployed or orphaned

people in their community. However, many simply don't give generously to the church.[583]

The only thing that can account for the fact that Africans give to other people but not to the church is that they have not been taught or expected to give to the church. After all, why would a thinking person give to something that is obviously funded with outside money? If there is a deficit, the outsiders should fix it.[584] Giving is not an intuitive thing in this situation. A psychological shift is needed, precipitated by intentional teaching on the part of Majority World leaders is needed in order to awaken congregations to the importance of sustainability and the long-term negative effects of depending on aid.

After being convicted in the area of tithing while on an international support-raising trip, Bafundi Mpofu, a Zimbabwean church elder and leader of a Christian school, went home with a vow to change things:

> He resolved to tithe himself. Furthermore, he preached on tithing at his local church in August 2003 upon his return to Zimbabwe...[and] all the leaders agreed to start tithing as an example for the rest of the congregation. He then began to spread the message to other churches. The results amazed him and the other elders. First, his church asked the American missionary to stop his contributions to their pastor, as they were prepared to carry his full salary....Beyond that, they support evangelism in their target area where they have planted ten new churches.[585]

In hindsight, Mpofu acknowledged that he had harbored wrong "assumptions about the limitations of what Zimbabwean Christians could do." Indeed, he had never had the opportunity to see what his countrymen could do because they had never before been convicted and challenged to give. There is a pessimism that is rampant among Majority World churches who receive funds from the West; they believe that what they could give is an insignificant pittance when compared with the vast sums flowing from Western coffers. When leaders teach congregations by example how they can give generously to God and His work, they will experience, like Mpofu's church, "a new sense of purpose, which in turn makes them better evangelists, as faith has produced fruit in giving and outreach."[586]

For those churches whose members find it nearly impossible to give monetarily to the church each month, a creative solution is offered by a church in Bolivia. The church wanted to be involved in mission to Equatorial Guinea, but was unsure how their small numbers would be able to support one of their own to go as a missionary. They eventually decided to split themselves up into thirteen groups, twelve called "January" and "February" and "March" all the way through the year, and a thirteenth called "Christmas." This way, families in the church did not have to struggle to give 10% every month but were able to spend a whole year preparing and saving so that they were able to give their full tithe during their designated month. This plan worked very well for the Bolivian church, and they were able to support a missionary family to go long-term to Equatorial Guinea.[587]

Perhaps some will continue to assert that cash is in such short supply in the Majority World that it is ludicrous to expect it to be given to the church. It should be noted, in response to this, that giving does not need to be limited to the giving of money. "In kind" offerings are also acceptable and should to be encouraged. This is especially helpful in rural congregations in which the majority of the members of the congregation are farmers. Schwartz relates a story of a pastor in Zambia who would visit the cattle herders in his congregation at regular intervals during the year to select 10% of the cows to be sold to benefit the church.[588] Livestock can also be given directly to missionaries in order to give them the ability to provide for themselves early on in the new communities to which they go.[589]

In Kenya, churches regularly raise money to plant new churches by hosting an event at which they auction off local produce donated by the farmers in the congregation or they buy meals prepared by the women in the congregation. Everything that is earned is used for ministry, and the events are also excellent for fellowship and community building.[590] When a Rwandan church caught the vision of giving beyond mere cash, they brought in such an abundance of fruits and vegetables "that the church had to assign a previously unemployed person to collect and sell the produce the church was given."[591]

Even simpler but worth mentioning is the idea that pastors can accept animals, produce, and other necessary items from the congregation in lieu of a salary (either at times or all the time). This allows the congregation to provide for their pastor from the literal and metaphorical fruit of their hands without needing to give cash.

Redeeming Business for Kingdom Purposes

Unemployment raises an interesting idea in Schwartz's mind: he says that some of the tithes that are missing from the African church coffers are the tithes of unemployed people, since they often have little or nothing to give. In order to increase the amount that the church is able to do through the tithes that she receives, those in the church should make it their business to help each other find gainful employment.

Rather than buying into the sacred/secular divide, Christian leaders should teach their people to serve the Lord in whatever profession he calls them to – whether medicine or farming or sales or church-planting. As more Christians get intentionally involved in the workplaces of African societies, there will likely be two beneficial results: there will be more funds available for the work of the church and there will be less corruption in the world because of the light that Christians bring with them in all their dealings.

Those African Christians who are already in business should be encouraged to have a "charitable mentality" toward the church and to use their businesses for Kingdom purposes.[592] Tentmaking may be a key strategy to be used by Majority World churches in order to make their ministries and missions efforts sustainable. Brant speculates that tentmaking "might involve building up the capacity of the sending churches to send more missionaries...might involve helping the receiving church develop its capacity" and also might be used by missionaries to "supplement their income."[593] Missionaries can be encouraged to "learn skills that would help them to generate income – and maybe provide a service for the communities to which they go." Indeed, "entrepreneurial" endeavors should be encouraged,[594] whether they are started to earn a livelihood (which in turn would produce a tithe) or whether they are started with the express purpose of supporting the work of the church.[595]

Rift Valley Vision – A Potential Ethiopian Prototype

A case study of special significance is given by Howard Brant in the section of his article on sustainable funding. Rift Valley Vision (RVV) is "a new mission society" indigenous to Ethiopia which has been having exciting success with moving toward local funding:

> RVV is unique in that the first year's operating and salary costs were covered by World Vision Ethiopia. But within that first year, they were able to build the capacity they need to be self-supporting. They found ways of building vision into the existing Christian NGOs in Ethiopia (like World Vision and Prison Fellowship), not to get support from the NGO itself – but rather the Christian workers in the NGO have pledged to support Rift Valley Vision from their (usually significantly higher) salaries. They also found Christian affinity groups like the Ethiopian Christian Pilots Association and challenged them to take on the support of

some of the missionaries. They have been able to activate the Ethiopian Diaspora in South Africa and other countries to support their programs.

While purists may protest that RVV should have started as a self-supporting entity from the beginning and that churches rather than individuals should support them, Brant is correct in asserting that "RVV is breaking new ground here" and is proposing a practical and creative "way ahead for new emerging missions." While it may not be a perfect solution that they have come up with, it is a start, and it should serve as an inspiration to other Majority World (especially Ethiopian) mission efforts.

Next Steps for Ethiopia Toward Sustainable Funding

Ethiopia is at a crucial crossroads. The burgeoning evangelical church is growing in size and opportunities for mission abound. This nation has the potential to become a major missionary sending nation within this generation, but in order to do so she must overcome spiritual, psychological, and societal barriers in the area of finances. This chapter will end with practical suggestions for next steps in order overcome those barriers for the glory of God and the good of the unreached peoples in Ethiopia and beyond who have yet to hear the Gospel.

Overcoming Spiritual Barriers

Any current of true and lasting change starts in the hearts of people, and the movement for sustainability in mission is no different. Leaders must first focus on spiritual renewal, encouraging church members to give generously, for everything they have was given to them by God and He has richly blessed them. When people are reawakened to how much they have been given by God, giving generously to His work is the natural result.

Bold teaching on tithing is needed, as it was needed in many of the case studies mentioned above. When the Ethiopian church is reawaked to the biblical principle of giving sacrificially of what we have to God and His mission, the church will be blessed and Gospel will be pushed forward into the furthest corners of Ethiopia and beyond. Just because Westerners often give money to subsidize Ethiopian church programs (this is another issue that should be dealt with in another paper), this does not mean that Ethiopian Christians are freed from the responsibility and privilege of giving.

Giving to God is as much about the heart and attitude of the giver and what the giving does to him as it is about the amount of money and what it is used to do. God's people are called to be joyful givers,[596] so if Ethiopians are not being challenged to live up to this standard, they are missing out on part of what God calls them to in terms of character. Regardless of what Westerners do or how much money the Ethiopian Evangelical Church already has or does not have, Ethiopians must be sensitized to the fact that if they hold back what is rightfully God's, they are robbing God of his due and they are robbing themselves of the incredible opportunity to get closer to Him by sacrificing their possessions as a way to participate in His mission.[597]

Overcoming Psychological Barriers

This spiritual renewal requires a shift in psychological perspective that may need to be gradual because it is so drastic. Ethiopian Christians have relied on aid in many ways and for many years, and so local sustainability may not be immediately attractive or may seem initially impossible. This is where solid teaching by Christian leaders on the dangers of dependence and the benefits of the biblical way of sustainability must come in. Leaders should inspire their congregations to look at what

Ethiopians have, not what they lack. When Ethiopians begin to look inside their country and their community to find solutions to problems and answers to questions, they will see the richness that has been often ignored because of the indiscriminate influx of foreign subsidies.

The enthusiasm that is possible for local initiatives was seen in the flurry of excitement and nearly universal participation of Ethiopians in a recent government bond program to raise money to build a dam across the Abay River [Blue Nile] in order to enable irrigation and harness electrical power to be used within the country and to be sold to neighboring countries. There was excited talk about this unified effort and huge goal on the streets of Addis, newspapers will filled with updates on progress, and even churches had special offerings given in a celebratory fashion specifically to help the government towards their goal. If this much enthusiasm was garnered for a secular mission, how much more will the people of God rise up to participate in the mission of God when they are inspired and challenged to do so!

The mission of God is not necessarily widely understood in Ethiopian churches, where, as mentioned before, 97% of churches are not mobilized for missions. Teaching on the world's need for the Gospel is crucial, particularly the fact that many unreached people groups exist within the borders of Ethiopia, not to mention the many who have never heard the name of Jesus throughout the rest of the 10/40 Window and in other locations around the globe.

Ethiopia has a history of isolationism and cultural homogeneity, which has served her well in many regards, but it also makes her at times self-focused and not in-tune with the needs of other places. The problems at home have also often kept her from being cognizant of the problems abroad. Being preoccupied with the growth and flourishing of the Gospel in the populous areas at home has often kept her from being interested in the growth and flourishing of the Gospel abroad or even in the rural, tribal locations within her borders. Teaching on the universal Church would likely lift the eyes of Ethiopian congregations and would ignite them in passion for missions, and as a result, transform them into people who give generously, as well as people who pray and people who go.

Overcoming Societal Barriers

The majority of Ethiopians do not have an abundance of discretionary cash on hand. This is not truly a problem unless cash is the only thing that people are encouraged to tithe. Rural agricultural Ethiopians can be encouraged to give a portion of their produce or livestock to the church to be sold for profit or given to the pastor, as discussed previously. They can also offer to serve the pastor and his family by taking on some of the work that must be done in his fields.

Some pastors and other church leaders should consider being bivocational, serving the church during the evenings and weekends and delegating excess responsibilities to a team of others whom he mentors. Ethiopian missionary church planting teams can be made up of one or a few people who devote themselves to sharing the Gospel, while several others farm for the subsistence of the missionary team or take up employment in the community in order to support the team. Missionary trainees should be taught vocational skills like hairdressing, IT, animal husbandry, etc.; this is already being done at some Ethiopian missionary training schools and should be continued and expanded. Those who already have professional degrees should be encouraged to use them in pioneer mission situations in order to gain acceptance within the community and support themselves at least until the church is established in that area (and perhaps even after).

It remains to be seen what will happen when Ethiopia is reawakened to her responsibility and privilege to sustain her own ministry and mission to the ends of the earth. Brant is right in forecasting that the Majority World missions movement is "too big to be supported by Western discretionary giving."[598] If this movement is to reach its potential – if Ethiopia is to reach her potential – a local means of sustainable funding must be found. Spiritual, psychological, and societal barriers must be torn down and the seemingly new yet ancient paradigm for self-reliant ministry and mission must be resurrected.

Without sustainable funding, it is safe to say that the vision of Ethiopia becoming a major missionary sending nation will never happen. With sustainable funding, and with the grace of God which is already so evident within her, however, the potential of Ethiopia to contribute to the fulfillment of the Great Commission is stunning and within reach. This issue is worthy of the Majority World's – and Ethiopia's – full attention, for the future of modern missions depends upon it.

CONCLUSION

In this book, we have attempted to chart a way forward for Ethiopia towards major missionary involvement. We have examined her great potential and the great barriers that are currently blocking her way. Talking about barriers and actively working to remove them are very different things, however. A few people -- like we four -- can brainstorm and talk about removing barriers, but when it comes to removing them we need many more people to join the cause.

We call upon pastors and leaders to disciple those under your charge to be disciple makers themselves, with eyes toward Great Commission fulfillment.

We call upon young people to not "let anyone look down on you because you are young, but set an example for the believers" (1 Tim 4:12 NIV).

We call upon business people to have a kingdom mindset, not mistakenly thinking that fulfilling the Great Commission is only for "full time" workers.

We call upon people living and working cross-culturally in Ethiopia to help remove barriers in ways that empower and inspire Ethiopians to cross cultures with the Gospel themselves.

Many hands make light work. And we are all held in the big hands of God, which are powerful enough to take our small efforts and make them great and world-changing, for His glory. "He has made everything beautiful in its time" (Ecc 3:11).

And we pray with the Psalmist: "May the favor of the Lord our God rest upon us; establish the work of our hands for us – yes, establish the work of our hands" (Ps 90:17).

ENDNOTES

[1] William J. Larkin Jr., "Mission in Luke," in *Mission in the New Testament: An Evangelical Approach*, eds. William J. Larkin, Jr. and Joel F. Williams (Maryknoll, NY: Orbis Books, 2002), 158-162; Marvin J. Newell, *Commissioned: What Jesus Wants You To Know as You Go* (N.p., Church Smart Resources, 2010), 45-46; K.P. Yohannan, *Revolution in World Missions* (Carrollton, TX: GFA Books, 2004), 111-115.

[2] Christopher R. Little, "ICS 6030: Biblical Theology of Mission" (Lecture, Columbia International University Seminary and Graduate School of Ministry, Columbia, SC, 2013).

[3] Christopher J. H. Wright, *The Mission of God: Unlocking the Bible's Grand Narrative* (Downers Grove, IL: InterVarsity Press, 2006), 36.

[4] David J. Bosch, "Reflections on Biblical Models of Mission," in *Toward the Twenty-First Century in Christian Mission*, ed. James M. Phillips and Robert T. Coote (Grand Rapids, MI: Wm. B. Eerdmans, 1993), 176.

[5] Ibid., 175.

[6] Ibid., 180.

[7] Wright, *The Mission of God*, 127.

[8] David M. Howard Jr., *Joshua: An Exegetical and Theological Exposition of Holy Scripture*, The New American Commentary, ed. E. Ray Clendenen (Nashville, TN: B & H Publishing Group, 1998), 103.

[9] Ibid., 104; Richard D. Nelson, *Joshua* (Louisville, KY: Westminster John Knox Press, 1997), 50.

[10] Howard, *Joshua*, 104.

[11] Trent C. Butler, *Joshua*, Word Biblical Commentary, eds. David A. Hubbard and Glenn W. Barker (Mexico City: Thomas Nelson, Inc., 1983), 35.

[12] Walter C. Kaiser, *Mission in the Old Testament: Israel as a Light to the Nations*, 2nd ed. (Grand Rapids, MI: Baker Academic, 2012), 39.

[13] Howard, *Joshua*, 103.

[14] Douglas J. Moo, *The Letter to James*, Pillar New Testament Commentary, ed. D.A. Carson (Grand Rapids, MI: Wm. B.

Eerdmans Publishing Company, 2000), 143; Donald W. Burdick, "James," in *The Expositor's Bible Commentary*, ed. Frank E. Gaebelein, 12 vols. (Grand Rapids, MI: Wm. B. Eerdmans Publishing Company, 1981), 185.

[15] Gareth L. Cockerill, *The Epistle to the* Hebrews, NICNT, ed. Gordon Fee (Grand Rapids, MI: Wm. B. Eerdmans Publishing Company, 2012), 584-585.

[16] E. John Hamlin, *Joshua* (Grand Rapids, MI: Wm. B. Eerdmans Publishing Company, 1983), 18.

[17] Burdick, "James," 185; Luke T. Johnson, "James," in *The New Interpreters Bible,* ed. Leander E. Keck (Nashville, TN: Abingdon Press, 1998), 199; James LaGrand, *The Earliest Christian Mission to 'All Nations' in the Light of Matthews's Gospel*, 2nd ed. (Grand Rapids, MI: Wm. B. Eerdmans Publishing Company, 1995), 175; Scot McKnight, *The Letter of James*, NICNT, ed. Gordon Fee (Grand Rapids, MI: Wm. B. Eerdmans Publishing Company, 2011), 256-257.

[18] Johnson, "James," 199.

[19] Leon Morris, "Hebrews," in *The Expositor's Bible Commentary*, ed. Frank E. Gaebelein, 12 vols. (Grand Rapids, MI: Zondervan, 1981), 128-129.

[20] David Oginde, "Joshua," in *Africa Bible Commentary*, 2nd ed., ed. Tokunboh Adeyemo (Grand Rapids, MI: Zondervan, 2010), 262.

[21] Donald A. Hagner, *Encountering the Book of Hebrews: An Exposition* (Grand Rapids, MI: Baker Academic, 2002), 152-153.

[22] Donald H. Madvig, "Joshua," in *The Expositor's Bible Commentary*, rev. ed., ed. Frank E. Gaebelein, 12 vols. (Grand Rapids, MI: Zondervan, 1992), 262.

[23] Ibid.

[24] Donald Guthrie, *Hebrews*, Tyndale New Testament Commentary, ed. Leon Morris (Grand Rapids, MI: Wm. B. Eerdmans, 1983), 242.

[25] Paul Ellingworth, *The Epistle to the Hebrews*, NIGTC, eds. I. Howard Marshall and Donald A. Hagner (Grand Rapids, MI: Wm. B. Eerdmans Publishing Company, 1993), 622.

[26] Ibid.

[27] Wright, *The Mission of God*, 127.
[28] Ibid.
[29] Ibid.
[30] Ellingworth, *The Epistle to the Hebrews*, 622.
[31] Ibid.
[32] Ralph P. Martin, *James*, Word Biblical Commentary, ed. Bruce M. Metzger (Colombia: Thomas Nelson, Inc., 1998), 97.
[33] Charles Van Engen, *God's Missionary People: Rethinking the Purpose of the Local Church* (Grand Rapids, MI: Baker Books, 1991), 81.
[34] Timothy C. Tennent, *Invitation to World Missions: A Trinitarian Missiology for the Twenty-first Century* (Grand Rapids, MI: Kregel Publications, 2010), 202.
[35] Inclusivists adhere that a Christian represents those who profess and embrace Christ as their Lord, whereas a believer "has only experienced Christ implicitly and does not even realize that he or she has been saved by Christ." Yet it is appropriate to mention that inclusivists acknowledge that "...a Christian and a believer....[both] are saved through the completed work of Christ on the cross." Ibid.
[36] Ibid.
[37] Craig L. Blomberg and Mariam J. Kamell, *James*, Zondervan Exegetical Commentary on the New Testament, ed. Clinton E. Arnold (Grand Rapids, MI: Zondervan, 2008), 140.
[38] Solomon Andria , "James," in *Africa Bible Commentary*, 2nd ed., ed. Tokunboh Adeyemo (Grand Rapids, MI: Zondervan, 2010), 1539.
[39] Tennent, *Invitation to World Missions*, 202.
[40] Little, "ICS 6030" Lecture.
[41] Mordechai Cogan and Hayim Tadmor, *II KINGS: A New Translation with Introduction and Commentary*, The Anchor Bible (USA: Doubleday & Company, Inc., 1988), 66.
[42] R.D. Patterson and Hermann J. Austel, "1 & 2 Kings," in *The Expositor's Bible Commentary*, rev. ed., ed. Frank E. Gaebelein, 12 vols. (Grand Rapids, MI: Zondervan, 1988), 189.
[43] Paul R. House, *1, 2 Kings: An Exegetical and Theological Exposition of Holy Scripture*, The New American Commentary,

ed. E. Ray Clendenen (Nashville, Tennessee: Broadman & Holman Publishers, 2003), 271-272

[44] Kaiser, *Mission in the Old Testament*, 42.

[45] Little, "ICS 6030" Lecture.

[46] House, *1, 2 Kings*, 272.

[47] Gina Hens-Piazza, *1-2 Kings*, Abingdon Old Testament Commentaries, ed. Frederick Carl Eiselen (Nashville, TN: Abingdon Press, 2006), 259.

[48] Volkmar Fritz, *1 & 2 Kings*, trans. Anselm Hagedorn (Minneapolis, MN: Fortress Press, 2003), 259.

[49] Slave girl → Naaman's wife → Naaman → King of Syria → King of Israel (because he did not know what YHWH could do, 2 Kgs 5:6-8).

[50] House, *1, 2 Kings*, 273.

[51] Ibid.

[52] Hens-Piazza, *1-2 Kings*, 261.

[53] Maier quoted in Kaiser, *Mission in the Old Testament*, 47.

[54] Steven C. Hawthorne, "The Story of His Glory," in *Perspectives on the World Christian Movement: A Reader*, 4th ed., eds. Ralph D. Winter and Stephen C. Hawthorne (Pasadena, CA: William Carey Library, 2009), 50.

[55] William J. Larkin, Jr., *Acts*, IVPNTC, ed. Grant R. Osborne (Downers Grove, IL: IVP Academic, 2011), 154.

[56] Ibid., 163.

[57] Ibid., 163-164.

[58] John Piper, *Let the Nations Be Glad: The Supremacy of God in Missions* (Grand Rapids, Michigan: Baker Academic, 2003), 135-136.

[59] Tennent, *Invitation to World Missions*, 202.

[60] John R.W. Stott, *The Message of Acts*, The Bible Speaks Today, ed. John Stott (Downers Grove, IL: InterVarsity Press, 1994), 199.

[61] Tennent, *Invitation to World Missions*, 202.

[62] William J. Larkin, Jr., "Mission in Luke," in *Mission in the New Testament: An Evangelical Approach*, eds. William J. Larkin, Jr. and Joel F. Williams (Maryknoll, NY: Orbis Books, 2002), 155, 172-173.

[63] William J. Larkin, Jr., "ICS 6010: Acts in Historical, Theological and Missiological Perspective" (Lecture, Columbia International University Seminary and School of Ministry, Columbia, SC, 2013).
[64] Little, "ICS 6030" Lecture.
[65] Larkin, "ICS 6010" Lecture.
[66] Eckhard J. Schnabel, *Early Christian Mission: Jesus and the Twelve*, 2 Vols. (Downers Grove, IL: InterVarsity Press, 2004), 711.
[67] Ibid.
[68] David J. Hesselgrave, *Paradigms in Conflict: 10 Key Questions in Christian Missions Today* (Grand Rapids, MI: Kregel Publications, 2005), 122.
[69] Schnabel, *Early Christian Mission: Jesus and the Twelve*, 711.
[70] Stott, *The Message of Acts*, 277.
[71] Ibid.
[72] Ibid., 280.
[73] William J. Larkin, Jr., *Culture and Biblical Hermeneutics: Interpreting and Applying the Authoritative Word in a Relativistic Age* (Eugene, OR: Wipf and Stock Publishers, 2003), 298.
[74] Stott, *The Message of Acts*, 280.
[75] Larkin, *Acts*, 253.
[76] Ibid.
[77] Larkin, *Culture and Biblical Hermeneutics*, 319.
[78] Stott, *The Message of Acts*, 281.
[79] Larkin, *Culture and Biblical Hermeneutics*, 319.
[80] Ibid.
[81] Ibid.
[82] William J. Larkin, Jr., "ICS 6024: Biblical Contextualization Segment Study Guide" (Lecture, Columbia International University Seminary and School of Ministry, Columbia, SC, 2012).
[83] Larkin, *Acts*, 256.
[84] Stott, *The Message of* Acts, 281.
[85] Ibid.
[86] Larkin, *Acts*, 258.
[87] Ibid., 259.

[88] Ibid., 258.
[89] Ibid., 259.
[90] Andreas J. Kostenburger and Peter O'Brien, *Salvation to the Ends of the Earth: A Biblical Theology of Mission* (Downers Grove, IL: InterVarsity Press, 2001), 152.
[91] Larkin, *Acts*, 260.
[92] Ibid.
[93] Contextualization should not always be about finding ideas or concepts that are parallel to the culture the missionary is trying to reach with the gospel. It should also be about new concepts or ideas that are not familiar to the culture as can be gleaned from Paul's missionary orthopraxy in verse 19.
[94] Hesselgrave, *Paradigms in* Conflict, 100.
[95] Ibid., 102.
[96] Ibid., 103.
[97] William J. Larkin, Jr., "Mission in Acts," in *Mission in the New Testament: An Evangelical Approach*, eds. William J. Larkin, Jr. and Joel F. Williams (Maryknoll, NY: Orbis Books, 2002), 180.
[98] Ibid., 107.
[99] The term biblical Christianity is used here as opposed to Western Christianity which carries with it connotations of imperialism, capitalism, naturalism, postmodernism and other – *isms* and which tries to monopolize the nations through homogenization.
[100] Little, "ICS 6030" Lecture.
[101] Indeed, a handful of churches are striving to reach out to the prostitutes in their areas, yet most of them are merely focused on delivering the gospel message and making converts while overlooking the fact that the former prostitutes need equipping in life skills. This would help prevent the former prostitutes from relapsing by enabling them to find ways to generate income.
[102] This false dichotomy is one area Ethiopian theologians need to address through teaching, preaching and writing.
[103] Tribe-based churches are not bad by themselves so long as they do not have a tribalistic or ethnocentric mentality that makes them aloof, reluctant and antagonistic toward other tribes.

[104] How to relate with the EOTC members and the reasons to share the gospel with them is dealt with in-depth in chapter 3 of this book.
[105] Tibebe Eshete, *The Evangelical Movement in Ethiopia: Resistance and Resilience* (Waco, TX: Baylor University Press, 2009), 234.
[106] Ibid.
[107] The way internet evangelism and discipleship is used in Ethiopia in recent years is discussed in chapter 12 of this book.
[108] Tibebe Eshete, *The Evangelical Movement in Ethiopia: Resistance and Resilience* (Waco, Texas: Baylor University Press, 2009), 16.
[109] Jacques A. Blocher and Jacques Blandenier, *The Evangelization of the World: A History of Christian Mission*, trans. Michael Parker (Pasadena, CA: William Carey Library, 2013), 49; Bruce M. Metzger, *The Bible in Translation: Ancient and English Versions* (Grand Rapids, MI: Baker Academic, 2001), 44; Paul R. Spickard, and Kevin M. Cragg, *A Global History of Christianity: How Everyday Believers Experienced Their World* (Grand Rapids, MI: Baker Academic, 1994), 133; Philip Jenkins, *The Next Christendom: The Coming of Global Christianity*, 3rd ed. (New York, NY: Oxford University Press, 2011), 25; Steven Kaplan, *The Monastic Holy Man and the Christianization of Early Solomonic Ethiopia* (Wiesbaden: Steiner, 1984), 15.
[110] Eshete, *The Evangelical Movement in Ethiopia*, 16; Blocher and Blandenier, *The Evangelization of the World*, 49; Metzger, *The Bible in Translation*, 44; Stephen Neill, *A History of Christian Missions*, rev. Owen Chadwick (London, England: Penguin Books Ltd., 1986), 46-47; Girma Bekele, *The In-Between People: A Reading of David Bosch through the Lens of Mission History and Contemporary Challenges in Ethiopia* (Eugene, OR: Pickwick Publications, 2011), 146-148; Michael A. Knibb, *Translating the Bible: The Ethiopic Version of the Old Testament* (New York, NY: Oxford University Press, 1999), 11-12; Edward Ullendorff, *Ethiopia and the Bible: The Schweich Lectures* (New York, NY: Oxford University Press, 1968), 11; Kaplan, *The Monastic Holy Man*, 15.

[111] Ibid., 17; Metzger, *The Bible in Translation*, 44-45; Spickard & Cragg, *A Global History of Christianity*, 133.
[112] Harold G. Marcus, *A History of Ethiopia* (Los Angeles, CA: University of California Press, 1994), 7.
[113] Eshete, *The Evangelical Movement in Ethiopia*, 16-24.
[114] Bekele, *The In-Between People*, 148-149.
[115] Eshete, *The Evangelical Movement in Ethiopia*, 16.
[116] Ibid., 16.
[117] Ullendorf, *Ethiopia and the Bible*, 31; See also Mikre-Sellassie G/Ammanuel, *The Early Translation of the Bible into Ethiopic/Geez* (Addis Ababa, A.A: Birhanina Selam Printing Press, 2008), 59.
[118] Bekele, *The In-Between People*, 148.
[119] G/Ammanuel, *The Early Translation of the Bible*, 80-84; Bekele, *The In-Between People*, 148.
[120] Kaplan, *The Monastic Holy Man*, 17; Ullendorf, *Ethiopia and the Bible*, 37; Gustav Arén, *Evangelical Pioneers in Ethiopia: Origins of the Evangelical Church Mekane Yesus* (Uppsala: Offsetcenter ab, 1978), 41.
[121] Metzger, *The Bible in Translation*, 45; Eshete, *The Evangelical Movement in Ethiopia*, 17; Kaplan, *The Monastic Holy Man*, 17; Stuart Bergsma, *Rainbow Empire: Ethiopia Stretches Out Her Hands* (Grand Rapids, MI: Eerdmans, 1932), 208-209.
[122] Knibb, *Translating the Bible*, 2-3; Metzger, *The Bible in Translation*, 45; Kaplan, *The Monastic Holy Man*, 17; G/Ammanuel, *The Early Translation of the Bible*, 75; Ullendorf, *Ethiopia and the Bible*, 37-38; Philip Jenkins, *The Lost History Of Christianity: The Thousand – Year Golden Age of the Church in the Middle East, Africa, and Asia – and How It Died* (New York, NY: HarperCollins Publishers, 2008), 55.
[123] G/Ammanuel, *The Early Translation of the Bible*, 85; Knibb, *Translating the Bible*, 3.
[124] G/Ammanuel, *The Early Translation of the Bible*, 87.
[125] Knibb, *Translating the Bible*, 14.
[126] Ibid., 23-24; Kaplan, *The Monastic Holy Man*, 17.
[127] Eshete, *The Evangelical Movement in Ethiopia*, 48, 247.
[128] Ibid., 66; Also Arén, *Evangelical Pioneers in Ethiopia*, 36.

[129] Arén, *Evangelical Pioneers in Ethiopia*, 48; Eshete, *The Evangelical Movement in Ethiopia*, 66.

[130] Eshete, *The Evangelical Movement in Ethiopia*, 125; Ullendorf, *Ethiopia and the Bible*, 67; Spencer J. Trimingham, *The Christian Church and Missions in Ethiopia (including Eritrea and the Somalilands)* (New York, NY: World Dominion Press, 1950), 24.

[131] Eshete, *The Evangelical Movement in Ethiopia*, 67; Ullendorf, *Ethiopia and the Bible*, 65-66; Bekele, *The In-Between People*, 156 n37; Arén, *Evangelical Pioneers in Ethiopia*, 42-43.

[132] Eshete, *The Evangelical Movement in Ethiopia*, 67; Ullendorf, *Ethiopia and the Bible*, 66-67.

[133] Arén, *Evangelical Pioneers in Ethiopia*, 44; See also Bergsma, *Rainbow Empire*, 261-263.

[134] Eshete, *The Evangelical Movement in Ethiopia*, 126.

[135] Ullendorf, *Ethiopia and the Bible*, 67.

[136] Eshete, *The Evangelical Movement in Ethiopia*, 126.

[137] Ullendorf spells Tigriña as "Tigriña" or in a short form "Tña" in order to differentiate it from Tigre, the official language of Eritrea. It is also important to mention that Tigriña and Tigre language Bible translations were superintended by the Swedish Evangelical Mission almost at the same period. Ullendorf notes that:
> The first instalment [sic] of the Scriptures in *Tigre* was printed in 1889 at the Swedish Mission Press at Monkullo, some ten miles from Massawa. It was the Gospel of St. Mark and had been translated into Tigre by Täwåldä Mädhən and Dawit Emmanuel, under the supervisión of Dr. C Winquist. In 1902 the entire New Testament in Tigre was printed at the Swedish Mission Press at Asmara. (Ullendorf, *Ethiopia and the Bible*, 71).
> See also Trimingham, *The Christian Church and Missions*, 43.

[138] Ibid., 62.
[139] Ibid., 70.
[140] Ibid., 69
[141] Ibid.
[142] Trimingham, *The Christian Church and Missions*, 43.
[143] Ibid., 67.

[144] Ibid.; Wolbert G.C. Smidt, "The role of the former Oromo slave Pauline Fathme in the foundation of Protestant Oromo mission," in *Ethiopia and the Mission: Historical and Anthropological Insights*, eds. Verena Böll et al. (Münster: LIT VERLAG Münster, 2005), 77; Arén, *Evangelical Pioneers in Ethiopia*, 73.

[145] Kebede Hordofa Janko, "Missionaries, enslaved Oromo and their contribution to the development of the Oromo language: an overview." In *Ethiopia and the Mission: Historical and Anthropological Insights*, eds. Verena Böll et al. (Münster: LIT VERLAG Münster, 2005), 64.

[146] Ibid., 64.

[147] Ibid., 64-65.

[148] Smidt, "The role of the former Oromo slave," 92; See also Janko, "Missionaries, enslaved Oromo and their contribution," 65.

[149] Eshete, *The Evangelical Movement in Ethiopia*, 72; also Bergsma, *Rainbow Empire*, 264.

[150] Eshete, *The Evangelical Movement in Ethiopia*, 72, 74; Janko, "Missionaries, enslaved Oromo and their contribution," 66-67.

[151] F. Peter Cotterell, *Born at Midnight* (Chicago, IL: Moody Press, 1973), 105; Raymond J. Davis, *Fire on the Mountains: The Story of a Miracle – the Church in Ethiopia* (Grand Rapids, MI: Zondervan Publishing House, 1966), 162-163.

[152] Davis, *Fire on the Mountains*, 163.

[153] Cotterell, *Born at Midnight*, 105, 161.

[154] Ibid., 50-51; E. Paul Balisky, *Wolaitta Evangelists: A Study of Religious Innovation in Southern Ethiopia, 1937-1975* (Eugene, OR: Pickwick Publications, 2009), 113.

[155] Davis, *Fire on the Mountains*, 162.

[156] Cotterell, *Born at Midnight*, 161.

[157] Eshete, *The Evangelical Movement in Ethiopia*, 295-296.

[158] Ibid., 293.

[159] Ibid., 294.

[160] Trimingham, *The Christian Church and Missions*, 44. Also The Bible Society of Ethiopia announces on its website that it has been working on various languages, though it is not up-to-date:
> i) Amharic Study Bible Project: (51% completed), ii) Afar OT Translation Project: (95% completed), iii)

Anuak OT Translation Project: (98% completed), iv) Arsi-Bale Oromo Bible Adaptation Project: (26% completed), v) Guji Oromo Bible Translation Project: (72% completed), vi) Hadiyya OT Translation Project: (72% completed), vii) Kambatta OT Translation Project: (71% completed), viii) Konso OT Translation Project: (60% completed), ix) Maale Bible Translation Project: (89% completed), x) Sidama OT Translation Project: (83% completed), xi) Tigrinya Bible Adaptation Project: (92% completed), xii) East Oromo OT Project (began in 2010), xiii) Geez Bible Project (began in 2011) and xiv) Amharic Bible a Catholic Edition (to being in the near future). The goal of BSE in carrying out these translation projects is to access BIBLE FOR ALL in every language every Ethiopian understands. Thus BSE has daunting and very demanding task ahead to raise the number of languages at least to 10 with the whole Bible. In the coming years we strive to complete the current ongoing translation projects, and reach 70% of the Ethiopian population with the whole Bible in their native languages. So the vision and goal of translation office in the coming five years would be to complete the Anuak (nearly completed), Afar, Guji, Sidama, Kambatta, Hadiyya, Male, and Konso Bible projects. In 2015, we shall have the whole Bible in twelve languages:- Amharic, [Afan] Oromo, Tigrigna [Tigriña], Wolayita, Gurage, Anuak, Afar, Male, Sidama, Hadiyya, Kambatta and Konso languages. (Haileyesus Engedashet, "Bible Translation Projects," *Translation*, last revised March 3, 2011, accessed April 05, 2014, http://biblesociety-ethiopia.org/?page_id=632).

[161] Balisky, *Wolaitta Evangelists*, 316. Yet, there are still fifteen languages without any Scripture in Ethiopia. These are: Argobba, Bambassi, Bussa, Chara, Dime, Gayil, Hozo, Inor, Kistane, Kwama, Libido, Mursi, Opuuo, Oyda, Seze. See Wycliffe, *Languages Without Scripture* poster. But in reality, more than twenty languages are Bibleless in Ethiopia. Ethiopia has eight full

Bibles, twenty three New Testaments and close to three dozen portions in the vernaculars.

[162] Steve Strauss, "Creeds, Confessions, and Global Theologizing: A Case Study in Comparative Christology," in *Globalizing Theology: Belief and Practice in an Era of World Christianity*, ed. Craig Ott and Harold A. Netland (Grand Rapids, MI: Baker Academic, 2006), 142 n1.

[163] Ibid., 149.

[164] Bryan M. Litfin, *Getting To Know the Church Fathers: An Evangelical Introduction* (Grand Rapids, MI: Brazos Press, 2007), 245.

[165] Donald Crummey, *Priests and Politicians: Protestant and Catholic Missions in Orthodox Ethiopia 1830-1868* (London: Oxford University Press, 1972), 15.

[166] Strauss, "Creeds, Confessions, and Global Theologizing," 148-149.

[167] Crummey, *Priests and Politicians*, 15.

[168] Strauss, "Creeds, Confessions, and Global Theologizing," 149.

[169] Steve Strauss, *Perspectives on the Nature of Christ in the Ethiopian Orthodox Church: A Case Study in Contextual Theology* (Pasadena, CA: William Carey International University Press, 2014), 85.

[170] Crummey, *Priests and Politicians*, 21.

[171] Ibid., 15.

[172] Litfin, *Getting To Know the Church Fathers*, 245.

[173] Strauss, "Creeds, Confessions, and Global Theologizing," 152; also Bekele, *The In-Between People*, 155.

[174] Strauss, "Creeds, Confessions, and Global Theologizing," 149-150.

[175] Eshete, *The Evangelical Movement in Ethiopia*, 74.

[176] Ibid.

[177] Ibid. For example, Saint Estifanos (Stephen) challenged Zara Yaqob, and later *Aleqa* Meseret challenged the EOTC Christological position that added extra-biblical doctrines using their Ge'ez and Amharic Scriptures. Saint Estifanos' biblically informed Christology came into play before the arrival of Western Protestant missionaries. This does not mean that Scriptures in the vernaculars solely contributed to the understanding of Christ and

his work, however. Both Western and Non- Western theological educators had their own contribution as well. But in the end, the Scriptures in the vernaculars take the lion's share in shaping the Christological understanding of Ethiopian believers. Ibid., 44-45; Bekele, *The In-Between People*, 234-235. John S. Mbiti shares this sentiment with regard to the vital role of the Bible in the vernaculars, John S. Mbiti, *Bible and Theology in African Christianity* (Nairobi: Oxford University Press, 1986), 28.

[178] Ibid., 52.
[179] Ibid., 53.
[180] Tsega Endalew, "Protestant mission activities and persecution in Bahər Dar, 1968-1994: a chronicle," in *Ethiopia and the Mission: Historical and Anthropological Insights,* eds. Verena Böll et al. (Münster: LIT VERLAG Münster, 2005), 214-215.
[181] Trimingham, 24; see also Eshete, *The Evangelical Movement in Ethiopia,* 54, 114.
[182] Cotterell, *Born at Midnight*, 153.
[183] Ibid., 162; Davis, *Fire on the Mountains*, 163.
[184] Eshete, *The Evangelical Movement in Ethiopia,* 52.
[185] Ibid., 88.
[186] Mbiti, *Bible and Theology*, 28.
[187] Kwame Bediako, *Christianity in Africa: The Renewal of a Non-Western Religion* (Maryknoll, NY: Orbis Books, 1995), 62.
[188] Eshete, *The Evangelical Movement in Ethiopia,* 114-116, 119.
[189] Ibid., 120.
[190] A. F. Matthew, trans., *The Teaching of the Abyssinian Church As Set Forth by the Doctors of the Same* (Westminster, London: The Faith Press Ltd., 1936), 35.
[191] Ibid., 38.
[192] Cotterell, *Born at Midnight*, 153.
[193] Philip Jenkins, *The New Faces of Christianity: Believing the Bible in the Global South.* (New York, NY: Oxford University Press, 2006), 42-43.
[194] Mbiti, *Bible and Theology*, 35-36.
[195] Ullendorf, *Ethiopia and the Bible*, 5.
[196] For detailed impact of the Old Testament on various areas of the EOTC as well as Ethiopians at large, see Ullendorf 73-130; also G/Ammanuel, *The Early Translation of the Bible*, 56-58.

[197] Eshete, *The Evangelical Movement in Ethiopia*, 19.
[198] Bekele, 152, 166; for detail on the connection of Ethiopian kings with the Solomonic Dynasty see also Miguel F. Brooks, trans. and ed. *Kebra Nagast (The Glory of Kings): The True Ark of the Covenant* (Asmara, Eritrea: The Red Sea Press, Inc., 1996); Ullendorf, *Ethiopia and the Bible*, 82; G/Ammanuel, *The Early Translation of the Bible*, 52-53.
[199] Ullendorf, *Ethiopia and the Bible*, 82.
[200] Ibid., 83-85.
[201] EOTC members even swear by them, saying, "*Arba aratun*" (I swear by the forty four arks).
[202] Ullendorf, *Ethiopia and the Bible*, 84-85.
[203] Ibid., 83.
[204] Mersha Alehegne, "The Orthodox-Protestant relationship in Ethiopia: a glimpse on interaction, attitude, causes of disharmony, consequences, and some solutions," in *Ethiopia and the Mission: Historical and Anthropological Insights*, eds. Verena Böll et al. (Münster: LIT VERLAG Münster, 2005), 204.
[205] Matthew, *The Teaching of the Abyssinian Church*, 65.
[206] Cotterell, *Born at Midnight*, 153.
[207] Davis, *Fire on the Mountains*, 162.
[208] Cotterell, *Born at Midnight*, 149.
[209] Endalew, "Protestant mission activities and persecution," 213.
[210] Alehegne, "The Orthodox-Protestant relationship in Ethiopia," 203-204.
[211] Endalew, "Protestant mission activities and persecution," 214-215.
[212] Eshete, *The Evangelical Movement in Ethiopia*, 234-235.
[213] Ibid., 246; See also Ibid., 278-283 for detail on how music was used to resist Marxism-Leninism.
[214] Ibid., 277.
[215] Ibid., 163.
[216] Ibid., 100-101; Bekele, 242-243.
[217] Bekele, 242.
[218] Eshete, *The Evangelical Movement in Ethiopia*, 86.
[219] Ibid., 127.
[220] Ibid., 86.
[221] Ibid., 126.

222 Ibid., 159.
223 Ibid., 172.
224 Ibid., 88.
225 Ibid., 89.
226 Ibid.; Steven Kaplan comments regarding the spiritual realm and the expectation of godly men to address it in the Ethiopian context could show that Ethiopians are very aware of the demonic world and the need to be delivered from it: "The Ethiopian hagiographies portray the holy men as coming to the aid of their disciples and followers in a multitude of ways: driving out demons, healing the sick, warding off dangerous animals....No areas of Ethiopian life was free from Satan's influence. However, it is in and around the royal court that claims of satanic activity appear to have been most concentrated." Kaplan, *The Monastic Holy Man*, 70-71; See also Ullendorff, *Ethiopia and the Bible* 79-82. Also Abbebe Kifleyesus, a critic of Pentecostals, notes the blossoming power encounter and deliverance ministry in Addis Ababa. Abbebe Kifleyesus, "Zännət lä Geta. Flaunt fancy for Christ's celebrity: Pentecostal proselytation and identity formation in Addis Ababa," in *Ethiopia and the Mission: Historical and Anthropological Insights*, eds. Verena Böll et al. (Münster: LIT VERLAG Münster, 2005), 135-137.
227 Jenkins, *The New Faces of Christianity*, 103.
228 Eshete, *The Evangelical Movement in Ethiopia*, 90.
229 Ibid., 128-129.
230 Ibid., 177.
231 Ibid., 176.
232 Ibid., 177.
233 Taddesse Tamrat quoted in Mersha Alehegne, "The Orthodox-Protestant relationship in Ethiopia: a glimpse on interaction, attitude, causes of disharmony, consequences, and some solutions," in *Ethiopia and the Mission: Historical and Anthropological Insights*, eds. Verena Böll et al. (Münster: LIT VERLAG Münster, 2005), 203.
234 For instance, it is imperative to share the gospel with liberal "Christians" in America who claim to be evangelicals (those who believe in the *evangel*) but who deny the authority of the

Bible and its teaching, and also to the Catholics (not all but the majority in countries like Italy or the Vatican is wrapped up by tradition, superstition, Mariology and saints worship rather than the Bible and Christ) who have no idea about biblical Christianity. Or even sharing the gospel to the nominal Evangelical Christians in the continent of Africa is essential.

[235] Alehegne "The Orthodox-Protestant relationship in Ethiopia," 198.
[236] Eshete, *The Evangelical Movement in Ethiopia*, 16.
[237] Ibid.
[238] Ibid., 17.
[239] Because of *ergocentric* theology, that is salvation by works, the Church has focused on doing good deeds to the exclusion of preaching the gospel in recent years. Thus the Church has become inward focused. Another contribution to the inward focus of the Church is that the EOTC fought Islam, the Jesuits and other foreign interferences for centuries. These encounters have made the church to be inclined toward self-preservation rather than salvation-propagation. This has indeed contributed to the dwindling of the missionary zeal in the EOTC compared to the earlier periods. On the other hand, the evangelicals, in reaction to the works-based *soteriology* and also probably due to the influence of the western missionaries dichotomistic view of faith and works especially in some mission founded churches, have focused on preaching the gospel alone and not demonstrating their faith in works. Hence they neglected the whole person. See also Bekele, *The In-Between People*, 411-412; Eshete, *The Evangelical Movement in Ethiopia,* 24. Emmanuel Abraham also depicts this western dichotomistic tendency. He indicates that preaching alone was replaced by another extreme end in the pendulum: development alone. He states:

> The new emphasis was on social action, community development in nation-building. Proclamation of the Gospel had become a side-issue which should be reserved to those who might have a special concern for the spiritual welfare of people....These two extreme positions were equally harmful to the local Churches in Developing Countries which see it as their obligation to

serve the whole man. It had been suggested that false piety was responsible for the old imbalance [proclamation alone] and a sense of guilt for the new imbalance [social action alone] in the assistance to the work of the Church. (Emmanuel Abraham, *Reminiscences of My Life* [Asmara, Eritrea: The Red Sea Press, Inc., 2011], 293).

[240] Zara Yaqob means the Seed of Jacob.

[241] Eshete, *The Evangelical Movement in Ethiopia*, 19.

[242] "Steven Kaplan argues that the king's motivation for eradicating magic was political, for he sought to attack and weaken the position of a general class of rebels, deviants, and heretics opposed to him who used magic to undermine his authority." Ibid., 367, n18.

[243] Ibid., 19-20.

[244] For example, Isa 49:23 is a classic verse used by the EOTC to show that the nations (Kings and Queens) will bow and worship Mary. Every verse that mentions Zion in the Old Testament is considered by the EOTC to be Mary in the Old Testament. The "elect lady" in 2 John is also taken by the EOC to be Mary, the mother of Jesus.

[245] In recent years, however, the younger generation of EOC seems to pick up the Bible for instruction, or so as to display that the Bible is not only for Evangelicals alone. This is also facilitated because of the revival in education that is happening in various demographics of the society. Yet sadly, the literature that are available are not necessarily helpful in general. The streets of Addis are filled with book vendors on every corner, yet most of the books are pornographic, anti-Christian (like Dan Brown's kind), or self help books that are written *by* and *to* Westerners on psychology, money, sex or positive thinking. There is a literature starvation that is fed with junk and the burden lies on Ethiopian writers to take this opportunity and provide helpful, thoughtful, thought provoking, and contextual literature so as to save the country from immoral, frivolous, irrelevant and uncontextual literature. For potential topics for aspiring Ethiopian authors, see Nigusse Bulcha's *Weqtawi-*

Zelalemawi: Yeseminar Tsihufoch Sibisib (Addis Ababa: Rehobot Atamiwoch, Hamle 2005 E.C.), 54-55.

[246] Daniel falling on his face before Gabriel in Dan 8:17 and also Gabriel's conversation with Daniel 9:21-23 are taken as a ground for the worship of angels in the EOC theology. Both Michael and Gabriel have days set apart for them for worship in the EOC.

[247] The EOTC clergy as well as its members point out that salvation is earned through good works, using the Biblical text Jas 2:14-26. See footnote 20 for the proper relationship of faith and works.

[248] Eshete, *The Evangelical Movement in Ethiopia*, 34.

[249] Bekele, *The In-Between People*, 409-410.

[250] Eshete, *The Evangelical Movement in Ethiopia*, 21.

[251] Ibid., 23.

[252] It is vital to understand what the Bible teaches about the relation between works, faith and salvation in the Ethiopian milieu. Their relation can be depicted in three ways: "Roman Catholic Church [also EOTC]: Faith + Works (Merit) = Salvation; Protestant: Faith = Salvation + Works; NT/Paul: Faith + Works (manifestations) (or a faith declared by works (cf. *Rom. 1:5; 16:26; Jam. 2:17, 24, 26*)) = Salvation." A common misconception among Protestants is that faith is absolutely divorced from works, and can stand by its own. Probably, this is a reaction to legalism. Christopher R. Little, "ICS6030" Lecture.

[253] Eshete, *The Evangelical Movement in Ethiopia*, 44.

[254] Ibid.

[255] Ibid.

[256] Ibid., 45; Bekele, *The In-Between People*, 234.

[257] Bekele, *The In-Between People*, 235.

[258] Alehegne, "The Orthodox-Protestant relationship in Ethiopia," 203.

[259] John 1:1, 14; 16:33; 20:28; Col 1:15-20; 2:15; Heb 4:14; Titus 2:13; 1John 3:8.

[260] Edward Ullendorf, *Ethiopia and the Bible: The Schweich Lectures*, (New York, NY: Oxford University Press, 1968), 15.

[261] Philip Jenkins, *The Next Christendom: The Coming of Global Christianity* 3rd ed. (New York, NY: Oxford University Press, 2011), 26.

[262] John Stott, *The Message of Acts* (Downers Grove, IL: InterVarsity Press, 1990), 79.
[263] Ibid., 80.
[264] Ibid., 81.
[265] Ibid.
[266] Nigusse Bulcha also has excellent recommendations on how Evangelicals can interact with people from other religions, particularly with those in the EOTC/ECC. He suggests five strategies in conversing with them. I have translated his suggestions from Amharic into English below:
> First, we should strive to learn their religion….Second, we should strengthen our common creeds and values….Third, we should make a way to converse on our differences seriously….Fourth, let us avoid anything that displays arrogance and superiority complex…. Fifth, let us use the media properly for everyone is watching what we say. In other words, let us not use the media to degrade people from other faiths and let us use it for the benefit of man and for the glory of God. (Bulcha, *Weqtawi-Zelalemawi*, 18-21;).

[267] Marcion was a second century heretic who showed a disdain and a disregard for the Hebrew Bible, for he found the God who is depicted in the Hebrew Bible to be ferocious and ungracious, and thus inferior compared to the gracious, merciful and loving God of the New Testament. He used the New Testament as his sole source of theology. Roger E. Olson captures Marcion's thought succinctly:
> Marcion believed it necessary to strip away all vestiges of Judaism from Christianity—including the Hebrew Bible and its God, Yahweh. For him, the Old Testament had no validity for Christians whatever, and he considered the God described in it a tribal, bloodthirsty demigod who did not deserve Christian adoration or worship. Marcion's similarities to Gnosticism come out in his idea that the God of the Old Testament wrongly created matter and that matter is the cause of evil. For Marcion, the Old Testament Yahweh was more demonic than divine. (Roger E. Olson, *The Story of Christian*

Theology: Twenty Centuries of Tradition and Reform [Downer's Grove, IL: InterVarsity Press, 1999], 132-133).
In the same manner, Protestants, mostly Westerners, prefer the New Testament over the Old. In so doing, they imply the Old Testament's inferiority and uselessness for today. On the other hand, the EOTC relies heavily upon the Old Testament, even to the neglect of the New Testament. Wisdom literature, especially Psalms and the Pentateuch, are widely known, applied and gleaned from. Because of this, the Hebrew Bible is a good place to start a conversation with EOTC adherents. Eventually, one can connect the storyline of the Old Testament to that of the New Testament.

[268] In some areas this might not be true. There are some places where members of the EOTC practicing witchcraft but have no idea about the truth of Christianity.

[269] Central Statistical Agency, "Census 2007," CSA, http://www.csa.gov.et/pdf/Cen2007_firstdraft.pdf (accessed March 19, 2010).

[270] Hailu Mezegebu, "A Day in Bishoftu: Erecha a Quest for Spiritual Identity?" Originally published in Amhraic in *Addis Neger News*, October 2010, English translation at tinsae.org/index/?m=201010 (accessed March 19, 2010).

[271] Ibid.

[272] Asafa Jalata, "Oromo Peoplehood: Historical and Cultural Overview," *Sociology Publications and Other Works of the Tennessee Research and Creative Exchange* (March 2, 2010), 3.

[273] Ibid., 4.

[274] Ibid., 8.

[275] Ibid., 16-17.

[276] Ibid., 8.

[277] Ibid., 16-17.

[278] Ibid., 4-5.

[279] Brita Marie Servan, "Sacred Networks: Religion and Social Life Among the Oromo in Norway" (master's thesis, University of Bergen, 2008), 17.

[280] Ibid., 23-26.

[281] Jalata, "Oromo Peoplehood," 7.

[282] Thomas L. Friedman, *The Lexus and the Olive Tree: Understanding Globalization* (New York: Anchor Books, 2000), 9.
[283] Ibid., 9.
[284] Ibid., 42.
[285] Thabo Mbeki, "The African Rennaisance, South Africa and the World" (speech at the United Nations University, Tokyo, Japan, April 9, 1998).
[286] Desissa, Desalegn, "Traditional Oromo Religion," http://www.mikepalmer.co.uk/woodyplantecology/ethiopia/sacredgrove/oromo.html (accessed March 19, 2010).
[287] Mezegebu, "A Day in Bishoftu."
[288] Servan, "Sacred Networks," 22.
[289] Mezegebu, "A Day in Bishoftu."
[290] Jalata, "Oromo Peoplehood," 20.
[291] A. Scott Moreau, Gary R. Corwin, and Gary B. McGee, *Introducing World Missions: A Biblical, Historical and Practical Survey* (Grand Rapids, MI: Baker Academic, 2004), 13.
[292] Servan, "Sacred Networks," 78-79.
[293] Jalata, "Oromo Peoplehood," 10.
[294] Servan, "Sacred Networks," 20.
[295] Andy Crouch, *Culture Making: Recovering Our Creative Calling* (Downer's Grove, IL: IVP Books, 2008), 67.
[296] Ibid., 37.
[297] Ibid., 36.
[298] Bruce A. Koch, "The Surging Non-Western Mission Force," in *Perspectives on the World Christian Movement: A Reader*, 4th ed., eds. Ralph D. Winter and Steven C. Hawthorne (Pasadena, CA: William Carey Library, 2009), 370.
[299] Larry E. Keyes and Larry D. Pate, "Two-Thirds World Missions: The Next 200 Years," *Missiology: An International Review*, 21.2 (1993): 191.
[300] Todd Johnson and Sandra S.K. Lee, "From Western Christendom to Global Christianity," in *Perspectives on the World Christian Movement: A Reader*, 4th ed., eds. Ralph D. Winter and Steven C. Hawthorne (Pasadena, CA: William Carey Library, 2009), 387.

[301] Howard Brant, "Seven Essentials of Majority World Emerging Mission Movements," in *Missions in the Majority World: Progress, Challenges, and Case Studies*, ed. Enoch Wan and Michael Pocock (Pasadena, CA: William Carey Library, 2009), 44.
[302] Ibid, 39.
[303] *Columbia Electronic Encyclopedia*, 6th ed., s.v. "Menelik II."
[304] Robert Lundquist, "The Amhara (Amara) People of Ethiopia," Orville Jenkins, http://orvillejenkins.com/profiles/amhara.html (accessed April 17, 2013).
[305] Eshete, *The Evangelical Movement in Ethiopia*, 302.
[306] Aragaw Sisay, *Summer Missions 2012 Report* (Addis Ababa, Ethiopia: EvaSUE), 2012
[307] Jason Mandryk, *Operation World: The Definitive Prayer Guide to Every Nation*, 7th ed. (Colorado Springs: Biblica Publishing, 2009), 26.
[308] Ibid.
[309] Brant, "Seven Essentials of Majority World Emerging Mission Movements," 57.
[310] Mandryk, *Operation World*, 328.
[311] Timothy Kiho Park, "Korean Christian World Mission: The Missionary Movement of the Korean Church," in *Missions in the Majority World: Progress, Challenges, and Case Studies*, ed. Enoch Wan and Michael Pocock (Pasadena, CA: William Carey Library, 2009), 101-102.
[312] Mandryk, *Operation World*, 328.
[313] Brant, "Seven Essentials of Majority World Emerging Mission Movements," 45.
[314] Ben Naja, *Releasing the Workers of the 11th Hour* (Pasadena, CA: William Carey Library, 2007), 12.
[315] Ibid., 19.
[316] Theodore Williams, "Is Missionary Training Necessary for Two-Thirds World Missionaries?" in *Internationalising Missionary Training*, ed. William D. Taylor (Grand Rapids, MI: Baker, 1991), 23.
[317] Brant, "Seven Essentials of Majority World Emerging Mission Movements," 44.

[318] *Invitation to Cross-Cultural Theology: Case Studies in Vernacular Theologies* (Grand Rapids, MI: Zondervan, 1992), 17.
[319] Brant, "Seven Essentials of Majority World Emerging Mission Movements," 44.
[320] Tite Tienou, *The Theological Task of the Church in Africa*, 2nd ed. (Hong Kong: Africa Christian Press, 1990), 24.
[321] Ibid., 23.
[322] Ibid., 22-23.
[323] Ayuk A. Ayuk, "Portrait of a Nigerian Pentecostal Missionary," *Asian Journal of Pentecostal Studies* 8:1 (2005), 131.
[324] Sarojini Nadar, "Contextual Theological Education in Africa and the Challenge of Globalization," *The Ecumenical Review*, 59:2-3 (2007): 237.
[325] R. Paul Stevens and Brian Stelck, "Equipping Equippers Cross-Culturally: An Experiment in the Appropriate Globalization of Theological Education," *Missiology: An International Review* XXI.1 (1993), 31.
[326] Ibid., 34.
[327] Ibid., 33-34.
[328] Ibid., 35.
[329] Ibid., 37.
[330] Ibid., 36.
[331] Naja, "Releasing Workers for the 11th Hour," 56.
[332] Cephas N. Omenyo, "'The Spirit-Filled Goes to School': Theological Education in African Pentecostalism," *Ogbomoso Journal of Theology* XIII.2 (2008), 43.
[333] Ibid., 45-46.
[334] Cited in Omenyo, ibid., 54.
[335] Ibid.
[336] Tite Tienou, "The Training of Missiologists for an African Context," in *Missiological Education for the Twenty-First Century: The Book, the Circle, and the Sandals*, ed. J. Dudley Woodberry, Charles Van Engen, and Edgar J. Elliston (Eugene, OR: Wipf & Stock Publishers, 1997), 96.
[337] Ibid., 97.

[338] Robert W. Ferris, ed., *Establishing Ministry Training: A Manual for Programme Developers* (Pasadena, CA: William Carey Library, 1995), back cover.
[339] Ibid., 145.
[340] Ross Kinsler, *Diversified Theological Education: Equipping All God's People*, ed. Ross Kinsler (Pasadena, CA: William Carey Library, 2008), 27.
[341] Ibid., 28.
[342] Ibid., 27.
[343] Robert Brynjolfson and Jonathan Lewis, *Integral Ministry Training: Design & Evaluation* (Pasadena, CA: William Carey Library, 2006), viii.
[344] Ibid., 31.
[345] Ibid., 32.
[346] Ibid., 27.
[347] Ibid., 22.
[348] Ibid., 23.
[349] David Harley, *Preparing To Serve: Training for Cross-Cultural Mission* (Pasadena, CA: William Carey Library, 1995), 70-77.
[350] Brant, "Seven Essentials of Majority World Emerging Mission Movements," 46.
[351] Tite Tienou, "The Training of Missiologists for an African Context," 98.
[352] Ibid., 97.
[353] Ibid., 98.
[354] Brynjolfson and Lewis, *Integral Ministry Training*, 91.
[355] Ibid., 91-92.
[356] Margaretha Adiwardana, "Formal and Non-Formal Pre-Field Training: Perspective of the New Sending Countries," in *Too Valuable to Lose: Exploring the Causes and Cures of Missionary Attrition*, ed. William David Taylor (Singapore: World Evangelical Fellowship Missions Commission, 1997), 210.
[357] Edgar J. Elliston, *Introduction to Missiological Research Design* (Pasadena, CA: William Carey Library, 2011), 77.
[358] Ibid., 123.
[359] SBCE, *Shiloh Bible College Ethiopia: Prospectus* [n.d.: n.p., n.d.], 1.

[360] Brant, "Seven Essentials" (Pastors' Book Set), 29.
[361] Ibid, 5.
[362] Ibid., 2.
[363] Ibid., 6.
[364] Ibid., 3.
[365] Ibid., 1.
[366] Ibid.
[367] Ibid., 3.
[368] Ibid., 2.
[369] Ibid., 4.
[370] Ibid.
[371] Ibid., 2.
[372] Ibid., 4.
[373] EKSM, *Planning the Curricular Timetable* [Durame, Ethiopia: n.p., n.d.], 1.
[374] Brant, "Seven Essentials (Pastor's Book Set)," 21.
[375] Ibid., 2.
[376] Ibid., 3.
[377] Ibid., 2.
[378] Ibid., 3.
[379] Ibid.
[380] Ibid., 4-6.
[381] Ibid., 1.
[382] Ibid., 4-6.
[383] Ibid.
[384] Ibid., 4-6.
[385] The Evangelical Theological College, *Programme Catalogue* [Addis Ababa, Ethiopia: n.p., 2010-2011], 7.
[386] Ibid., 33.
[387] Ibid., 33-34.
[388] Ibid., 5.
[389] Ibid., 7.
[390] Ibid.
[391] Ibid., 6.
[392] Ibid., 33-34.
[393] Ibid., 5.
[394] Ibid., 43.
[395] Brynjolfson and Lewis, *Integral Ministry Training*, 141.

[396] FTLT, "About Us," FTLT, http://www.ftlt.org/mission-leadership-training-school (accessed July 28, 2013).
[397] Brynjolfson and Lewis, *Integral Ministry Training*, 163.
[398] FTLT, "Informal Training," FTLT, http://www.ftlt.org/mission-leadership-training-school/mission-leadership-training-school-2/informal-training (accessed July 28th, 2013).
[399] FTLT, "Formal Training and Curriculum," FTLT, http://www.ftlt.org/mission-leadership-training-school/mission-leadership-training-school-2/curriculum (accessed July 28, 2013).
[400] Ibid.
[401] Brynjolfson and Lewis, *Integral Ministry Training*, 163.
[402] FTLT, "Mission Leadership Training School," FTLT, http://www.ftlt.org/mission-leadership-training-school (accessed July 28th, 2013).
[403] FTLT, Formal Training and Curriculum," FTLT, http://www.ftlt.org/mission-leadership-training-school/mission-leadership-training-school-2/curriculum (accessed July 28, 2013).
[404] Brynjolfson and Lewis, *Integral Ministry Training*, 164-165.
[405] FTLT, Formal Training and Curriculum," FTLT, http://www.ftlt.org/mission-leadership-training-school/mission-leadership-training-school-2/curriculum (accessed July 28, 2013).
[406] FTLT, "Informal Training," FTLT, http://www.ftlt.org/mission-leadership-training-school/mission-leadership-training-school-2/curriculum (accessed July 28, 2013).
[407] Brynjolfson and Lewis, *Integral Ministry Training*, 163-164.
[408] NEMI, "Nigeria Evangelical Missionary Institute (NEMI)," NEMI, http://nemitoday.blogspot.com/2012/09/nigeria-evangelical-missionary.html (accessed July 28, 2013).
[409] Ibid.
[410] Ibid.
[411] Brynjolfson and Lewis, *Integral Ministry Training*, 152.

[412] NEMI, "Nigeria Evangelical Missionary Institute (NEMI)," NEMI, http://nemitoday.blogspot.com/2012/09/nigeria-evangelical-missionary.html (accessed July 28, 2013).
[413] Ibid.
[414] Ibid.
[415] Ibid.
[416] Brynjolfson and Lewis, *Integral Ministry Training*, 152.
[417] Brynjolfson and Lewis, *Integral Ministry Training*, 154.
[418] Seth Anyomi, "Attrition in Ghana," in *Too Valuable to Lose: Exploring the Causes and Cures of Missionary Attrition*, ed. William David Taylor (Pasadena, CA: William Carey Library, 2012), 166.
[419] Brynjolfson and Lewis, *Integral Ministry Training*, 155.
[420] Anyomi, "Attrition in Ghana," 166.
[421] Robert Brynjolfson and Jonathan Lewis, *Integral Ministry Training: Design and Evaluation* (Pasadena, CA: William Carey Library, 2012), 155.
[422] Ibid., 155.
[423] Ibid., 156.
[424] Ibid., 157.
[425] Ibid., 156.
[426] Ibid., 155.
[427] Ibid., 155.
[428] Ibid., 156.
[429] Jessica Udall, "Preparing Ethiopians for Cross-Cultural Ministry: Maximizing Missionary Training for Great Commission Impact" (Master's thesis, Columbia International University, 2013), 3-4.
[430] Sam Farzaneh and Bill McKenna, "Little Ethiopia," *BBC News*, 11 July 2013, 1, accessed March 27, 2014, http://www.bbc.co.uk/news/magazine-22803973.
[431] Aaron Matteo Terrazas, "Beyond Regional Circularity: The Emergence of an Ethiopian Diaspora," *Migration Information Source* (June 1, 2007): 1, accessed March 27, 2014, http://www.migrationinformation.org/profiles/display.cfm?ID=604.

[432] Jason Mandryk, *Operation World: The Definitive Prayer Guide to Every Nation*, 7th ed. (Colorado Springs, CO: Biblica, 2010), 328.
[433] "Countries of Birth for U.S. Immigrants, 1960-Present," *MPI Data Hub*, 2012, accessed May 31, 2014, http://www.migrationpolicy.org/programs/data-hub/us-immigration-trends#source.
[434] Farzaneh and McKenna, "Little Ethiopia."
[435] Perspectives Study Program, "Perspectives On the World Christian Movement," Perspectives on the World Christian Movement, March 28, 2014, accessed March 28, 2014, http://www.perspectives.org/.
[436] Abeneazer Gezahegn Urga, *Prayer and Evangelism: Inseparable Elements in Furthering the Gospel* (Addis Ababa: Andnet Printers, 2013), 79.
[437] Sam Farzaneh and Bill McKenna, "Little Ethiopia."
[438] "Habesha Student," Habesha Student, March 28, 2014, accessed March 28, 2014, http://www.habeshastudent.com/.
[439] The Jesus Film Project, "Jesus Film Store," The Jesus Film Project, March 28, 2014, accessed March 28, 2014, http://www.jesusfilmstore.org/.
[440] "Internet Usage Worldwide," Statista, accessed December 17, 2014, http://www.statista.com/topics/1145/internet-usage-worldwide/.
[441] Commander, "World Internet Usage Statistics by Continent," *Commander* (blog), August 5, 2014, accessed December 17, 2014. http://blog.commander.com/world-internet-usage-statistics-by-continent/.
[442] Dominique Baron, et al, "The Impact of Telecommunications Services on Doing Business in Ethiopia," *Addis Ababa Chamber of Commerce and Sectoral Associations*, 7. PDF. Accessed December 17, 2014, http://www.ethiopianchamber.com/Data/Sites/1/psd-hub-publications/the-impact-of-telecommunications-services-on-doing-business-in-ethiopia.pdf.
[443] Leonard Sweet, *Viral: How Social Networking is Poised to Ignite Revival* (Colorado Springs, CO: WaterBrook Press, 2012), 55.
[444] Ibid., 49.
[445] Craig Von Buseck, *Net Casters: Using the Internet to Make Fishers of Men* (Nashville, TN: B & H Publishing Group, 2010), 6.

[446] Dwight J. Friesen, *Thy Kingdom Connected: What the Church Can Learn from Facebook, the Internet, and Other Networks* (Grand Rapids, MI: Baker Books, 2009), 142.
[447] Von Buseck, *Net Casters*, 20-21
[448] Sweet, *Viral*, 10.
[449] Von Buseck, *Net Casters*, 7.
[450] Rob Haskell, "eVangelism: The Gospel and the World of the Internet," *Evangelical Review of Theology* 34.3 (July 2010), 284.
[451] Miheret Tilahun, "Millions Are Waiting for Answers," *My Generation for Christ* (blog), January 11, 2010, accessed November 11, 2014, https://www.gcx.org/miheret/2010/01/11/millions-are-waiting-for-answers/.
[452] Ibid., "Online Missionaries Retreat," *My Generation for Christ* (blog), August 26, 2011, accessed November 11, 2014, https://www.gcx.org/miheret/2011/08/26/online-missionaries-retreat/.
[453] Ibid., "Ministry Update," *My Generation for Christ* (blog), November 12, 2010, accessed November 11, 2014, https://www.gcx.org/miheret/2010/11/12/ministry-update/.
[454] Ibid., "Using Facebook to Bring the Good News," *My Generation for Christ* (blog), November 20, 2012, accessed November 11, 2014, https://www.gcx.org/miheret/2012/11/20/using-facebook-to-bring-the-good-news/.
[455] John Stott, "The Living God Is a Missionary God," in *Perspectives on the World Christian Movement*, 4th ed., eds. Ralph D. Winter and Steven C. Hawthorne (Pasadena, California: William Carey Library, 2009), 4.
[456] Thom S. Rainer, *Evangelism in the Twenty-First Century: The Critical Issues* (Wheaton, Illinois: Harold Shaw Publishers, 1989), 61.
[457] Peter Falk, *The Growth of the Church in Africa: Contemporary Evangelical Perspective* (Grand Rapids, MI: Zondervan, 1979), 292.
[458] Great Commission Ministry Ethiopia, "Background," The Great Commission Ministry Ethiopia. http://www.gcmethiopia.org.et/Htmlpages/jesus1.htm (accessed November 25, 2011).

[459] The Lausanne Congress on World Evangelization. "The Lausanne Covenant" in *Perspectives: On the World Christian Movement*, 4th ed., eds. Ralph D. Winter and Steven C. Hawthorne (Pasadena, California: William Carey Library, 2009), 766.
[460] Tsadiku Abido, "Two Historical Phenomena," (paper presented at an Ethiopian Full Gospel Believers' Church, Addis Ababa, Ethiopia, 2007).
[461] Roger Greenway, *Go and Make Disciples!: An Introduction to Christian Missions* (Phillipsburg, NJ: P&R Publishing, 1999), 106-07.
[462] Ibid., 108.
[463] Lemma Degefa, "Leadership Training," (lecture given at World Vision Ethiopia, Addis Ababa, Ethiopia, February 16, 2009).
[464] Miriam Adeney "'Is God Colorblind or Colorful?' The Gospel, Globalization and Ethnicity," in *Perspectives on the World Christian Movement*, 4th ed., eds. Ralph D. Winter and Steven C. Hawthorne (Pasadena, California: William Carey Library, 2009), 418.
[465] Samuel W. Kunhiyop, *African Christian Ethics* (Nairobi: WordAlive Publishers, 2008), 108.
[466] Charles Van Engen, "Is the Church for Everyone? Planting Multi-Ethnic Congregations in North America," *Global Missiology* 1.2 (October 2004): 3, accessed August 12, 2011, http://ojs.globalmissiology.org/index.php/english/issue//24.
[467] Robert Garrett, "The Gospels and Acts: Jesus the Missionary and His Missionary Followers," in *Missiology: An Introduction to the Foundations, History, and Strategies of World Missions*, eds. John Mark Terry, Ebbie Smith and Justice Anderson (Nashville, Tennessee: Broadman & Holman Publishers, 1998), 80.
[468] Norman E. Thomas, "The Church in Antioch," in *Mission in Acts: Ancient Narratives in Contemporary Context*, eds. Robert L. Gallagher & Paul Hertig (Maryknoll, New York: Orbis Books, 2004), 146.
[469] Arthur F. Glasser, "Apostle Paul and the Missionary Task," in *Perspectives on the World Christian Movement: A Reader*, 4th

ed., eds. Ralph D. Winter and Steven C. Hawthorne (Pasadena, California: William Carey Library, 2009), 150.
[470] Stephen B. Bevans and Roger P. Schroeder, *Constants in Context: A Theology of Mission for Today* (Maryknoll, NY: Orbis Book, 2004), 26.
[471] Eckhard Schnabel, *Paul the Missionary: Realities, Strategies and Methods* (Downer's Grove, IL: IVP Academic, 2008), 26-27.
[472] Thomas, "The Church in Antioch," in *Mission in Acts*, 153.
[473] Ibid., 147.
[474] Ibid.
[475] Ibid.
[476] Ibid.
[477] Ibid., 148.
[478] Ibid.
[479] Ibid., 149.
[480] Kent Hunter, *Foundations for Church Growth: Biblical Basics for the Local Church* (np: Church Growth Center, 1984), 80-81.
[481] Charles H. Dunahoo, *Making Kingdom Disciples: A New Framework* (Phillipsburg, New Jersey: P & R Publishing, 2005), 3.
[482] Thomas, "The Church in Antioch," in *Mission in Acts*, 149.
[483] Ponraj S. Devasahayam, *Church Planting Approach in Mission* (Salem, India: Bethel Bible Institute, 1987), 9-12.
[484] Thomas, "The Church in Antioch," in *Mission in Acts*, 151.
[485] Ibid., 151-52.
[486] Rick Warren, *The Purpose Driven Life: What on Earth am I Here For?* (Grand Rapids, Michigan: Zondervan, 2002), 118.
[487] Thomas, "The Church in Antioch," in *Mission in Acts*, 149-50.
[488] Orlando E. Costas, *The Church and Its Mission: A Shattering Critique from the Third World* (Wheaton, IL: Tyndale House Publishers, 1974), 35.
[489] Thomas, "The Church in Antioch," in *Mission in Acts*, 151.
[490] Ibid.
[491] Elmer L. Towns, "Overcoming Large Church Barriers of 1,000 People," in *The Everychurch Guide to Growth: How Any Plateaued Church Can Grow*, C. Peter Wagner, Thomas S.

Rainer and Elmer L. Towns (Nashville, Tennessee: B & H Publishers, 1998), 169.
[492] Robert Lionel Elkington, "A Missional Church Model," *SAGE* (7 November 2011): 7, accessed December 2, 2011, http://sgo.sagepub.com/content/early/2011/11/07/2158244011428086.
[493] C. Peter Wagner, *Your Church Can Grow: Seven Vital Signs of a Healthy Church* (Glendale, CA: Regal Books Division, 1976), 69.
[494] Lesslie Newbigin, *The Gospel in a Pluralist Society* (Grand Rapids, Michigan: Wm. B. Eerdmans Pub. Co., 1989), 235.
[495] Barje S. Maigadi, *Divisive Ethnicity in the Church in Africa* (Kaduna, Nigeria: Baraka Press, 2006), 205.
[496] Ibid., 205-06.
[497] Ibid., 207.
[498] Ibid., 208.
[499] Ibid., 208-209.
[500] Charles Van Engen, "Is the Church for Everyone? Planting Multi-Ethnic Congregations in North America," *Global Missiology* 1.2 (October 2004): 2-3, http://ojs.globalmissiology.org/index.php/english/issue//24 (accessed August 12, 2011).
[501] Donald A. McGavran, *Eye of the Storm: The Great Debate in Mission* (Waco, Texas: Word Books, 1972), 142.
[502] Donald A. McGavran, *Understanding Church Growth*, 3rd ed., rev. and ed. C. Peter Wagner (Grand Rapids, MI: Wm. B. Eerdmans Publishing Co., 1990), 164.
[503] Evangelical Churches Fellowship of Ethiopia, "Unity in Christ: The History of ECFE," Evangelical Churches Fellowship of Ethiopia, http://www.ecfethiopia.org/mission.htm (accessed October 9, 2011).
[504] The Lausanne Congress on World Evangelization, "The Lausanne Covenant," in *Perspectives: On the World Christian Movement*, 4th ed., eds. Ralph D. Winter and Steven C. Hawthorne (Pasadena, California: William Carey Library, 2009), 766.

[505] EvaSUE Alumni North America, *2014 Report, 2015 Plan: Send Me, Isaiah 6:8* (Santa Clarita, CA: EvaSUE North America, 2015), 3.
[506] Maigadi, *Divisive Ethnicity in the Church in Africa*, 251.
[507] Ibid., 252.
[508] Ibid.
[509] FOCUS-KENYA, *Staff Orientation and Training Manual* (Ruaraka, Kenya: FOCUS, 2008), 36.
[510] Ibid., 37.
[511] H. Wilbert Norton, Sr., "The Student Foreign Mission Fellowship Over Fifty-five Years," *International Bulletin of Missionary Research* (January 1993), 17.
[512] Ben Harder, "The Student Volunteer Movement for Foreign Mission and Its Contribution to 20th Century Mission," *Missiology* VIII.2 (April 1980), 141.
[513] Ibid, 146.
[514] Ibid., 141.
[515] Ibid., 144.
[516] Ibid., 142.
[517] Ibid., 149.
[518] Ibid., 145.
[519] Norton, "The Student Foreign Mission Fellowship," 17.
[520] Eshete, *The Evangelical Movement in Ethiopia*, 132.
[521] Ibid., 134.
[522] Ibid., 133.
[523] Ibid., 137.
[524] Ibid., 138.
[525] Ibid., 177.
[526] Ibid., 165.
[527] Ibid., 172.
[528] Ibid., 166.
[529] Ibid., 165.
[530] Ibid., 167.
[531] Ibid., 172.
[532] Unless otherwise noted, the remainder of the quotations are from these interviews.
[533] Steve Shadrach, "College Students: The Powerful 1%," *Mission Frontiers* (November-December 2009), 7.

[534] Howard Brant, "Seven Essentials," (Pastors' Book Set from Mission Conference, 2012), 15.
[535] S. Alkire, A Conconi, and J.M. Roche. "Multidimensional Poverty Index 2013: Brief Methodological Note and Results," Oxford Poverty and Human Development Initiative, Oxford University, http://www.ophi.org.uk/multidimensional-poverty-index/mpi-data-bank/mpi-data/ (accessed September 8, 2013).
[536] Dambisa Moyo. *Dead Aid: Why Aid is Not Working and How There Is a Better Way for Africa* (New York: Farrar, Straus and Giroux, 2009), 5.
[537] Central Intelligence Agency, "Ethiopia," *CIA World Factbook*, https://www.cia.gov/library/publications/the-world-factbook/geos/et.html (accessed June 5, 2014).
[538] Moyo, *Dead Aid*, 72.
[539] Brant, "Seven Essentials" (Pastor's Book Set), 26.
[540] Mandryk, *Operation World*, 329.
[541] Moyo, *Dead Aid*, 7.
[542] Ibid., 44.
[543] Robertson, McQuilkin, "Stop Sending Money! Breaking the Cycle of Mission Dependency," *Christianity Today* 43:3, 1999, 57.
[544] "Dependency Hinders Development: An Exploration of Receiving Relationships," in *Currents in Theology and Mission* 16:5, 1989, 347.
[545] Moyo, *Dead Aid*, 75.
[546] Ibid., xix.
[547] Ibid., 75.
[548] Ibid., 149.
[549] McQuilkin, "Stop Sending Money," 59.
[550] Brant, "Seven Essentials" (Pastor's Book Set) 25-26.
[551] Glenn Schwartz. *When Charity Destroys Dignity: Overcoming Unhealthy Dependency in the Christian Movement* (Bloomington, IN: AuthorHouse, 2007), 35.
[552] Ibid., 34.
[553] Ibid., 42.
[554] Robert Reese, *Roots and Remedies of the Dependency Syndrome in World Missions* (Pasadena, CA: William Carey Library, 2009), 117.

555 Ibid., 51.
556 Ibid., 24.
557 Ibid., 134.
558 Ibid., 135.
559 Thomas R. Walls, Review of *Mission in the Way of Paul: Biblical Mission for the Church in the Twenty-First Century*, by Christopher R. Little, *Missiology* 35, no. 1(January 2007): 112.
560 1 Corinthians 11:1 (New International Version).
561 Melvin Hodges, *The Indigenous Church: A Complete Handbook on How to Grow Young Churches* (Springfield, MO: Gospel Publishing House, 1976), 76-77.
562 Schwartz, *When Charity Destroys Dignity*, 1.
563 Reese, *Roots and Remedies*, 161.
564 Hodges, *The Indigenous Church*, 77.
565 Ibid., 79.
566 Schwartz, *When Charity Destroys Dignity*, 238.
567 Reese, *Roots and Remedies*, 112.
568 Schwartz, *When Charity Destroys Dignity*, 8.
569 I am aware that, particularly in urban areas, churches are required to construct buildings of a certain size and quality in order to meet urban planning standards. There is certainly nothing wrong with having a building, even a comfortable one. The issue I am trying to press is that of priority – if a church is fretting and focusing on her building fund to the neglect of her outreach, priorities must be realigned and the question must be asked: "Who are we trying to please – men or God?"
570 Hodges, *The Indigenous Church*, 83.
571 Brant, "Seven Essentials" (Pastors' Book Set), 28.
572 Reese, *Roots and Remedies*, 166.
573 Ibid., 166-167.
574 Schwartz, *When Charity Destroys Dignity*, 234.
575 Ibid., 159.
576 Ibid., 160.
577 Ibid., 266.
578 Ibid., 278.
579 Ibid., 43.
580 Brant, "Seven Essentials" (Pastor's Book Set), 15.
581 Ibid., xiv.

[582] Schwartz, *When Charity Destroys Dignity*, 161.
[583] Ibid., 153.
[584] Ibid., 112.
[585] Reese, *Roots and Remedies*, 169.
[586] Ibid., 170.
[587] Brant, "Seven Essentials" (Pastor's Book Set), 31-32.
[588] Schwartz, *When Charity Destroys Dignity*, 25.
[589] Reese, *Roots and Remedies*, 153.
[590] Schwartz, *When Charity Destroys Dignity*, 96.
[591] Ibid., 283.
[592] Ibid., 217.
[593] Brant, "Seven Essentials," (Pastors' Book Set), 32.
[594] Ibid., 29.
[595] Schwartz, *When Charity Destroys Dignity*, 99. When businesses are started to benefit the church, Schwartz cautions from experience that they should not actually be run *by* the church.
[596] 2 Corinthians 9:7.
[597] Reese, *Roots and Remedies*, 169.
[598] Brant, "Seven Essentials" (Pastor's Book Set), 27.

www.ingramcontent.com/pod-product-compliance
Lightning Source LLC
Chambersburg PA
CBHW071958220426
43662CB00009B/1180